OVERCOMING RACISM AND SEXISM

OVERCOMING RACISM AND SEXISM

Edited by
Linda A. Bell
and
David Blumenfeld

Rowman & Littlefield Publishers, Inc.

ROWMAN & LITTLEFIELD PUBLISHERS, INC.

Published in the United States of America
by Rowman & Littlefield Publishers, Inc.
4720 Boston Way, Lanham, Maryland 20706

3 Henrietta Street
London WC2E 8LU, England

British Cataloging in Publication Information Available

Library of Congress Cataloging-in-Publication Data

Overcoming racism and sexism / edited by Linda A. Bell and David
Blumenfeld.
p.   cm.
Includes bibliographical references and index.
1. Racism–United States. 2. Sexism–United States. 3. Afro
-Americans–Civil rights. 4. Women's rights–United States.
5. United States–Race relations. I. Bell, Linda A.
II. Blumenfeld, David, 1937–   .

E18615.094   1995   305.8—dc20   95–11998   CIP

ISBN 0-8476–8030–4 (cloth: alk. paper)
ISBN 0-8476–8031–2 (pbk.: alk. paper)

Printed in the United States of America

The paper used in this publication meets the minimum requirements of American National Standard for Information Sciences—Permanence of Paper for Printed Library Materials, ANSI Z39.48–1984.

Contents

PART III: PAIN AND ANGER: PRACTICAL OUTGROWTHS

A) Respecting the Pain of Others

B) Rethinking Anger

PART IV: WHERE DO WE GO FROM HERE?

Acknowledgments

This volume consists primarily of papers delivered at a conference ("Racism and Sexism: Differences and Connections") sponsored by the Department of Philosophy at Georgia State University in the Spring of 1992. We thank the conference participants for allowing us to reprint their essays and for agreeing that royalties derived from this volume should be paid to the Georgia State philosophy department for the purpose of sponsoring further conferences on ethical issues. We also wish to thank Clyde W. Faulkner (then Dean of the College of Arts and Sciences) for funding the conference, Judith Myrick and her staff in Continuing Education for managing registration, Henri Madigan for her careful attention to a host of important administrative details, and Edward Conner, Isadora Vardaros, Ernelle Fife, Ellen Logan, and Nancy Sullivan for their able editorial assistance.

In order to provide further context for some of the essays and to make the volume more suitable for classroom use, we have added a few other papers to this volume. These are: "The Problem of Speaking for Others," by Linda Martín Alcoff, *Cultural Critique* 20 (Winter 1991–92); "The Uncompleted Argument: Du Bois and the Illusion of Race," by Kwame Anthony Appiah, *Critical Inquiry* 12 (Autumn 1985); "'I Just See People': Exercises in Learning the Effects of Racism and Sexism" (with an appendix, "Why Dialogues are Difficult or 15 Ways a Black Woman Knows When a White Woman's Not Listening," by Marcia Houston), by Bernita Berry; "Some Reflections on Race, Racism, and Ethnicity," by Claudia Card; and "The Peculiar Position of a Woman of Color When World Fame Isn't Enough," by La Verne Shelton, *American Philosophical Association Newsletters* 91, no. 2 (Fall 1992). We thank these authors and gratefully acknowledge the permission of the American Philosophical Association, *Critical Inquiry*, and *Cultural Critique* to reprint the papers of Shelton, Appiah, and Alcoff. Finally, with her permission, we have reprinted Marilyn Frye's "White Woman/White Feminist: The Meaning of White" (from *Willful Virgin: Essays in Feminism 1976–1992* [Freedom, Calif.: The Crossing Press, 1992]), which is a revised version of a paper delivered at the Georgia State University Conference on Racism and Sexism.

Introduction

Linda A. Bell

That man over there says that woman needs to be helped into carriages and lifted over ditches. . . . Nobody ever helps me into carriages, or over mud-puddles or gives me any best place. And ain't I a woman?

Look at my arm! I have ploughed, and planted, and gathered into barns, and no man could head me! And ain't I a woman?

I would work as much and eat as much as a man, when I could get it, and bear the lash as well. And ain't I a woman?

I have borne thirteen children and seen em most all sold off to slavery, and when I cried out with my mother's grief, none but Jesus heard me! And ain't I a woman?

Sojourner Truth, 1851

Some Historical Connections
between Racism and Sexism

Questions concerning the relationship between racism and sexism have arisen in the United States in a number of ways. For those who heard and who continue to hear the anguished cry of a former slave who eloquently and courageously asked "Ain't I a woman?" at a women's rights meeting in Akron, Ohio, in 1851, the assumption that all women are affected in the same way by sexism becomes untenable. After all, as Sojourner Truth so deftly noted, she had not been helped into carriages or received any advantages whatsoever from the much touted gallantry of her day. Not even the most minimal respect for motherhood was accorded her as she

1

watched her children sold into slavery. And, yet, she asked, isn't she a woman?[1]

Truth's speech reveals a major hypocrisy in sexist claims about the fragility of women: this fragility allegedly rendered women unsuitable as voters and as holders of rights equal to those of men, but it did not—and was not intended to—apply to black women or even to poor white women. In her brilliant speech, this uneducated black woman was able to cut through sexist lies about the differences between men and women. She knew she could work as hard as most men, and eat as much, too, if she could get the food.

Moreover, she could acknowledge that there might be real differences among human beings; she simply could not see that these differences should have the consequences her opponents thought they should. In particular, if capacities such as intelligence were distributed unequally among human beings and if she happened to have less than another, the man who would prevent her from using her "half measure" is simply "mean." In arguing for women's rights, she was as audaciously ready to identify as a woman with Mary's role in producing the Christian's Jesus ("He came from God and a woman—*man* had nothing to do with it") as the heckling preacher was to identify as a man with God's having chosen a male form in which to be born as a human being.

A different problem is seen in the arguments of many who, though on the side of women's rights, lacked or rejected the awareness of women's differences from one another. Many of the economically privileged white women working and writing in the various women's movements have universalized their own condition, once again rendering women like Sojourner Truth invisible. Like the preachers and other men who heckled Truth, these privileged women have ignored the plight of less fortunate women.

On the other hand, far too often the case for women's rights has been supported with analogies to slavery. This strategy was no doubt especially tempting for early women's rights advocates as they moved from challenging slavery to promoting women's suffrage. Some were careful in their use of the analogy, recognizing clearly that the submission of women to men was substantially different from the slavery imposed on former Africans and their descendants in the United States. For example, in 1869 the British philosopher John Stuart Mill observed that men want *willing* slaves of women, which makes marriage a unique form of bondage. Even so, he says, "the law of servitude in marriage is a monstrous contradiction to all the principles of the modern world, and to all the experience through which those principles have been slowly and painfully worked out." Mill continues:

> [Marriage] is the sole case, now that Negro slavery has been abolished, in which a human being in the plenitude of every faculty is delivered up to the tender mercies of another human being, in the hope forsooth that this other will use the power solely for the good of the person subjected to it. Marriage is the only actual bondage known to our law. There remain no legal slaves, except the mistress of every house.[2]

Not all women's rights enthusiasts were as careful as Mill in their analogies of women's condition in marriage with that of black slaves. For black women, it must have been galling indeed to hear privileged white women proclaiming the identity of their situations with that of black slaves whose existence had often been so harsh.[3] Many of those white women had successfully used the "cult of the lady," the "cult of motherhood," and the domesticity movement to gain real power in the very homes where they made black women into overworked and underpaid workers, with no protection against workplace indignities, exploitation, and abuse, particularly sexual abuse by the males.[4]

Adding devastating injury to insult, the cults of the lady and of motherhood and the domesticity movement helped to buttress the protection-of-white-womanhood claims of lynchers and the view of hardworking—hence "unladylike"—black women as lustful, animalistic beings who provoked and hence deserved the sexual attacks of white men. Moreover, according to the perverse logic of victim-blaming, black women, who supposedly lacked the "higher" morality proper to their gender and were thereby unable to act as the necessary curbs on male lust, were held responsible for the allegedly unrestrained sexuality of black men. This rationale became such a widely circulated myth that it successfully hid from view—and continues to do so today—the facts uncovered by Ida B. Wells. In her extensive investigations of the 728 lynchings that had taken place in one decade, she found that women and children were among those lynched and that "[o]nly a third of the murdered Blacks were even *accused* of rape, much less guilty of it. . . ."[5] For both black women and black men, the usurpation of their experience by white women of means and influence must have been very painful, given the continued brutal oppression of blacks even after slavery was over. Alas, this usurpation of the black experience of slavery and oppression has continued in white feminist writings to the present day.[6]

Although the harm they suffered was severe and often fatal, black men and black women were hardly the only ones injured by the myths that white women used to liberate themselves from the absolute control of their husbands and that whites in general used to secure their power over blacks. Though they may have gained a modicum of power thereby, white women suffered in obvious ways from the myths of their purity and superior morality. At the very least, these myths locked well-off white women into their domestic roles as childbearers and moral exemplars and out of the possibility of sexual fulfillment and other human interests and achievements.

Moreover, apart from the fact that oppressors may suffer moral harm or dehumanization as a result of their oppression and dehumanization of others, surely white women suffered additional harm (as they continue to do today) from believing the myth of the black rapist. With its claim that black men are the rapists and white women the victims, this myth harms not only black women, by hiding attacks on them from social cognizance and legal recognition and making them even less likely to be reported than attacks on white women;[7] it also harms white women by denying the very real threat they face from those far likelier to rape them, namely, white male acquaintances, friends, and lovers/husbands. Surely, too, by helping to protect many white perpetrators of rape (as well as black rapists whose victims are black) and placing an even heavier burden of proof on the victims in the relatively few instances when rapists are actually accused and forced to stand trial, this myth creates a situation in which many men feel they can rape with relative impunity.

Another important problem is that even those who have fought racism have fallen into subtle ways of perpetuating it. Often, discussions in liberal circles have proceeded as though the notions of race and racism are perfectly clear. Racism too frequently has been seen as something practiced only by the rabid, such as Nazis and members of the Ku Klux Klan and White Citizens' Councils. This assumption camouflages and makes acceptable—even normal—not only nonrabid racism but also what has come to be called institutional racism: the ways in which social institutions such as language, the law, and the economy structure our conceptions and our treatment of others so as to insure the preservation of an oppressive status quo.

Discussions of race and racism have tended to concern themselves only with the experiences of black men, romanticizing[8] or ignoring, for example, the systematic rape of slave women by white slaveholders and the later lynchings of black women as well as black men, often under the same bogus claim of protecting white women's purity.[9] Once more black women are rendered invisible. In these discussions, a black woman might well rephrase Sojourner Truth's question and ask, "And ain't I black?" In fact, in the debate about whether black men or white women should get the vote first, Truth did register her objection against those, including Frederick Douglass, who contended that black men should be first: "There is a great stir about colored men getting their rights, but not a word about the colored women; and if colored men get their rights, and not colored women theirs, you see the colored men will be masters over the women, and it will be just as bad as it was before."[10] In the title of a book they edited in 1982—*All the Women Are White, All the Blacks Are Men, But Some of Us Are Brave*[11]—Gloria T. Hull, Patricia Bell-Scott, and Barbara Smith mock the way debates about both racism and sexism render black women invisible.

These are just some of the ways racism and sexism have intersected and buttressed one another. Thinkers have illuminated, analyzed, and critiqued various aspects of this intersection, and more remains to be done. The essays in this volume are a contribution to that ongoing discussion.

Essays in This Volume

Part I: Overview

In this section, Blanche Radford Curry looks at the so-called women's movement and laments the snail's pace at which it has progressed in terms of awareness and inclusiveness vis-à-vis race. She argues that we can have little hope for something better in the coming century if feminists, particularly white feminists, do not get beyond our own racism and then begin to attack the structures of oppression around us. In my response, I agree with her and use the occasion to explore the dynamics of a white woman responding to an essay written by a black woman. I try to show how difficult it is for whites to disconnect from white privilege, how easy it is to refocus attention on the problems of whites, and how this privilege even makes that refocusing seem quite virtuous.

Bernita C. Berry continues this discussion with a look at classes she taught the same semester at two women's colleges, one black, the other predominantly white. She observes how easily students in both classes were able to identify male privilege, how readily black students recognized white privilege, but how bemused and uncomfortable the white students were over claims that they have privilege. She includes a speech—"Why Dialogues Are Difficult or 15 Ways a Black Woman Knows When a White Woman's Not Listening"—in which the writer, Marsha Houston, Professor of Communication at Tulane University, itemizes ways she has heard white women identify with the experience of the less privileged so as to hide and deny their own privilege.

Part II: Racism and Sexism—Theoretical
Considerations

Writers in this section examine some theoretical aspects of racism and sexism. First, several thinkers probe the concept of race. Kwame Anthony Appiah analyzes W. E. B. Du Bois's efforts to understand and to amend nineteenth-century scientific and social views of race. According to Appiah, Du Bois at times seems to have acknowledged what Appiah sees as the truth about race, namely, "that there are no races: there is nothing in the world that can do all we ask 'race' to do for us."[12] Du Bois himself argued in his 1940 essay *Dusk of Dawn*: "It is easy to see that scientific definition of race is impossible; it is easy to prove that physical characteristics are not so inherited as to make it possible to divide the world into races; that ability is the monopoly of no known aristocracy; that the possibilities of human development cannot be circumscribed by color, nationality, or any conceivable definition of race."[13] According to Appiah, Du Bois did not complete his argument by jettisoning the notion of race. Instead, he persistently wavered between the biological conception of race and a sociohistorical notion. Du Bois's ultimate contribution to the debate over race was to offer the antithesis in what Appiah sees as the "classic" dialectic of reaction to racial prejudice. In opposition to the thesis denying difference (exemplified, for Du Bois, in "the American Negro's attempt to 'minimize race distinctions'"), Du Bois proposes the valorization of difference, arguing that each group has a unique and positive contribution to make in the history of civilization. Appiah sees a similar dialectic in feminism, with the denial of difference followed by a revaluing of the feminine, but he interprets Du Bois's proposal as still presupposing rather than escaping from the scientific or biological understanding of race. After all, Appiah argues, how else can we account for Du Bois's continued talk about "blood," common descent, and the features that follow from such descent?[14]

Lucius Outlaw, on the other hand, takes exception to Appiah's interpretation of Du Bois. In Outlaw's view, although Du Bois thought biology lends no credence to the concept of race, he nevertheless believed the concept should be retained, albeit under a new interpretation. Agreeing with Du Bois, Outlaw challenges Appiah's claim that there is no way to make the concept of race do what we want it to do. Outlaw concedes to Appiah that there is no *biological* basis for a distinction among races, but argues that Du Bois was reinterpreting the notion of race so that it no longer would involve the earlier biological assumption of natural kinds with fixed inherited essences (including moral and cultural traits and potentialities) and so that it would be able to take seriously history and sociology and even choice. In Outlaw's opinion, then, Du Bois was self-consciously—and defensibly—reinterpreting race as a socially constructed concept.

Stephen Prothero uses Du Bois's paper to come to substantially the same conclusion, namely, that race is an important, socially constructed concept, even if it has no basis in biology. Although race is a biological fiction, it is nonetheless the way human beings construct reality and see themselves. The question for Du Bois, as Prothero understands him, is not whether races exist but rather how they are to be interpreted. Recognizing, with Outlaw, that Du Bois's main concern was to detoxify and valorize the concept of race by seeing each race as having its own distinctive mission, Prothero proposes that Du Bois be read as a conjurer, adapting dangerous substances for his own therapeutic ends, namely, to fight racism, much as black preachers turned the very Bible used by the slave-masters to justify slavery into a condemnation of slavery and a support for freedom.

Another approach to the social construction of reality is that of Marilyn Frye, who coins the term "whitely" to create a way to discuss the destructive behaviors and attitudes of most privileged white people. She recognizes that "white," like "male," is simply a descriptive word. But just as feminists distinguish masculinity from maleness, so she uses "whiteliness" to characterize a normative concept, which she distinguishes from the descriptive concept of whiteness. Like masculinity, whiteliness is a deeply ingrained way of being in the world. While recognizing that not all whites need be whitely and that whiteliness is not necessarily limited to white people (and, in fact, may be more closely linked with class), she analyzes the features of this socially constructed combination of attitudes and behaviors. These include a "staggering faith" in one's own and other whitely people's righteousness, merit, pure motives, and lack of prejudice, as evinced mainly in knowing, following, and enforcing vis-à-vis others "the rules" of the dominant society. This sense of entitlement and authority hides from them their privilege as whites or justifies it when it becomes apparent. Frye's ultimate concern is to use this analysis as a tool to undermine these attitudes and behaviors and to end the domination and privilege that they support.

In responding to Frye, Victoria Davion uses her Jewish ethnicity to examine whiteliness and concludes that it may be an even more complex configuration of behaviors and attitudes than Frye's analysis suggests. Both white and a Jew, Davion notes that many of the features Frye characterizes as whitely are quite different from the primary attitudes and behaviors that Davion was taught. While not disputing that she learned the whitely behaviors, she proposes that she learned them not so much as a privileging identity but rather as a protective device that she could put on when she needed to divert attention from her being Jewish. Although these behaviors may have served as camouflage for her and others, she argues, those behaviors "fractured" and alienated her and were, therefore, harmful even as they may have been protective.

By considering issues of identity, Claudia Card links the analyses of Du Bois, Outlaw, Prothero, and Frye. While Card agrees with Du Bois, Outlaw, and Prothero that race is socially constructed and that its social constructedness does not thereby make it unreal, she, like Davion, expands this discussion by comparing and contrasting race with ethnicity. Rejecting simplistic notions of biological inheritance, she suggests that race and ethnicity may in fact come together in the notion of "heritage." This notion involves, in addition to a past, a cultural legacy—a legacy that connects one with traditions, which may bestow privileges and liabilities, and to which one can be disloyal even if one cannot elect to opt out of it. Individuals can be disinherited or alienated from this legacy. The cultural aspect of this heritage can be annihilated, for example, by the cultural genocide practiced by whites in the United States against both African Americans and Indians. It can also be appropriated by others. She links her analysis to Frye's discussion of whiteness and whiteliness, balancing the aspect of givenness in the reality of heritage with the element of choice—that, for example, individuals whose heritage confers privilege can choose whether or not to remain loyal to that heritage.

Laurence Thomas illuminates differences between racism and sexism by discussing two different kinds of abusive power arrangements. One of these, the capricious power arrangement, he finds at work in the Holocaust. Here power is used to manipulate and control the behavior of others, with no concern that they recognize its legitimacy. The second type, which he calls expectations-generating, involves a concern that those controlled recognize the legitimacy of the power exercised over them. Both slavery and sexism, according to Thomas, set up power arrangements of the second type. In these arrangements, those in control voluntarily refrain from harming those who comply, restraining themselves to gain the trust of those whose voluntary subservience is actively sought. Indeed, on Thomas's view, trust is required to secure the degree of voluntary subservience involved in sexism and in American slavery, just as it is essential to securing the norms that justify the dependent status of women and American slaves.

While slavery and sexism press trust into the service of immorality, Thomas observes, trust did not play a similar role in the Holocaust, where Nazis regarded the Jews as irredeemably evil. Instead, the power arrangements were capricious, generating no expectations that compliance would be met with any sort of restraint by those in power. Although the capricious power arrangements resulted in a great deal of compliance behavior, the compliance was based almost entirely on fear rather than trust. Because the Nazis' goal was the *extermination* of the Jews rather than the establishment of a social order in which Jews willingly accepted domination, there was little need to build Jewish trust or to get Jews to internalize norms justifying their subservience.

Thomas distinguishes racism from sexism by claiming that men receive their gender identity from sexual interaction with women, unlike women, who can derive their gender identity from the biological experience of motherhood. Simply fathering a child is not parallel since a woman gives birth and knows the child is hers.

Men, on the other hand, must rely on socially constructed experiences, which, in a heterosexually oriented society, are bound to lead
to a "macho" or dominating form of identity. Thus, Thomas sees a
deep tie between a heterosexually oriented society and sexism. Since
our society is likely to remain heterosexually oriented, Thomas argues,
sexism seems secure. Because racial identity involves no such dependence of one group on another, he concludes that racism may
be easier to eradicate than sexism.

   In responding to Thomas, David Blumenfeld takes exception to
the argument that since men depend for their gender identity on
their relations with women, sexism will be around as long as such
identity persists. First of all, it is not clear to Blumenfeld that in
our society men depend for their gender identity *exclusively* on their
relations with women. In fact, he believes, a good deal of current
male gender identity depends on men's relations with other men
(though, unfortunately, these relations commonly involve macho and
homophobic ideals). More important, however, even if men do depend for their gender identity on women, it does not follow that
every heterosexually oriented society must be sexist. Blumenfeld
denies Thomas's "deep tie" between the two by arguing for the
possibility of an egalitarian heterosexual ideal that forswears male
domination and rejects homophobia. If the ideal he defends is fea-
sible, then the battle against sexism is not linked per se to undoing
a heterosexually oriented society. The battle can also be won by
replacing macho gender identity with a more liberated and humane
masculine gender ideal.

Part III: Pain and Anger—Practical Outgrowths

   In this section, the pain and anger that arise in connection with
racism and sexism are the focus of attention. Elizabeth V. Spelman
analyzes the appropriation of others' pain, particularly that of black
slave women by white women seeking rights for themselves. She
also connects this with contemporary examples, such as recent designer-line "homelessness" fashions. Those who engage in such
exploitative sentimentality treat others as "spiritual bellhops," by
disingenuously creating the impression that they, too, have had similar
experiences.

   Spelman argues that experience cannot and should not be viewed
as incomprehensible to those not literally sharing it, but that it also
must not be appropriated by others in a way that denies the uniqueness

of the experience or renders invisible the original experience and those who have it. She elaborates on these dangers by showing how the experience of Jews in the Holocaust has been trivialized by the characterization of other disasters and calamities as "holocausts" and how the pain of black slaves has been appropriated by white women, an appropriation to which she disparagingly refers as "boomerang perception"—"I look at you and come right back to myself."[15] She proposes that the experience of individuals and groups subjected to oppression should be heard. It is important, too, she maintains, for others to *identify* with that experience in important and appropriate ways, but without treating it as *identical to* their own experience. The proper response to the pain of others respects differences, specifically the different ways different groups may be oppressed, yet sees even those differences as enabling us to grasp and to participate in a shared humanity. It neither appropriates the pain of others nor engages in what Spelman has called elsewhere an "Oppression Olympics," that is, an irrelevant effort to determine who has suffered most.

In her response to Spelman, Pamela M. Hall carefully distinguishes the two extremes discussed by Spelman, referring to them as "vicious particularity"—the view that each individual's experience is radically unique and incomprehensible to others—and "vicious generalization"—a move that collapses experiences with important differences into each other and thereby blurs the differences. Both are vicious: the former denies any commonality in the human condition and renders our stories of suffering wholly incommunicable, at least to those outside the circle of pain; the latter obliterates the singularity of the suffering, sometimes its gratuitousness, and always the aspect of it that is incommunicable. Hall then explores the possibility of a middle ground between the two extremes, a way of holding in tension the universality and the distinctiveness of the particular suffering.

Reflecting on her own experience of subordination in a system structured by racism and sexism, María Lugones turns our attention from pain to anger, noting that she has been taught to distrust and fear her own anger. Because she sees anger, properly understood and used, as an important source of change, she analyzes the major types of anger, dividing it into two kinds—first- and second-order anger. First-order anger is communicative, an anger that seeks "uptake" or acknowledgment by others—something like Aristotle's notion of righteous indignation, anger in accord with the "mean."

In the context of oppression, Lugones says, this anger demands respect from the oppressor. It thus presupposes and affirms a world of meanings and sense inhabited by both the oppressor and the oppressed, and to that extent it may constitute a trap for those who are oppressed, tying them into a status quo that is antagonistic to them and needs to be changed. Second-order anger, on the other hand, looks neither to others nor to the past. It cannot demand respect from an oppressor since there is no common ground or meaning—she refers to this as a shared world of sense—on the basis of which this demand can be understood and seen as intelligible. Lugones depicts this uncommunicative anger as rage.

Although Lugones maintains that first-order anger can fuel resistance, she proposes second-order anger, anger across worlds of sense (rage), as an even more fruitful source of resistance to oppression. Rejecting her earlier training to fear her own rage as out of control and irrational, she suggests that such second-order anger can be very important for the oppressed, opening as it does a space for them and, by pushing against walls, pointing toward a future in which those walls will be broken down. Affirming the power of rage leads Lugones to propose that her own fear of rage is itself a learned reaction that serves oppression and so must be unlearned.

In her response to Lugones, Bernadette Hartfield offers a sensitive and provocative illustration of these two kinds of anger by describing her own early experience of racism when, as a young Southern girl on a trip north, she was refused admission to a swimming pool on the ground that, although it was open to each and every white person, it was nonetheless "private." Even the white family turned away with her could not understand why she was so upset. Hartfield illustrates Lugones's first-order anger by pointing to the incapacitating tears of indignation over the racist disregard for the worth of a black child. Hartfield agrees with Lugones that this anger is quite different from—and far less useful than—anger that would make racists uncomfortable.

Part IV: Where Do We Go from Here?

The last two essays in the volume raise a question important to all of us, namely, how do we proceed to act in the world on the basis of a heightened consciousness of racism and sexism? Linda Martín Alcoff invites readers to think with her through some issues about speaking for others. She recognizes that well-intentioned advocates of social change have all too often and much too arrogantly made pronouncements about the situations and needs of others who have either not been allowed or not been encouraged to speak for themselves. Many have seen only a single danger to be avoided, namely, the arrogance of the privileged who improperly universalize their own experience or speak on behalf of rather than listening to others. Instead, with Spelman, Alcoff recognizes not only that danger but also another that is just as much to be avoided: the would-be insularity of those who try to restrict themselves to speaking only for others "like" them. She sees this as an unsuccessful attempt to find a challenge-proof position from which to speak. While the desire to avoid criticism should be rejected as unworthy, the attempt to achieve invulnerability is problematic in other ways. This attempt assumes the existence of a neutral position where one can stand, extricated from all ties with others in different locations. If we reject the liberal notion of autonomy, there is no such neutral position. Moreover, by dividing those who might otherwise be allies, the attempt undercuts political struggle. Finally, since location is neither one-dimensional nor a fixed essence, the attempt greatly oversimplifies the location of the speaker. Such oversimplification is especially problematic inasmuch as, given complex identities such as Alcoff's own (part Angla, part Latina), it prevents her from speaking even for groups of which she is a part, many others of whom may be unable, at the moment or even permanently, to speak for themselves.

Finally, La Verne Shelton continues the discussion begun by Alcoff by challenging all of us to think of our responsibility for creating a better world. If blacks leave whites to work out the whites' problems of racism and if whites leave blacks to solve their own, much will be ignored and little is likely to be accomplished. Her challenge is a double one: that what goes on in the world is *our* problem and that, at the very least, each of us has internalized too much for us to consider racism and sexism merely the problems of others.

Alcoff's and Shelton's essays thus take us back to the point made by other authors in this volume: that racism and sexism affect everyone, dictating where we can safely go, what we can safely do, and what we can safely think and feel, even about ourselves. Racism and sexism prescribe not just how we react and how we think of ourselves but also our places and possibilities within the social and economic world. While the other essays show how differently individuals of different groups are thought of as well as affected by racism and sexism, collectively the essays in this volume demonstrate that these oppressive behaviors and conditions are everyone's problems. They show how important it is that we understand racism, sexism, and their interconnections as a first step in overcoming them and thereby creating a better world.

Notes

While contributing valuable suggestions and helpful editing to this introduction as well as throughout the volume, David Blumenfeld has been more than just a careful critic for this introduction, often suggesting more felicitous phrasings, and sometimes completely rewriting, to make what I was trying to say more readable or to summarize the various authors' views more clearly.

1. According to Paula Giddings [*When and Where I Enter: The Impact of Black Women on Race and Sex in America* (New York: Bantam Books, 1985), 54], the white women at the meeting had not wanted Truth to speak for fear that this would associate their cause with "'abolitionists and niggers.'" Although Truth rescued the meeting by taking control away from hecklers and ultimately had the white women responding with (in the words of one participant) "'streaming eyes and hearts beating with gratitude,'" Giddings observes that "Gratitude did not extend, however, to realizing that Black women had advanced ideas which would help all women."

2. John Stuart Mill, "From *The Subjection of Women*," in *Visions of Women*, ed. Linda A. Bell (Clifton, N.J.: Humana Press, 1983), 289 and 295.

3. It was common for white women to claim to *be* slaves. For some striking examples of such claims to identity, see Elizabeth V. Spelman's essay in this volume.

4. See Angela Y. Davis, *Women, Race & Class* (New York: Vintage Books, 1983), 91–93.

5. Giddings reports that from newspaper accounts and interviews with eyewitnesses, Wells discovered: "[m]ost were killed for crimes like 'incendiarism,' 'race prejudice,' 'quarreling with Whites,' and 'making threats'" (*When and Where I Enter*, 28).

6. Spelman cites bell hooks's objection, in her *Feminist Theory: From Margin to Center*, to the claim of "common oppression" made by conservative and liberal women in the United States. See note 7 of Spelman's chapter in this volume.

7. Davis examines statistics and the myth of the black rapist in *Women, Race & Class* (see 172–201).

8. Davis quotes as an example Eugene D. Genovese's treatment of the rape of slave women by whites as "miscegenation" and, from the point of view of the men, portraying as a "tragedy" the fact that "[m]any white men who began by taking a slave girl in an act of sexual exploitation ended by loving her and the children she bore," but were confronted by a "terrible pressure to deny the delight, affection and love that often grew from tawdry beginnings" (*Women, Race & Class*, 25).

9. For a discussion of the importance of the daring and revealing investigations of Ida B. Wells into the lynchings that were taking place, see Giddings's account in *When and Where I Enter*, 89–94.

10. Sojourner Truth's statement at the 1867 Equal Rights Association convention is quoted by Davis in *Women, Race & Class*, 83. Fairness to Douglass demands that we recognize that he did actively support the franchise for black—and white—women as well. But he thought it unlikely that the white male power structure would be prepared to extend the franchise so widely all at once. And, he reasoned, if a choice had to be made between black male suffrage and white female suffrage, then the vote should go to black men, because women were not attacked with the same deadly force simply for being women as were blacks simply for being blacks (see Davis's discussion of this on page 82).

11. *But Some of Us Are Brave* (Old Westbury, N.Y.: Feminist Press, 1982).

12. Anthony Appiah, "The Uncompleted Argument: Du Bois and the Illusion of Race," 75.

13. W. E. B. Du Bois, *Dusk of Dawn: An Essay toward an Autobiography of a Race Concept* (New York: Schocken, 1968 [1940]), 137.

14. Appiah, 63–64.

15. Elizabeth V. Spelman, *Inessential Woman: Problems of Exclusion in Feminist Thought* (Boston: Beacon Press, 1988), 12.

Part I

Overview

1

Racism and Sexism: Twenty-First-Century Challenges for Feminists

Blanche Radford Curry

What will it take to get beyond our current conflicting standpoints about racism and sexism so that African American and white feminists can work together in effective twenty-first-century transformative coalition? My thoughts about this topic began at a regional philosophy conference involving comments about oppression, racism, and sexism from a white female philosopher. What she meant by oppression is very like the definition given by Arthur Brittan and Mary Maynard in *Sexism, Racism and Oppression*.[1] The oppressed are "those who are . . . coerced by others. Their freedom of action is limited by the superior power of those who are in a position to ensure their compliance."[2] What she meant by racism and sexism is very like the definitions given by Audre Lorde in *Sister Outsider*. Racism is defined as "the belief in the inherent superiority of one race over all others and thereby the right to dominance" and sexism is defined as "the belief in the inherent superiority of one sex over the other and thereby the right to dominance."[3] The white feminist philosopher at the conference rejected the claim that African American women are more oppressed than white women and that racial oppression is greater than sexual oppression. Another white female philosopher, however, expressed the opposite position. Both of them, as well as others, were quite vocal in pointing out personal experiences and in giving arguments in support of one or the other of these two frequently asserted positions. I thought to myself that we could continue this mode of discussion at length and still not resolve the issue. As an African American female philosopher, I too could share virulent and subtle experiences of racism and sexism and formulate other arguments in support of each position. However, I thought, surely all of us are aware that our individual experiences do not adequately support or undermine cultural analyses.

The problem African American and white feminists need to address involves much more than reciting our various personal experiences and arguments about racism and sexism in support of one or the other of these two positions. Why are we still struggling with each other over partial perspectives? This is déjà vu. The twenty-first century is upon us. Will the blinders about racism and sexism never come off for some African American and white women? How can we get beyond these two opposing and inadequate positions? Is greater political solidarity between African American and white women possible in our struggles against racism and sexism? It is my position that our minimal progress is related, in part, to many African American and white women's differing "standpoints" about racism and sexism. Of greater significance is many African American and white women's denial of each other's standpoints. For many African American women, most white women deny racism as well as important differences between African American and white women that are manifested by racism and sexism. For many white women, most African American women deny the significance of sexism as compared to racism. Examples of each of these standpoints are well documented. In this essay I address several typical examples of African American and white women's standpoints about racism and sexism. Then I consider how we can resolve this impasse by confronting our differing standpoints and widening our perspective on oppression.

African American Women's Standpoints on Racism

When considering African American women's standpoints on racism, we find overwhelming past and present evidence of white women's denial and betrayal at various levels, beginning with the historical struggles of liberation by African Americans and white women. During the 1800s, many white women supported the liberation struggles of African Americans. There was an alliance between the liberation struggles of African Americans and white women suffragists. However, even amid this alliance there were realities of racism among white women. One notable example was the shunning of Sojourner Truth at the National Women's Right Convention in 1851. Several of the white women suffragists were fearful of being embarrassed by Sojourner Truth's "speech" and leery of a speech from an African American woman. But it was Sojourner Truth's remarkable speech, "Ain't I a Woman?," and the vigor with which she delivered it that made the convention the historical event that it is today. She challenged white men when she, in effect, said, "You say Jesus was a man, but wasn't he born of a man and a woman?" She challenged both white women and men when she asked, "Ain't I a woman?" And, of course, she defined the vision for feminists when she exclaimed, "If the first woman God ever made was strong enough to turn the world upside down all alone, these women together ought to be able to get it right side up again! And now they are asking to do it, the men better let them."[4]

With the passage of the Fifteenth Amendment to the Constitution in 1870 granting African American men the right to vote, white women abandoned their alliances with African Americans and formed the National American Women's Suffrage Association (NAWSA) in 1890. Examples of racism by white women became more blatant. The association viewed passage of the Fifteenth Amendment as an insult to white women and openly condoned racism. Their position was stated by Belle Kearney in 1903: "Just as surely as the North will be forced to turn to the South for the nation's salvation, just so surely will the South be compelled to look to its Anglo-saxon women as the medium through which to retain the supremacy of the white race over the African."[5] This was a statement from white women that they valued their whiteness above their sex. After all, as has often been pointed out, sexual exploitation notwithstanding, both the white woman and the white man had the power to discriminate against African Americans.[6] Also implicit in Kearney's remarks was white women's view of African American women as African Americans rather than women—not as a group separate and distinct from African American men and belonging to a larger group of "women" in this society.[7] Moreover, the fact that passage of the Fifteenth Amendment did not empower African American men with the same voting power as white men was not of importance to these white women, nor was the Fifteenth Amendment seen as important as the Nineteenth Amendment for woman suffrage.[8]

Another late 1800s example of racism on the part of white women was the General Federation of Women's Clubs' racial and class shunning of African American women, which necessitated the formation in 1895 of a parallel but separate African American women's club: National Association of Colored Women (NACW). At the organizational meeting for the NACW, African American women adopted specific philosophies that distinguished their association from its white counterpart:

> Our woman's movement is woman's movement in that it is led and directed by women for the good of women and men, for the benefit of *all* humanity, which is more than any one branch or section of it. We want, we ask the active interest of our men, and, too, we are not drawing the color line; we are women, American women, as intensely interested in all that pertains to us such as all other American women; we are not alienating or withdrawing, we are only coming to the front, willing to join any others in the same work and cordially inviting and welcoming any others to join us.[9]

The motto of the National Association of Colored Women was "Lifting As We Climb."

These examples of racism by white women are typical of the 1800s through the early 1900s. In discussing the history of racism within the women's movement and the formation of a separate African American women's organization, Rosalyn Terborg-Penn points out that "discrimination against Afro-American women reformers was the rule rather than the exception within the women's rights movement from the 1830s to 1920."[10] The same observation is made by Angela Davis. In pointing out three distinct waves of the women's movement—the 1840s, the 1960s and the 1980s—she notes that we still have the same concerns as we begin the 1990s: "Black women are still compelled to expose the invisibility to which we have been relegated, in both theory and practice, within larger sectors of the established women's movement."[11] In an article addressing women's liberation and black civil rights, Catherine Stimpson writes:

> I believe that women's liberation would be much stronger, much more *honest* and ultimately more secure if it stopped comparing white women to Blacks so freely. . . . It perpetuates the depressing habit white people have of first defining the Black experience and then making it their own. . . . Perhaps more dangerous, the analogy evades, in the rhetorical haze, the harsh fact of white women's racism.[12]

Much of the recent feminist literature by African American women offers examples of racism in the women's movement. Among the many articles are: bell hooks's "Racism and Feminism: The Issue of Accountability," Pauline Terrelong Stone's "Feminist Consciousness and Black Women," and Elizabeth F. Stone's "Black Women, White Women: Separate Paths to Liberation." We find other examples in books by African American women, such as *Black Women, Feminism and Black Liberation: Which Way?*, by Vivian V. Gordon; *Woman Power*, by Cellestine Ware; and *Women, Race & Class*, by Angela Davis.

In addition to the examples of racism found in the women's movement, similar instances occur in other situations. One example involves school desegregation, wherein too frequently white mothers who support equality among the sexes reject desegregation as tantamount to destroying their "ethnic purity." Another instance of this self-interest, discussed by Audre Lorde, involves white mothers' parenting practices. They teach their children to marry "right"—that is, white—and to hate the right people—that is, non-whites.[13] Similarly, we find, too often, white women challenging various affirmative action decisions by charging "reverse discrimination." They maintain that their entrance, for example, to law or medical school, has been denied because of focus on ethnic minorities. In such cases, white women make their whiteness primary. In discussing white women's racism in "Feminist Consciousness and Black Women," Pauline Terrelong Stone writes:

> Racism is so ingrained in American culture, and so entrenched among white women, that Black [women] have been reluctant to admit that anything affecting the white [woman] could also affect them. Indeed, many Black women have tended to see all whites regardless of sex, as sharing the same objective interest and clearly the behavior of many white women vis-à-vis Blacks has helped to validate this reaction.[14]

Other notable situations that reveal racism on the part of white women include white feminist literature. In "Racism and Feminism: A Schism in the Sisterhood," Margaret A. Simons examines several major feminist works by white women and concludes: "In reviewing the work of [white] feminist theorists, one is struck by the relative lack of attention given to racism and the oppression of minority women. . . . Minority women remain invisible in most contemporary feminist theory, including most articles in feminist philosophy."[15] Among the white feminists' works examined by Simons are *The Second Sex*, by Simone de Beauvior; *Sex Equality*, edited by Jane English; *Feminism and Philosophy*, edited by Mary Vetterling-Braggin et al.; *Philosophy of Women*, edited by Mary Mahowald; *Feminist Frameworks*, edited by Alison M. Jaggar and Paula Rothenbery Struhl; *Notes from the Second Year*, edited by Shulamith Firestone; and *Notes from the Third Year*, edited by Anne Koedt. Among the points that Simons makes in her examination of these works are the following: that the ethnocentrism of de Beauvoir's perspective reflects insensitivity toward the experiences of women in other cultures, that the experiences of minority women are not defined as major theoretical questions, and that discussions of minority women, where they occur at all, are related only to concrete problems.[16] Simons qualifies her conclusion, noting that minority women are not always invisible in works by white feminists. She calls our attention to *Woman in Sexist Society: Studies in Power and Powerlessness*, edited by Vivian Gormick and Barbara K. Moran, and *Voices from Women's Liberation*, edited by Leslie Tanner, two anthologies in women's studies which include articles by and about women of color. However, Simons notes further, "[B]ut the insights offered by these authors seldom seem to be accepted by other feminists. And the sense of cultural isolation continues. A profoundly disturbing example of this phenomenon can be seen in the very influential 1970 feminist anthology, *Sisterhood is Powerful*."[17] Accordingly, we continue at a tortoise's pace toward minimizing our concerns about racism.

A further issue of concern related to white feminist literature is the funding of research. It is not unusual for white women to receive grant monies to do research on African American women. However, the same is not true for African American women. Indeed, bell hooks states that she "can find no instance where Black women have received funds to research white women's history. . . ." Moreover, while she acknowledges that some work about African American women by white women is significant, she questions whether, given the pressure to publish in academe, their scholarly motivation always involves sincere interest or rather the taking advantage of an available market.[18]

A related issue of concern involves women's studies programs, which represent, in part, an extension of the women's movement and involve substantial research about women. Although there is an awareness of the need to address racism and other "isms," the leadership of women's studies continues to be mostly white women. In this respect, women's studies remains white women's studies.[19] Similarly, considering the curriculum and who takes the classes, the center remains white women, while the margins remain African American women. The course topics and specific focuses reflect the standpoints of white, middle-class, heterosexual, Christian women. Responses to theoretical or practical questions about the exclusion of African American women's standpoints are usually the same despite the diversity of the questions. Likewise, the major course texts are frequently about white women and written by white women. Moreover, instances of limited course offerings reflecting the standpoints of African American women are often challenged by the white women enrolled in them. It is not unusual for them to claim knowledge of African American women's standpoints without collaborative dialogue with African American women, including professors. Similarly, texts on African American women are frequently criticized as unclear or as maintaining questionable theses. This concern about exclusion in women's studies programs is clearly outlined in "The Costs of Exclusionary Practices in Women's Studies" by Maxine Baca Zinn, Lynn Weber Cannon, Elizabeth Higginbotham, and Bonnie Thornton Dill. They discuss two examples of the incomplete, incorrect, and self-perpetuating applications of feminist theory resulting from the exclusion of women of color from feminist theory. One involves the idea that emphasis on the shared experiences of women has obscured the important differences among us. The other involves the claim that "failure to explore fully the interplay of race, class, and gender has cost the field the ability to provide a broad and truly complex analysis of women's lives and of social organization."[20]

In examining language for instances of racism on the part of white women, we must focus not on blatant remarks that most of us would consider racial, but rather on the presumption of "whiteness." Seldom do white women refer to themselves in racial terms. When "women" is used, it usually means white women. The same is the case for "feminist." We normally presume that it means white feminist. Bell hooks argues that "such a custom, whether practiced consciously or unconsciously, perpetuates racism in that it denies the existence of non-white women in America."[21] A similar example of this custom is white women's references to themselves and others. For instance, white women speak and write of "women and minorities," "white and African American women." It is the idea that whiteness is first, whether implicit, as in "women and minorities," or explicit, as in "white and African American women." Some may respond, in all honesty, that this habit is not *intended* to perpetuate racism. However, if we acknowledge the possibility that this habit does perpetuate racism, even if it is not intended, then why the problem with giving up the habit? In some cases, we use alphabetical orderings of persons' names to avoid sexism or to avoid suggestions of ranking. The same is true for our discussion of corporations, various awards, and the like. Why not "African American and white women"? The concern about language in this context is analogous to the concern about gendered language.

Differences for African American Women

When we consider African American women's standpoint about racism and sexism, we find that certain "differences" are indeed evident for African American women, differences which on one hand distinguish them from white women and on the other hand reveal similarities between them. The differences manifested by racism and sexism for African American women do not involve an "additive analysis" of racism and sexism. It is not the idea that sexism represents a further oppression for African American women. Elizabeth Spelman explains, in "Theories of Race and Gender: The Erasure of Black Women," that it is "quite misleading to say simply that black women and white women both are oppressed as women, and that a black woman's oppression as a black is thus inseparable from her oppression as a woman because she shares the latter but not the former, with the white woman."[22] It is a *different* oppression rather than a *further* oppression that the black woman experiences.

More is involved in combining racism with sexism than simply the sum in an additive analysis. Indeed, many critical factors are overlooked in such an analysis. Realities of racism and sexism make it apparent that the differences for African American women are "not merely arithmetic," as Barbara Smith indicates.[23] Germane to these differences for the African American woman is the phenomenon of a "both/or" orientation. Deborah K. King describes this as the "act of being simultaneously a member of a group and yet standing apart from it—a state of belonging and not belonging."[24] This situation of contradictions and "otherness" for the African American woman is described by Bonnie Thornton Dill as the "dialectics of

Black womanhood."[25] Frances Beale refers to it as "double jeopardy,"[26] and Alice Walker calls it "the condition of twin 'affliction.'"[27] As Patricia Hill Collins states: "On certain dimensions Black women may more closely resemble Black men, on others, white women and still others, Black women may stand apart from both groups."[28]

Realities of racism and sexism which reflect differences for the black woman are evident in the African American movement, the women's movement, and daily life in general. In discussing the black movement and the women's movement, Shirley Chisholm points out that black women find themselves at the tail end. Neither the black movement nor the women's movement in this country has addressed the political problems of blacks who are female.[29] Similarly, bell hooks states that "When Black people are talked about, sexism militates against the acknowledgment of the interest of Black women; when women are talked about racism militates against a recognition of Black [women's] interest."[30] It is necessary for African American women to have alliances with both movements if we are concerned about racial equality and women's rights, for neither movement adequately considers both cases of oppression.

This reality of the necessity for African American women's alliances with both the black movement and the women's movement is a rejection of the position that African American women can divorce race from sex, or sex from race. It is also a reality that reveals dimensions of the African American woman's existence that resemble those of the African American man. Among these dimensions is racism, which African American women and men have shared and still share, although sometimes in different ways. Elizabeth F. Hood explains that "Racism . . . affects the psychological structures of Black people without separating them from each other."[31] This dimension of racism shared by African American women and men demands that the African American woman consistently evaluate it in relation to other legitimate conflicts within the African American community. Sexism sometimes represents one such legitimate conflict. "It is easy," Audre Lorde notes, "for Black women to be used by the power structure against Black men, not because they are men, but because they are Black."[32]

African American Women's Standpoints on Sexism

When we consider white women's claims that African American women fail to acknowledge the importance of sexism, we do find considerable confirmation of this. This widespread denial of sexism by African American women is based on the ideas that sexism is secondary to racism, that sexism cannot be destroyed until racism is destroyed, and that the impact of racism for African American women is far greater than that of sexism. Realities of sexism that support this denial are evident as early as the historical liberation struggles of African Americans in the nineteenth and early twentieth centuries. African American women readily declared that racism was far more oppressive than sexism. The view was expressed in several ways:

> The idea [was] that Blackness was by far more difficult and energy-draining than femaleness. . . . [B]oth racism and sexism exploit Black women. . . . Racism, however, destroys Black women, Black men and their offsprings. . . . Sexism enslaves, racism destroys. . . . [Racism] destroys [Black] culture and prevents [Blacks] from maintaining economically and socially stable communities.[33]

The same ideas about sexism and racism continued for the African American woman during the civil rights movement of the 1960s. In the aftermath of the movement, many African American women began to reassess the claim that racism is more oppressive than sexism. Questions were asked of African American males. Where was the African American male support for Shirley Chisholm during her campaign for the U. S. presidency? Where was the African American male support for the recognition and honoring of Barbara Jordan, Eleanor Holmes Norton, Alice Walker, Nannie Burroughs? Why was the African American male advocating revolution by day and sleeping with white women at night? Why was the African American male blaming the African American woman for all the problems in the African American community? Why was the African American male ignoring the atrocities suffered by African American women and their contributions to the history they shared? Why was the African American woman two steps behind the African American male, rather than in step with him?[34]

The heightening of African American women's consciousness in the late 1960s and early 1970s has not been substantially sustained. We have examples today that reflect the African American woman's denial of sexism. One such example was discussed by bell hooks during a talk for African American university women in the late 1980s. She related how astonished she was when these women suggested that sexism was not a political issue of concern to African American women, that the serious issue was racism.[35] Similarly, we find some African American women who will argue that the brutal sexist domination of the African American woman by the African American man as portrayed in *The Color Purple* by Alice Walker[36] has no basis in reality. While *The Color Purple* is a work of fiction, Nellie McKay[37] and others remind us that literary works by African American women often reflect their lived experience. Moreover, there are autobiographical works that address sexism in the lives of African American women. One historical example is Harriet Wilson's *Our Nig, or Sketches from the Life of a Free Black in a Two Story White House, North Showing that Slavery Shadows Fall Even There.*[38] Shall African American women insist on denying other widespread sexism during the institution of slavery?[39] Only recently, since the Anita Hill-Clarence Thomas hearings, have African American women begun to acknowledge sexism more.[40]

In addition to pointing to African American women's denial of the significance of sexism, some white women make a further claim about sexism that many African American women rightly deny, namely, that sexism is more fundamental than racism. The soundness of this claim, however, has been extensively questioned by Elizabeth V. Spelman. She begins by pointing out the "habit of speaking comparatively about sexism and racism, sexism or racism," which is related to the fact that feminism followed antiracist activities. Such comparisons, Spelman explains, "often culminate in questions about which form of oppression is more fundamental." She continues her analysis of this claim by outlining what it means and examining arguments in support of it. She states that "several different though related things" are meant when saying "sexism is more fundamental than racism," namely:

It is harder to eradicate sexism than to eradicate racism.

There might be sexism without racism but not racism without sexism. Any social and political changes which eradicate sexism will have eradicated racism, but social and political changes which eradicate racism will not have eradicated sexism.

Sexism is the first form of oppression learned by children.

Sexism is historically prior to racism.

Sexism is the cause of racism.

Sexism is used to justify racism.

Sexism is the model for racism.[41]

The arguments examined by Spelman are those expressed by Richard Wasserstrom, Laurence Thomas, Mary Daly, Kate Millet, Shulamith Firestone, and other leading proponents of the position that sexism is more fundamental than racism. In discussing Wasserstrom's arguments, Spelman points out that "his description of women does not apply to the Black woman, which implies that being Black is a more fundamental fact about her than being a woman." Regarding Thomas's arguments, Spelman says, "Thomas' description of sexism in relations between women and men leaves out the reality of racism in relations between blacks and whites." In the case of Daly's position, Spelman asserts that her "theory relies on an additive analysis [which] fails to describe adequately Black women's experience."[42] Regarding the position of Millet and Firestone, Spelman states that their analysis of "power" in support of their claim ignores the fact that institutionally based power in our society belongs to white males, not black males.[43] Spelman and other white feminist theorists have criticized as a dangerous mistake the claim that sexism is more fundamental than racism. Regarding the tendency to make this claim, Margaret S. Simons notes that, "Analyses by white feminists often de-emphasize the differences in women's situations in an effort to point out the shared experiences of sexism. [Too] often [white] feminist theorists [draw] analogies between the situations of oppressed minorities and white women without sufficient attention to the dissimilarities. . . ."[44] This tendency is related to what Adrienne Rich has termed "white solipsism":

> [T]o think, imagine and speak as if whiteness described the world . . . not the consciously held belief that one race is inherently superior to all others, but a tunnel-vision which simply does not see nonwhite experience or existences as precious or significant, unless in spasmodic, impotent guilt-reflexes, which have little or no long-term continuing momentum or political usefulness.[45]

For white feminists to ignore or distort ways in which African American women's experiences of oppression are different from those of white women is a form of solipsism, according to Spelman. It is a reality that within our society we ascribe differences between African American women and white women on the basis of culture. Likewise, it is a reality that these differences greatly influence the "kinds of life we lead or we have."[46] As Elizabeth F. Hood notes, "[T]here are substantive differences between the treatment accorded Black and white women, regardless of the individual white woman's feelings about her personal life style. [T]hey are more acceptable to society at large, and therefore, are in positions to influence, if only indirectly, the decisions of those in power."[47]

Confronting Our Realities

African American and white women's denial of each other's standpoints about racism and sexism suppresses our struggles against the intertwined oppressions of racism and sexism. We cannot begin to conceptualize the appropriate transformative responses to racism and sexism if we refuse to confront these realities. When we choose not to confront both racism and sexism, we reveal our unwillingness to work realistically to change these realities. It is a limited scope of vision and a lack of understanding that impede our liberation from racism and sexism. We are reminded by Audre Lorde that "it is not [the] differences between us that are separating us. It is rather our refusal to recognize those differences."[48] If African American and white women are to overcome racism and sexism, we must first of all confront these realities. This involves an ongoing conscious commitment on our part to make this choice.

It is not enough for us to know of racism and sexism, however; we must go beyond knowing to confronting these realities. This means bridging the gap between knowing and acting upon our knowledge. It requires engaging in actions that reflect our honesty about these realities. Our choice to confront both realities—racism and sexism—involves a matter of what Patricia Hill Collins calls an ethics of personal accountability: "[P]eople are expected to be accountable for their knowledge claims. . . . [It is] essential for individuals to have personal positions on issues and assume full responsibility for arguing their validity. . . . [It involves] utilizing emotion, ethics, and reason as interconnected, essential components in assessing knowledge claims."[49] This same position is taken by Margaret A. Simons. She reminds us: "[E]fforts on a theoretical level are not sufficient. We must extend our efforts to a personal and practical level as well. . . . As feminists, we must . . . confront racism. . . , as well as sexism, on both a personal and theoretical level. . . ."[50]

When we are able to confront both racism and sexism, we will begin to understand that oppression is far greater and more complex than racism and sexism alone. We will discover that our different standpoints on racism and sexism are only partial perspectives which are reconcilable. We will realize, as Audre Lorde points out, that human differences are not a matter of "simplistic opposition, superior-inferior, dominant-subordinate, good-bad."[51] Racism and sexism represent only two of the multilayered systems of oppression. Among the others are class, age, religion, ethnicity, and sexual orientation. We will begin to realize that the systems of oppression are intertwining, interlocking, and interconnecting, that an olympics of oppression is not possible. We usually encounter two or more systems of oppression at a given time. Too frequently we assume that one or two systems of oppression are the primary source of all oppression. This misconception sometimes causes us to support other systems of oppression. Indeed, in some instances we are the oppressor, while in others we are the oppressed.

Our reconceptualization of oppression as multilayered systems of inequities which operate at varying levels will provide us with a perspective for addressing the total reality of oppression, rather than only limited aspects. It will also become evident that there is a common thread between the multilayered systems of oppression, namely, power. That is, not reason but power as domination is a precondition of oppression that determines our social, economic, and political decisions. Thus, perspective will be provided for considering each other's standpoints without giving up our own or denying another's. As Elsa Barkley Brown explains, "[A]ll people can learn to center in another experience, validate it, and judge it by its own standards without need of comparison or need to adopt that framework as their own. Thus, one has no need to 'decenter' anyone in order to center someone else; one has only to constantly, appropriately, 'pivot the center.'"[52] It will become apparent that there is no need to perceive our differences as separating us. Rather, our differences represent multiple strengths which complement our commonalities. María Lugones and Elizabeth V. Spelman point out the urgent need for new transformative models to accommodate the rapidly changing circumstances of our society.[53] Both African American and white women are concerned about equal pay for equal work, the right to choose abortion, legal protection against domestic violence and rape, status of the homeless, adequate health care, federally subsidized day care, entry into traditionally male careers, quality education for all children, and the threat of nuclear war. Likewise, many of us concur that some males are indeed allies in our struggles against all systems of oppression. Differences are simply differences, no more or less. As Catharine A. MacKinnon states, differences cut both ways: just as you are different from me, I am different from you.[54] Johnnetta B. Cole's vision of a time "when differences will no longer make a difference"[55] can become a possibility. We can become empowered significantly to impact oppression through our knowledge, consciousness, and politics, if confronting reality is a criterion of our perspective.[56] Herein lie the twenty-first-century challenges for feminists, African American and white together.

Notes

I am indebted to Linda A. Bell, Earnest L. Curry, Judith M. Green, Lucius Outlaw, and Margaret S. Simons for their helpful comments on earlier drafts of this essay.

1. Arthur Brittan and Mary Maynard, *Sexism, Racism and Oppression* (New York: Basil Blackwell, 1984).

2. Ibid., 1.

3. Audre Lorde, *Sister Outsider* (New York: The Crossing Press, 1984), 115.

4. Sojourner Truth, "And Ain't I a Woman?," Women's Rights/Suffrage Convention, Akron, Ohio, May 29, 1851. Reprinted in *Women's America: Refocusing the Past*, 3rd ed., ed. Linda K. Kerber and Jane Sherron De Hart (Oxford: Oxford University Press, 1991).

5. Belle Kearney, quoted by Aileen Kraditor, *The Ideas of the Woman Suffrage Movement 1890–1920*, (New York: Columbia University Press, 1965), 202.

6. Elizabeth Hood, "Black Women, White Women: Separate Paths to Liberation," *Black Scholar* (April 1978): 45–56.

7. For other examples of African American women not being recognized *as women*, see Angela Davis's *Women, Race & Class* (New York: Vintage Press, 1981) and bell hooks's *Ain't I a Woman: Black Women and Feminism* (Boston: South End Press, 1981).

8. For a substantial discussion of numerous restrictions attached to the Fifteenth Amendment, white women's racial attack on it, white men's call for a repeal of it, and the significance of it to the Nineteenth Amendment for woman suffrage, see chapters 2, 3, and 4 of Bettina Aptheker's *Woman's Legacy: Essays on Race, Sex, and Class in American History* (Amherst: University of Massachusetts Press, 1982) and Eric Foner's *Reconstruction: America's Unfinished Revolution, 1863–1877* (New York: Harper & Row, 1988).

9. Josephine St. Pierre Ruffin, "The Beginnings of the National Club Movement," in *Black Women in White America: A Documentary History*, ed. Gerda Lerner (New York: Vintage Books, 1972), 443.

10. Rosalyn Terborg-Penn, "Discrimination Against Afro-American Women in the Women's Movement, 1830–1920," in *The Afro-American Woman: Struggles and Images*, ed. Rosalyn Terborg-Penn and Sharon Harley (Port Washington, N.Y.: Kennikat Press, 1987), 17.

11. Angela Y. Davis, *Women, Culture and Politics* (New York: Random House, 1989), 21.

12. Catherine Stimpson, "Thy Neighbor's Wife, Thy Neighbor's Servants: Women's Liberation and Black Civil Rights," in *Women in Sexist Society: Studies in Power and Powerlessness*, ed. Vivian Gormick and Barbara K. Moran (New York: New American Library, 1971), 650.

13. Lorde, *Sister Outsider*, 119.

14. Pauline Terrelong Stone, "Feminist Consciousness and Black Women," in *Women: A Feminist Perspective*, ed. Jo Freeman (Mountain View, Calif.: Mayfield, 1979), 583.

15. Margaret A. Simons, "Racism and Feminism: A Schism in the Sisterhood," *Feminist Studies* 5, no. 2 (1979): 384–401.

16. Ibid., 387–89. This is an excellent analysis in support of her thesis.

17. Ibid., 390.

18. hooks, *Ain't I a Woman*, 10.

19. Maxine Baca Zinn, Lynn Weber Cannon, Elizabeth Higginbotham, and Bonnie Thornton Dill, "The Costs of Exclusionary Practices in Women's Studies," *Signs* 11, no. 2 (1986): 290–303.

20. Ibid.

21. hooks, *Ain't I a Woman*, 8.

22. Elizabeth V. Spelman, "Theories of Race and Gender: The Erasure of Black Women," *Quest* 5, no. 4 (1982): 36–62. For additional discussion of the "additive analysis," see Angela Davis's "Reflections on the Black Woman's Role in the Community of Slaves," *The Black Scholar* 3, no. 4 (December 1971): 2–15.

23. Barbara Smith, "Notes for Yet Another Paper on Black Feminism or Will the Real Enemy Please Stand Up," *Conditions* 5 (1979): 123–27.

24. Deborah K. King, "Multiple Jeopardy, Multiple Consciousness: The Context of a Black Feminist Ideology," *Signs* 14, no. 1 (1988): 42–72.

25. Bonnie Thornton Dill, The Dialectics of Black Womanhood," *Signs* 4, no. 3 (1979): 543–55.

26. Frances Beale, "Double Jeopardy: To Be Black and Female," in *The Black Woman: An Anthology*, ed. Toni Cade (New York: New American Library, 1970).

27. Alice Walker, "One Child of One's Own: Meaningful Digression Within the Work(s)—An Excerpt," in *All the Women Are White, All the Blacks Are Men, But Some of Us Are Brave*, ed. Gloria T. Hull, Patricia Bell Scott, and Barbara Smith (New York: Feminist Press, 1982), 40.

28. Patricia Hill Collins, "The Social Construction of Black Feminist Thought," *Signs* 14, no. 4 (1989): 745–73.

29. Shirley Chisholm, *Unbought and Unbossed* (New York: Avon, 1970).

30. hooks, *Ain't I a Woman*, 7.

31. Hood, "Black Women, White Women," 48–49.

32. Lorde, *Sister Outsider*, 118.

33. Hood, "Black Women, White Women," 48–55.

34. Included among the books that address these questions and similar ones are the following: Bettina Aptheker, *Woman's Legacy: Essays on Race, Sex, and Class* (Amherst: University of Massachusetts Press, 1982), Chapter 7; Toni Cade, *The Black Woman: An Anthology* (New York: New American Library, 1970); Septima Poinsetta Clark, *Ready from Within* (New Jersey: Africa World, 1990); Shirley Chisholm, *Unbought and Unbossed* (New York: Avon, 1990); Jacqueline Jones, *Labor of Love, Labor of Sorrow: Black Women, Work, and the Family from Slavery to Present* (New York: Basic Books, 1985); Daniel Patrick Moynihan, *The Negro Family: The Case for National Action* (Washington, D.C.: GPO, 1965); LaFrances Rodgers-Rose, *The Black Woman* (Newbury Park, Calif.: Sage, 1980); and Michele Wallace, *Black Macho and the Myth of the Myth of the Superwoman* (New York: Dial, 1979).

35. bell hooks, *Talking Back: Thinking Feminist, Thinking Black* (Boston: South End Press, 1989), 37–38.

36. Alice Walker, *The Color Purple* (New York: Washington Square Press, 1982).

37. Nellie McKay, "Reflections on Black Women Writers: Revising the Literary Canon," in *Feminism: Anthology of Literary Criticism*, ed. Robyn Warhol and Diane Price Herndl (New Brunswick, N.J.: Rutgers University Press, 1991).

38. Harriet Wilson, *Our Nig, or Sketches From the Life of a Free Black in a Two Story White House, North Showing that Slavery Shadows Fall Even There* (Boston: George C. Rand and Avery, 1859; 2nd edition, New York: Vintage, 1983).

39. For other discussions of sexism and the institution of slavery, see Charles Ball, *Slavery in the United States: A Narrative of the Life and Adventures of Charles Ball, a Black Man* (Lewiston, Pa.: John W. Shugert, 1836); E. Franklin Frazier, *The Negro in the United States* (Chicago: University of Chicago Press, 1939); bell hooks, *Ain't I A Woman: Black Women and Feminism*; and La Frances Rodgers-Rose, *The Black Woman*.

40. See Toni Morrison's "Introduction: Friday on the Potomac" and Paula Giddings's "The Last Taboo" in *Race-ing Justice, En-gendering Power: Essays on Anita Hill, Clarence Thomas, and the Construction of Social Reality*, ed. Toni Morrison (New York: Pantheon Books, 1992).

41. Spelman, "Theories of Race and Gender," 37–38.

42. Ibid., 39, 41–42. For other examples of the "additive analysis," see Angela Y. Davis's "Reflections on the Black Woman's Role in the Community of Slaves" and Barbara Smith's "Notes For Yet Another Paper on Black Feminism or Will the Real Enemy Please Stand Up."

43. Spelman, "Theories of Race and Gender," 48–51. For additional analysis of the positions of Mary Daly, Kate Millet, and Shulamith Firestone, see

Margaret A. Simons's "Racism and Feminism: A Schism in the Sisterhood," 391–96.

44. Simons, "Racism and Feminism," 387–92.

45. Adrienne Rich, *On Lies, Secrets and Silence* (New York: Norton, 1979), 299.

46. Spelman, "Theories of Race and Gender," 55–56.

47. Hood, "Black Women, White Women," 47.

48. Lorde, *Sister Outsider,* 115.

49. Collins, "Black Feminist Thought," 768–69.

50. Simons, "Racism and Feminism," 397–99.

51. Lorde, *Sister Outsider,* 114.

52. Elsa Barkley Brown, "African-American Women's Quilting: A Framework for Conceptualizing and Teaching African-American Women's History," *Signs* 14, no. 4 (Summer 1989): 921–29.

53. María Lugones and Elizabeth V. Spelman, "Have We Got a Theory for You! Feminist Theory, Cultural Imperialism and the Demand for 'The Woman's Voice,'" *Woman's Studies International Forum* 6 (1983): 573–81.

54. Catharine A. MacKinnon, *Feminism Unmodified: Discourses on Life and Law* (Cambridge: Harvard University Press, 1987), 51.

55. *All American Women: Lines That Divide, Ties That Bind*, ed. Johnnetta B. Cole (New York: Free Press, 1986).

56. For examples of collaborative coalition models that begin to address the twenty-first-century challenges for African American and white feminists, see Judith M. Green and Blanche Radford Curry, "Recognizing Each Other Amidst Diversity: Beyond Essentialism in Collaborative Multi-Cultural Feminist Theory," *Sage: A Scholarly Journal on Black Women* 1. VIII, no. 1 (Summer 1991): 39–49; and Blanche Radford Curry, Judith Mary Green, Suzan Harrison, Carolyn Johnston, and Linda Lucas, "On the Social Construction of a Women's and Gender Studies Major," in *Gender and Academe: Feminist Pedagogy and Politics*, ed. Lagretta T. Lenker and Sara N. Deats (Lanham, Md.: Rowman & Littlefield, 1994), 3–18.

2

The Allure and Hold of Privilege: A Response to Blanche Radford Curry

Linda A. Bell

Responding to Blanche Radford Curry's presentation is both a pleasure and a challenge. On the one hand, it is particularly pleasurable to respond to analyses of important problems, especially when these are framed by a concern to envision and work for a less oppressive future society. On the other hand, and basically because of my fundamental agreement with what she says, an adequate response is a real challenge. I will try to explain what I mean by both of these comments, since particularly the second is likely to seem cryptic and mystifying to many. My remarks must be seen partially as a concurrence with and reiteration of Curry's paper and partially as a fairly privileged white woman's elaboration of, expansion of, and attempt to personally come to grips with some of Curry's major points.

I agree with Curry that the racist history of the so-called women's movement is discouraging. I am also disheartened by the classism and homophobia evinced by the movement. Too often white women have used the prerogatives accruing to them because of their whiteness, their class status, and even their heterosexuality to define issues of sexism and other problems facing "women." Too often white feminists have used labels like "women" and even "feminist" in ways that exclude not only females who are black, or Hispanic, or Asian, or Native American, but also white females who may be poor or lesbian or old or not able-bodied.

We must begin our discussions of feminist theory with the recognition of race and class as well as gender. Nonwhite and non-
privileged voices have been raised long enough and loudly enough
that we who are white and privileged no longer have any excuse
worthy of consideration for repeating in our own ways the arrogance of privilege—if indeed there ever was any acceptable excuse.

This brings me to my second point: why I believe it is important
but difficult for a white feminist to engage with Curry in critique
of the historical and continuing arrogance of white feminists, an
arrogance particularly distressing as we face a new century. I believe it is extremely important for whites to concur with this analysis and to educate ourselves on the links between racism and sexism
and on the very different ways sexism affects individuals of different races.

The task of educating ourselves and others is not an easy one.
Recently, two of my colleagues enthusiastically attacked a report
on the status of women faculty at Georgia State University. Their
attack focused on a point they were obviously proud of themselves
for having seen, namely, that the report discussed racism on campus as well as sexism. This, they claimed, was a major flaw, in
effect, a serious overstepping of the committee's "mandate" to
consider the status of "women." I asked, sarcastically and without
properly crediting Sojourner Truth, "Were black women, then, not
women?"

The problem I see is that too many white feminists are quite
aware when our male colleagues in academe and elsewhere use such
words as "whites," "humans," and, more offensively, "men" and
"mankind," in such a way as not to include us. We are generally,
however, not as attuned to the slights involved when these colleagues
and even we ourselves, like my male colleagues, use these and other
alleged "universals" in ways that exclude people of color. We are
even less aware of the ways in which the resulting invisibility of
large numbers of women and men jeopardizes their livelihoods, their
health, their happiness, and sometimes their very lives.

Educating others and ourselves is only the beginning. To move
into the twenty-first century with any reasonable hope for improve-
ment over what has gone before, we must focus attention on the
ways in which differences inevitably feed into systems of oppression in a complex system like ours, where hierarchies involving
domination form and inform, sometimes subtly, other times blatantly,

the most fundamental institutions and all of us to the extent that we participate in them.[1]

Like Curry, I agree with Audre Lorde that differences alone do not separate us. Nor are they, as many would have us believe, the root of hierarchy and domination. Rather, differences are just that, differences, no more and no less.[2] As Catharine MacKinnon notes, they cut both ways: to the extent that you are different from me, I am different from you.[3] It is only when we take those on one side as somehow representing or establishing the norm against which others are measured that hierarchy emerges and domination finds its support. Unfortunately, we live in a culture that takes the fairly well off, white, young, able-bodied, heterosexual male as the norm. In court cases, women are seen as asking for special treatment, for example, when they ask insurance programs to include maternity benefits. Even if the women point to such facts as the programs' benefits for hair transplants, they are still likely to lose. The transplants are justified as not parallel to maternity because, after all, transplants are covered for women as well as for men! Comparable reasoning that pregnancy benefits could be provided for men as well as women apparently is dismissed as just more special pleading. Heaven forbid that black women ask for coverage of medical problems tending to affect only blacks or, even worse, only black women!

The problem with the way this presumption affects all of us is that it is pervasive, insidious, and tempting. Our court system, our academic disciplines, and our very discourse constitute those who differ from the presumed norm as somehow in the wrong. This is what Simone de Beauvoir means when she says that woman is constituted as the other and as the second sex[4] (her point could be—and obviously needs to be—extended to apply to similar moves with respect to race). This presumption is made without fanfare and usually without any explicit acknowledgment thereof. In fact, sometimes we must cut through a great deal of data, justification, and rhetoric before we begin to realize that a norm has been presumed and that absolutely nothing else warrants the specific treatment of a particular individual or group.

The presumption of this norm offers some temptation even to those of us who differ from the norm. White women have succumbed to this temptation, and black women, though more consistently excluded, are, I think, not totally immune to the temptation. Because the norm is itself quite complex, many can partially identify with it. Although, for example, I am not male, I am white and can try to claim all of the cultural advantages of whiteness. Someone else, though not white, can, by virtue of being male, claim all of the prerogatives of maleness. Yet another, neither white nor male, could at least identify with the able-bodiedness or heterosexuality included in the norm, thereby laying claim to whatever advantages these aspects of "normalcy" may offer. The prerogatives offered to those who do not fit all of the aspects of the norm are not equal, are frequently though perhaps unequally subject to revocation because of the ways individuals do *not* fit, and are more often than not sops offered to the enormous number of individuals ultimately designated as "other" by the norm. Bell hooks makes this last claim when she discusses the attempt by black men to gain a share of power through affirming their maleness and at the expense of their black sisters.

Recognizing the ways in which difference connects with power in our society is necessary. If difference generally connects, as it does with black women, with lack of power and with oppression, lives may depend on this recognition. If, on the other hand, difference places individuals, for example, white women, on the side of power vis-à-vis particular individuals or groups, an acknowledgment of this power is necessary even if we try to renounce the power and place ourselves as equals with those to whom society gives less or perhaps no power. It is, as Marilyn Frye observes, those with power who have the prerogative to place themselves as equals with others.[5] Such an attempt must be acknowledged as an exercise of power at the same time that it seeks a divestiture from this power.

If feminists could only borrow Dorothy's ruby slippers and click our heels together while uttering the incantation "There is no inequality among women," we could ignore the problem. However, since we do not live in Oz and cannot rely on such magic, white feminists must acknowledge the intricate ways sexism and racism connect in ourselves and not just the ways they intersect in black women. It is an inescapable fact in our society that white women by virtue of being white share in the power accruing to whiteness in ways black women never can. This fact is inescapable even though it is also true that class and other factors also intersect with race and gender and result in radically different distributions of power even among white women. Marilyn Frye has discussed this in some detail, in this volume and elsewhere, but I reiterate it, partly because I believe it must be repeated until it receives the recognition it deserves, and partly because I think we continue, however inadvertently, to take white women as a norm unless we explicitly see not just black women but also white women as products of the intersection of race and gender. Alice Walker refers to the black woman's situation in this intersection as "the condition of twin afflictions,"[6] and Frances Beale calls it "double jeopardy."[7] Perhaps we should coin parallel terms for white women, but terms clearly affirming the conflicting power claims we must make about them: that white women are in jeopardy vis-à-vis white men and yet are able, in turn, to place those who are nonwhite in jeopardy.

Realistic hope for a better tomorrow requires not just clear-sighted analysis of the situations in which a complex system of oppression places individuals and groups. Our analysis must go beyond this to develop visions of a better society and strategies for moving our society in that direction. With even our imaginations fettered by the hierarchies and oppressions structuring our present society, we need to learn to dream beyond those restrictions, always, of course, subjecting our dreams to critical analysis. At the same time, we must develop strategies with which to subvert and undo the hierarchies and oppressions. These strategies must include, as Curry has recognized, clear consciousness of the ways we ourselves are embedded in these hierarchies and how our activities often unwittingly perpetuate them.

Finally, a bit of reflection on my remarks is in order. As I have built on Curry's paper, drawing from an assortment of feminist theorists, including bell hooks, Catharine MacKinnon, Marilyn Frye, María Lugones, Elizabeth V. Spelman, and Audre Lorde, I have become increasingly uncomfortable. My discomfort stems not from what I have said, all of which I firmly believe, but from my uncertainty concerning how what I argue applies to my own case as a white woman responding to the presentation of a black woman.

I began this response agreeing with Curry. As I have tried to place my agreement in a broader feminist analysis, I realize I have thereby left to some extent her initial concern with the dynamics between black women and white women. Although I believe I have done no more than develop a bit further "the multilayered systems of oppression" to which she refers, I am especially ill at ease with my claim that both black and white women may find temptations within the complex norm structuring our society and supporting existing dominations. I tried to distance myself from and ward off likely consequences of that recognition by indicating that the gains are not likely to be either equal or to the same degree irrevocable for different individuals, depending on which of the criteria specified by the norm they "meet" and try to use to gain privilege.

There remain, however, two dangers from which I have not freed my remarks. First, my remarks can be used too easily by whites to free themselves from the need to recognize their own power positions in the complex hierarchies structured by racism and sexism. From my experience I know that as soon as racists and sexists hear remarks such as I have made, they begin to weave them into justifications of their racism, sexism, and use of power to oppress others. I have heard too many whites smugly affirm that blacks are racist, too, without acknowledging that white, not black, racism structures the relations, opportunities, and power differentials within the society. Similarly, I have listened with dismay while discussions of male violence toward women and children have turned to women's battering and their abuse of children, ignoring and thus mystifying the structures of power and privilege that support even when they do not condone such violence by men but not by women.

Consequently, I feel it necessary to reiterate: nothing I have said warrants any oppression by one who is white and who uses power accruing to her or him by virtue of that whiteness.

Second, I do not wish to use my own white privilege to refocus the discussion and thus deflect the primary concern expressed in a presentation by a black woman. While I am forced by my own logic to admit that everything I have said is itself an exercise of my inescapable privilege, I want this concluding reflection on my earlier remarks and on the dynamic between Curry and myself at least to move in the direction of dismantling the effects of the privilege that ultimately must be abolished.

Unfortunately, in a situation where racism structures all of our lives and all of our interactions, even this concluding reflection may deflect the concern from illegitimate and unacceptable power and the exercise thereof to the problems white women face when they try to relate nonoppressively to those who are not white. It is all too easy to use white privilege to move the discussion to how difficult it is for white women (and men) to be politically correct.

Even worse, such discussion by whites is problematic since white privilege undercuts it by allowing us to take or receive too much credit for our effort. When a black person calls attention to white privilege and demands that we do something about it, she is not likely to receive much in the way of reward or congratulations for her efforts. She is more likely to be regarded as abrasive and demanding. On the other hand, when a white person accepts the challenge and tries to become aware of and to alter the privilege, the very privilege she disputes insidiously undermines her efforts by making those efforts seem generous and praiseworthy. When whites engage in the labor to which Curry points us, we must recognize that what we do is neither generous nor praiseworthy. Morally speaking, it is a minimum response for those with illegitimate power to develop an awareness of that power and to work to undermine the institutions that confer it.

In conclusion, I affirm both the necessity and the difficulty of developing, acting on, and altering the positions of power and privilege to which attention has been called. The difficulty of this task does not justify inaction. True, in an oppressive society, it is difficult—even impossible—to have truly clean hands and to *be* politically correct. Rather than lapsing into a litany of "poor, pitiful me," though, white women and men must resolve to get on with the twofold task Curry has pointed out to us: first, the theoretical clarification of the power structures informing virtually every aspect of our society and, second, the political dismantling of those structures. As she says, only then can we realistically hope for anything better in the coming century.

Notes

1. Diane L. Fowlkes, in her book *White Political Women: Paths from Privilege to Empowerment* (Knoxville: University of Tennessee Press, 1992), refers to this system as "complex domination."

2. Audre Lorde, *Sister Outsider* (Trumansburg, N.Y.: The Crossing Press, 1984).

3. Catharine A. MacKinnon, *Feminism Unmodified: Discourses on Life and Law* (Cambridge, Mass.: Harvard University Press, 1987), 51.

4. Simone de Beauvoir, "From *The Second Sex*," in *Visions of Women*, ed. Linda A. Bell (Clifton, N.J.: Humana Press, 1983), 441.

5. Marilyn Frye, "On Being White: Thinking Toward a Feminist Understanding of Race and Race Supremacy," in *The Politics of Reality: Essays in Feminist Theory* (Trumansburg, N.Y.: The Crossing Press, 1983), 110–27.

6. Alice Walker, "One Child of One's Own: Meaningful Digression Within

the Work(s)—An Excerpt," in *All the Women Are White, All the Blacks Are Men, But Some of Us Are Brave*, ed. Gloria T. Hull, Patricia Bell Scott, and Barbara Smith (New York: Feminist Press, 1982), 40.

7. Frances Beale, "Double Jeopardy: To Be Black and Female," in *The Black Woman: An Anthology*, ed. Toni Cade (New York: New American Library, 1970), 90–100.

3

"I Just See People": Exercises in Learning the Effects of Racism and Sexism

Bernita C. Berry

Are you White? middle class? college educated? How does racism affect you? Are you male? How does sexism affect you? Most majority group members (White males and females in terms of race, and men in general in terms of sex) can probably give at least one example of how racism and sexism affect members of minority groups (people of color and women in general). If members of the majority group are asked to give an example of how racism affects Whites or how sexism affects men, most would have problems comprehending the question. This is because in the United States majority group members are taught that they are *not* the recipients of racism or sexism. Whites and men are aware that racism and sexism are facts of life for certain groups of people in society. Many are ignorant of the sources of racism and sexism while at the same time denying that they are the beneficiaries of privileged status. Since White people and men are not, as such, members of minority groups, it is difficult for many of them to see how much they are affected by these 'isms.'

An important caveat is necessary here. It is true that women as a group have less power than men and groups such as Latinos, African Americans, and Native Americans have less power than Whites. The critical point here is that skin color privilege takes precedence over sex for White women, and male privilege takes precedence over race and ethnic identity for minority group males.[1] White women tend to downplay their race while enjoying it benefits, but they highlight the disadvantages associated with their sex. Minority males tend to focus on the negative consequences of their minority status while discounting the benefits accruing to them through a patriarchal social structure.

"I just see people; I don't see color." This statement and others like it, made by well-meaning and often well-educated White people, reflect a deeply hidden effect of racism. This statement reduces socially significant human differences to invisibleness and meaningless hype whereby one does not have to acknowledge what one does not see, that is, race and sex. Ultimately this statement means that the twin evils of racism and sexism may be reality for other people—"those minorities"—but they do not exist for the speaker.

This is apparent to me in the college classroom. The following class assignments, which I designed, demonstrate to students that everyone in society is affected by racism and sexism but not everyone is *consciously* aware of this. This is especially the case for males (sexism) and Whites (racism). Minority males and White females believe that White males are the only perpetuators and sustainers of racism and sexism. Few members of either of these privileged groups question the structure of a system that allows males to dominate women and allows Whites to dominate all minorities. White women, if they are "proper feminists," point the finger at White men (White "boys"), while African American men and Latino men see "the White man" as the problem. Women students, particularly at a women's college, may define themselves as feminists, but their attitudes and behaviors reflect racist tendencies. Further, White women become defensive when minority group women point out their racism to them.

"They Really Didn't Mean Anything by It"

Students enrolled in an introductory sociology class (all were women and all but two were White) were asked to observe the expressed attitudes and behaviors of their family members and close friends for a few days, looking for subtleties of racism. Some of the students were quite surprised to find that the people they love and respect exhibit prejudice and discrimination. Some were quick to rationalize these attitudes and behaviors as being caused by being born in the South ("they're from the South and they learned this growing up"), as a personality quirk, or as not really meaning anything (prejudicial). Students were not asked to look for instances of sexism; however, a few did include examples in their written reports. I deliberately did not include sexism in this exercise because it has been my experience that more, if not all, of the focus will be given to sexism, which tends to make racism seem less consequential to White women. Students have remarked in class that they are more aware of racism since having done the exercise.

"I Have No Problem with Dating Black Men"

I taught a gender course at a predominantly Black women's college while employed at a predominantly White women's college. Both colleges are in a major metropolitan area in the southern United States. A student in my class at the Black college suggested an exercise in which the Black campus students could have some interaction with the White campus students, since both are at women's colleges. I asked students at the White college if any would be willing to visit the Black college campus. Nine out of approximately thirty students made the trip to the Black college campus (including one student's mother and another student's daughter). All but three of the students from the White college were White. There were seven students enrolled in my class at the Black college; all were African American. I presented the group with a list of topics for discussion suggested by the students at the Black college. These included a local newspaper article on feminism and rape, the definition of feminism, *Playboy* magazine's pictorial presentation of women on women's college campuses, and male–female relationships. The latter two topics received considerable discussion. However, when the discussion changed to male–female relationships, two or three or the White women mentioned that they had dated or didn't mind dating Black men. I observed an immediate wall of silence and hostility from the Black women. For example, some of the Black students shifted in their seats, raised their eyebrows, or had discernible eye contact with each other. The White women were oblivious to this as they pointed out that they saw no difference in dating White men or Black men. "I didn't see his race; I just saw someone I liked." The session, which went a little overtime, ended with the White students feeling good about the experience and the Black students feeling angry.

In my next class session with the Black students, we discussed their feelings about and observations of what had transpired in the previous class session with the White students. They all said they left the class feeling angry. When asked why, one student explained that she purposely came to a predominantly Black college to get away from White people (her elementary and high school experiences were with White students). Others questioned why the White women students would think that their dating Black men would bond them to Black women. They were also angry with themselves for *not* pointing this out to the White women. There was a general feeling in the group that they did not want to carry out the second part of the exercise, which involved the Black students visiting the White college campus. I insisted that we complete the exercise as planned, and one week later the Black students traveled to the White college campus. I asked the same students from the White college who had attended the first session at the Black college campus to attend this session. Only two students (both White) were able to do so.

Prior to the session I gave each group of students a handout written by Marsha Houston, entitled "Why the Dialogues Are Difficult or 15 Ways a Black Woman Knows a White Woman's Not Listening,"[2] The discussion began with some general questions about campus life at the White college. Most of the discussion centered on the handout. The Black women talked much more than the White women. When we had completed our discussion of the handout, I asked if anyone had other comments or thoughts they would like to share. One of the Black students said she was upset by statements White students had made in the first session. The White students did not ask her to explain.

The next morning, I was met by one of the White women who was in the last class session with the Black students. She explained that she had not been able to figure out what was said at the first session to make the Black women upset. I asked her how she felt about having visited the Black college campus. She said it was fine and wanted to do it again. I asked her how she thought the Black women felt about the session. She said she cold not tell anything was wrong. I then told her about White women dating Black men. After about an hour, she was able to see partially why this angered Black women and placed distance between Black women and White women. She wanted me to give her *the* answer so that she would not make *that* mistake again. She left my office feeling better now that she had an answer to her question, but I had the feeling that she still did not fully understand the issues.

"What Do You Mean?"

In my classes on race and ethnicity and social problems, I noticed that when students are questioned about the effects of racism on minorities and the effects of sexism on women they can usually provide an answer. When they are asked about the effects of racism on Whites or the effects of sexism on men, there is a look of puzzlement on their faces. One student asked, "What do you mean?" I asked the students if they thought racism affected White people. They were hesitant to answer, although they did agree that racism affects Whites, but not in the same way that it affects, for example, African Americans. A similar situation occurred when I asked whether sexism affects men. It was at this point that I decided to make this a class assignment. Students were asked, first, to delineate, purely on the basis of their own life experiences thus far, the effects of racism on Whites and the effects of sexism on men, and then to find men to answer the sexism question and Whites to answer the racism question. The men could be any race and ethnic group and the Whites could be female or male. Students submitted a written report and the assignment was discussed in class. Some students said this was the hardest assignment they had ever had. When asked why, they said it was something they had never thought about. This was especially the case for racism affecting Whites. Underlying feelings of guilt and defensiveness were prominent in the students' written reports.

Discussion

These class exercises helped students become aware of how they and others in society are affected by racism and sexism. Some students said they had become more attuned to their own attitudes and behaviors and those of their family and friends. Some have been moved to the point where they now discuss, question, challenge, and confront racist and sexist behaviors in others while working on their own attitudes and behaviors. Not all students enjoyed these assignments, but the assignments certainly satisfied my objective of challenging the students' thinking.

Racism and sexism have never been nor will they ever be problems just for members of minority groups. Minority groups are not the "cause" of the differential treatment they experience. But by ignoring the effects of racism and sexism on majority group members, we continue to view inequality as something that happens only to minorities. In other words, as long as whites see racism as something that happens to people of color and they are unaffected by this, they will not examine their behavior toward people of color or even their existence in relation to people of color. This is especially the case if their behavior is not explicitly racist. "I treat all people the same whether they're Black, White, blue or polka-dotted." Since blue or polka-dotted people do not exist, the point is moot. We live in a society that values Whites over Blacks, and males over females, with institutions structurally reflecting this hierarchy. When children grow up in a society that treats White male presidents as normal and the possibility of a woman, Latina, African, Jew, or Arab president as abnormal, how can they not be adversely affected in their outlook? Patriarchy and White supremacy are the major culprits that have distorted White people's taken-for-granted view of themselves as "normal" and engendered men's belief that divine intervention (or was it inspiration?) created their position of dominance.

It is imperative that we as a society begin to acknowledge that racism and sexism do indeed affect majority group members. I agree that White men are not affected by these twin evils in the same way as are minority group members. However, to say that White men are not affected at all is untrue. White males see certain positions as exclusively theirs and authority and power as rightfully their domain. This gives White males a false sense of who they are (consciously and unconsciously) while maintaining a dangerous precedent in society.

The demographics of the United States are changing: populations of people of color are increasing; young, upwardly mobile, educated Whites are having fewer children or choosing to remain childless; and White men will not be able to hold all positions of power forever because their relative numbers are dwindling and people of color and women are moving into power positions. It is hoped that this will not be White women replacing White men or men of other racial and ethnic groups replacing White men. As people of color and women increase their numbers in positions of power and authority, they will do well not to perpetuate the White male model.

Notes

I would like to thank Tina Pippin, Martha Rees, and Linda Bell for their helpful comments and constructive critiques. An earlier version of this paper was presented at the Enhancing Teaching Conference, Charleston, South Carolina, in February 1993.

1. For a perceptive analysis of White privilege and its relationship to male privilege, see Peggy McIntosh, "White Privilege: Unpacking the Invisible Knapsack," in *Peace and Freedom* (July–August, 1989): 10–12.

2. This essay by Marsha Houston lets Black women know they are not alone when experiencing any one of the fifteen ways she has compiled. When I presented this paper to the Black women students, there was immediate identification with its content. Marsha Houston, "Why the Dialogues Are Difficult or 15 Ways a Black Woman Knows When a White Woman's Not Listening," presented at Spelman College.

Appendix

Why the Dialogues Are Difficult or 15 Ways a Black Woman Knows When a White Woman's Not Listening

Marsha Houston

These are some of the ways in which, during ordinary conversations or public discussions, I have observed white women deny black women's experiences of womanhood or redefine them in white women's terms.

You know she's not listening when the topic is racism and . . .

1. She calls you "confrontational."
   (Although blacks and whites have different communication styles, especially when involved in argument or debate, cutting off discussion unless the other person adopts your style is a vicious means for silencing them, denying their experience, and generally avoiding the discussion of the very issues which divide us.)

2. She tries to convince you that racism is:
   {i}   a figment of your imagination.
   {ii}   not as important to women's lives as sexism.
   {iii}   no different in form or effect from the occasional "hard times" everybody experiences in America.

3. She asserts that she's not prejudiced because she doesn't "see color" (that is, race); she just sees "human beings."

This is what I call the fallacy of "generically packaged" people. It assumes that people can or should be perceived as devoid of sex, race, height, weight, physical ability, age, socioeconomic class, gender, ethnicity and all other innate and socially learned characteristics that define them as fully human beings. In my experience, anyone who feels she must "ignore" or "overlook" any human characteristic does so because she *judges* that characteristic as negative.

To "overlook" another woman's race is to make a negative (that is, racist) judgment about her.

4. She projects the prospect of racial equality into some distant, imaginary future by telling you that "amalgamation of the races" through intermarriage is the "only way" to really improve race relations.

5. She sees black people, not racism, as a "problem" to be "solved." This "problem people" perspective strikes me as much like that which Hitler took toward the Jews.

You know she's not listening when the topic is scholarship about black women . . .

6. You delineate the effects of the dual oppression of racism and sexism, and she criticizes you for "defining the problem" but not telling how to "solve" it.

7. She insists that you *translate* your research on black women into terms with which she feels comfortable, which she is willing to accept, terms that challenge none of her preconceptions or misconceptions.

8. She asks you to explain why some black women you don't know behaved toward her in a way she didn't like or couldn't comprehend in some situation in which you were not present.

The perception is that, because you study black women, you should be able to explain the behavior of *every* black woman toward *every* white person in *every* situation—even if all you know about the black woman in question is that she is black and female!

9. She "studies" black women but refuses to associate with them and/or to regard any of them as her intellectual peers.

You know she's not listening when the subject is your own experiences as a black woman and . . .

10. She tells you that you "don't talk like a black woman," or are in some other way atypically black.
    This is the "you're the exception" ploy, a "divide and conquer" strategy.

11. She says she understands *your* experience as a member of a "minority group" because
    {i}   her parents are European immigrants.
    {ii}   she's physically handicapped.
    {iii} she's a lesbian.
    {iv}   she's overweight.
    {v}   she once attended a wedding/funeral/party in a black community and she was the only white woman there.
    Similar experiences are not *the same* experiences; they can mask important *differences* that should be respected and appreciated.

12. She says she understands your experience as a "woman of color" because she has a close friend who's Chinese-American/Puerto Rican/Mexican-American, etc.
    The experiences of women of color are *not* interchangeable.

13. She assures you she understands the black female experience because:
    {i}   she was raised by this "wonderful" black nanny "who was just like one of the family."
    {ii}   she's married to/sleeping with a black man (or a black woman).
    {iii} she watches the "Cosby Show" (and just lo-oves Felicia Rashad) or "Oprah."
    {iv}   she read *The Color Purple* or saw *The Women of Brewster Place*, etc., etc.

14. She assures you she understands black women's experiences with black men because:

{i}   she's married to/sleeping with a black man.

{ii}   she watches "Oprah" or the "Cosby Show" (and just lo-oves Bill).

{iii}   she read *The Color Purple* or saw *The Women of Brewster Place*, etc., etc.

{iv}   she attended *one* lecture (or many lectures), took one course, etc.

I call this one the "quick fix" fallacy, the misconception that one can learn about women of another ethnic group quickly and vicariously, that is, without interacting with any real-life female members of that group and without engaging in a life-long commitment.

15. She assumes that you *expect* her to *understand* your experience in the same way that she does her own, when all you want is that she respect and appreciate your experience, which is all one outside your "culture" can do.

Part II

Theoretical Considerations

4

The Uncompleted Argument: Du Bois and the Illusion of Race

Kwame Anthony Appiah

Contemporary biologists are not agreed on the question of whether there are any human races, despite the widespread scientific consensus on the underlying genetics. For most purposes, however, we can reasonably treat this issue as terminological. What most people in most cultures ordinarily believe about the significance of "racial" difference is quite remote, I think, from what the biologists *are* agreed on. Every reputable biologist will agree that human genetic variability between the populations of Africa and Europe and Asia is not much greater than that within those populations, though *how much* greater depends, in part, on the measure of genetic variability the biologist chooses. If biologists want to make interracial difference seem relatively large, they can say that "the population of genic variation attributable to racial differences is . . . 9–11%."[1] If they want to make it seem small, they can say that for two people who are both Caucasoid, the chances of difference in genetic constitution at one site on a given chromosome are currently estimated at about 14.3 percent, while for any two people taken at random from the human population, they are estimated at about 14.8 percent. (I discuss why this is considered a measure of genetic difference in the next section.) The statistical facts about the distribution of variant characteristics in human populations and subpopulations are the same, however the matter is expressed. Apart from the visible morphological characteristics of skin, hair, and bone, by which we are inclined to assign people to the broadest racial

categories—black, white, yellow—there are few genetic characteristics to be found in the population of England that are not found
in similar proportions in Zaire or in China; and few (though more)
that are found in Zaire but not in similar proportions in China or in
England. All this, I repeat, is part of the consensus.[2] A more familiar part of the consensus is that the differences between peoples in
language, moral affections, aesthetic attitudes, or political ideology—those differences which most deeply affect us in our dealings with each other—are not biologically determined to any significant degree.

These claims will, no doubt, seem outrageous to those who confuse the question of whether biological difference accounts for our
differences with the question of whether biological similarity accounts for our similarities. Some of our similarities as human beings in these broadly cultural respects—the capacity to acquire human
languages, for example, or, more specifically, the ability to smile—
are to a significant degree biologically determined. We can study
the biological basis for these cultural capacities and give biological explanations of our exercise of them. But if biological difference between human beings is unimportant in these explanations—
and it is—then racial difference, as a species of biological difference,
will not matter either.

In this essay I discuss the way in which W. E. B. Du Bois—who
called his life story the "autobiography of a race concept"—came
gradually, though never completely, to assimilate the unbiological
nature of races. I have made these prefatory remarks partly because it is my experience that the biological evidence about race is
not sufficiently known and appreciated but also because the fore-
going statements are important in discussing Du Bois. Throughout
his life, Du Bois was concerned not just with the meaning of race
but with the truth about it. We are more inclined at present, however, not to express our understanding of the intellectual development of people and cultures as a movement toward the truth; I sketch
some of the reasons for this at the end of the essay. I begin, therefore, by saying what I think the rough truth is about race, because,
against the stream, I am disposed to argue that this struggle toward
the truth is exactly what we find in the life of Du Bois. He can
claim, in my view, to have thought longer, more engagedly, and
more publicly about race than did any other social theorist of our
century.

"The Conservation of Races"

Du Bois's first extended discussion of the concept of race is in "The Conservation of Races" (1897), a paper he delivered to the American Negro Academy in the year it was founded. The "American Negro," he declares, has "been led to . . . minimize race distinctions" because "back of most of the discussions of race with which he is familiar, have lurked certain assumptions as to his natural abilities, as to his political, intellectual and moral status, which he felt were wrong." He continues: "Nevertheless, in our calmer moments we must acknowledge that human beings are divided into races," even if when we "come to inquire into the essential difference of races we find it hard to come at once to any definite conclusion." For what it is worth, however, the "final word of science, so far, is that we have at least two, perhaps three, great families of human beings—the whites and Negroes, possibly the yellow race."[3]

Du Bois is not, however, satisfied with the final word of nineteenth-century science. For, as he thinks, what matter are not the "grosser physical differences of color, hair and bone" but the "differences—subtle, delicate and elusive, though they may be—which have silently but definitely separated men into groups."[4]

> While these subtle forces have generally followed the natural cleavage of common blood, descent and physical peculiarities, they have at other times swept across and ignored these. At all times, however, they have divided human beings into races, which, while they perhaps transcend scientific definition, nevertheless, are clearly defined to the eye of the historian and sociologist.
>
> If this be true, then the history of the world is the history, not of individuals, but of groups, not of nations, but of races. . . . What, then, is a race? It is a vast family of human beings, generally of common blood and language, always of common history, traditions and impulses, who are both voluntarily and involuntarily striving together for the accomplishment of certain more or less vividly conceived ideals of life.[5]

We have moved, then, away from the "scientific"—that is, biological and anthropological—conception of race to a sociohistorical notion. Using this sociohistorical criterion—the sweep of which certainly encourages the thought that no biological or anthropological definition is possible—Du Bois considers that there are not three but eight "distinctly differentiated races, in the sense in which history tells us the word must be used."[6] The list is an odd one: Slavs, Teutons, English (both in Great Britain and America), Negroes (of Africa and, likewise, America), the Romance race, Semites, Hindus, and Mongolians.

> The question now is: What is the real distinction between these nations? Is it the physical differences of blood, color and cranial measurements? Certainly we must all acknowledge that physical differences play a great part. . . . But while race differences have followed mainly physical race lines, yet no mere physical distinctions would really define or explain the deeper differences—the cohesiveness and continuity of these groups. The deeper differences are spiritual, psychical, differences—undoubtedly based on the physical, but infinitely transcending them.[7]

Each of the various races is "striving, . . . in its own way, to develop for civilization its particular message, its particular ideal, which shall help to guide the world nearer and nearer that perfection of human life for which we all long, that 'one far off Divine event.'"[8] For Du Bois, then, the problem for the Negro is the discovery and expression of the message of his or her race.

> The full, complete Negro message of the whole Negro race has not as yet been given to the world.
>   The question is, then: how shall this message be delivered; how shall these various ideals be realized? The answer is plain: by the development of these race groups, not as individuals, but as races. . . . For the development of Negro genius, of Negro literature and art, of Negro spirit, only Negroes bound and welded together, Negroes inspired by one vast ideal, can work out in its fullness the great message we have for humanity.
>   For this reason, the advance guard of the Negro people—the eight million people of Negro blood in the United States of America—must soon come to realize that if they are to take their just place in the van of Pan-Negroism, then their destiny is *not* absorption by the white Americans.[9]

Du Bois ends by proposing his Academy Creed, which begins with words that echo down almost a century of American race relations:

> 1. We believe that the Negro people, as a race, have a contribution to make to civilization and humanity, which no other race can make.

2. We believe it the duty of the Americans of Negro descent, as a body, to maintain their race identity until this mission of the Negro people is accomplished, and the ideal of human brotherhood has become a practical possibility.[10]

What can we make of this analysis and prescription? On the face of it, Du Bois's argument in "The Conservation of Races" is that "race" is not a scientific—that is, biological—concept. It is a sociohistorical concept. Sociohistorical races each have a "message" for humanity—a message which derives, in some way, from God's purpose in creating races. The Negro race has still to deliver its full message, and so it is the duty of Negroes to work together—through race organizations—so that this message can be delivered.

We do not need the theological underpinnings of this argument. What is essential is the thought that through common action Negroes can achieve, by virtue of their sociohistorical community, worthwhile ends which will not otherwise be achieved. On the face of it, then, Du Bois's strategy here is the antithesis in the classic dialectic of reaction to prejudice. The thesis in this dialectic—which Du Bois reports as the American Negro's attempt to "minimize race distinctions"—is the denial of difference. Du Bois's antithesis is the acceptance of difference, along with the claims that each group has its part to play; that the white race and its racial Other are related not as superior to inferior but as complementaries; and that the Negro message is, with the white one, part of the message of humankind.

I call this pattern the classic dialectic for a simple reason: we find it in feminism also—on the one hand, a simple claim to equality, a denial of substantial difference; on the other, a claim to a special message, revaluing the feminine Other not as the helpmeet of sexism, but as the New Woman. Because this *is* a classic dialectic, my reading of Du Bois's argument is a natural one. I believe that it is substantially correct. But to see that it is correct, we need to make clear that what Du Bois attempts, despite his own claims to the contrary, is not the transcendence of the nineteenth-century scientific conception of race—as we shall see, he relies on it—but rather, as the dialectic requires, a revaluation of the Negro race in the face of the sciences of racial inferiority. We can begin by analyzing the sources of tension in Du Bois's allegedly sociohistorical conception of race, which he explicitly sets over against the scientific conception. The tension is plain enough in his reference to "common blood"; for this, dressed up with fancy craniometry, a dose of melanin, and some measure for hair-curl, is what the scientific notion amounts to. If he has fully transcended the scientific notion, what is the role of this talk about "blood"?

We may leave aside for the moment the common "impulses" and the voluntary and involuntary "strivings." These must be due either to a shared biological inheritance, "based on the physical, but infinitely transcending" it; to a shared history; or, of course, to some combination of these. If Du Bois's notion is purely sociohistorical, then the issue is common history and traditions; otherwise, the issue is, at least in part, a common biology. We shall know which only when we understand the core of Du Bois's conception of race.

The claim that a race generally shares a common language is also plainly inessential: the "Romance" race is not of common language nor, more obviously, is the Negro. And "common blood" can mean little more than "of shared ancestry," which is already implied by talk of a "vast family." At the center of Du Bois's conception, then, is the claim that a race is "a vast family of human beings, . . . always of common history [and] traditions." So, if we want to understand Du Bois, our question must be: What is a family of common history?

We already see that the scientific notion, which presupposes common features in virtue of a common biology derived from a common descent, is not fully transcended. A family can, it is true, have adopted children, kin by social rather than biological law. By analogy, therefore, a vast human family might contain people joined not by biology but by an act of choice. But it is plain that Du Bois cannot have been contemplating this possibility: like all of his contemporaries, he would have taken for granted that race is a matter of birth. Indeed, to understand the talk of "family," we must distance ourselves from its sociological meaning. A family is almost always culturally defined only through either patrilineal or matrilineal descent. But if an individual drew a "conceptual" family tree back over five hundred years and assumed that he or she was descended from each ancestor in only one way, it would have more than a million branches at the top. Although in such a case many individuals would be represented by more than one branch—that far back we are all going to be descended from many people by more than one route—it is plain that either a matrilineal or patrilineal conception of our family histories drastically underrepresents the biological range of our ancestry. Biology and social convention go startlingly different ways. Let's pretend, secure in our republicanism, that the claim of the queen of England to the throne depends partly on a single line from one of her ancestors nine hundred years ago. If there were no overlaps in her family tree, there would be more than fifty thousand billion such lines, though there have never been that many people on the earth; even with reasonable assumptions about overlaps, there are millions of such lines. We chose one line, even though most of the population of England is probably descended from William the Conqueror by *some* uncharted route. Biology is democratic: all parents are equal. Thus, to speak of two people as being of common ancestry requires that before some historical point in the past, a large proportion of the branches in their respective family trees coincided.[11]

Already, then, Du Bois requires, as the scientific conception does, a common ancestry (in the sense just defined) with whatever—if anything—that ancestry biologically entails. But apparently this does not commit him to the scientific conception, for there are many groups of common ancestry—ranging from humanity in general to narrower groups such as the Slavs, Teutons, and Romance people taken together— which do not, for Du Bois, constitute races. Thus, Du Bois's "common history," which must be what is supposed to distinguish Slav from Teuton, is an essential part of his conception. The problem is whether a common history can be a criterion that distinguishes one group of human beings—extended in time—from another. Does adding a notion of common history allow us to make the distinctions between Slav and Teuton or between English and Negro? The answer is no.

Consider, for example, Du Bois himself. As the descendant of Dutch ancestors, why doesn't his relationship to the history of Holland in the fourteenth century (which he shares with all people of Dutch descent) make him a member of the Teutonic race? The answer is straightforward: the Dutch were not Negroes; Du Bois is. But it follows from this that the history of Africa is part of the common history of African Americans not simply because African Americans descended from various peoples who played a part in African history but rather because African history is the history of people of the same race.

My general point is this: in order to recognize two events at different times as part of the history of a single individual, we have to have a criterion for identity of the individual at each of those times, independent of his or her participation in the two events. In the same way, when we recognize two events as belonging to the history of one race, we have to have a criterion for membership in the race at those times, independent of the participation of the members in the two events. To put it more simply: sharing a common group history cannot be a criterion for being members of the same group, for we would have to be able to identify the group in order to identify *its* history. Someone in the fourteenth century could share a common history with me through our membership in a historically extended race only if something accounts both for his or her membership in the race in the fourteenth century and for mine in the twentieth. That something cannot, on pain of circularity, be the history of the race. Whatever holds Du Bois's races together conceptually cannot be a common history; it is only because they are bound together that members of a race at different times can share a history at all. If this is true, Du Bois's reference to a common history cannot be doing any work in his individuation of races. And once we have stripped away the sociohistorical elements from Du Bois's definition of race, we are left with the true criterion.

Consequently, not only the talk of language, which Du Bois admits is neither necessary (the Romance race speaks many languages) nor sufficient (African Americans and Americans generally speak the same language) for racial identity, must be expunged from the definition; now we have seen that talk of common history and traditions must go too. We are left with common descent and the common impulses and strivings that I put aside earlier. Since common descent and the characteristics that flow from it are part of the scientific conception of race, these impulses are all that remain to do the job that Du Bois had claimed for a sociohistorical conception: namely, to distinguish his conception from the biological one. Du Bois claims that the existence of races is "clearly defined to the eye of the historian and sociologist."[12] Since biology acknowledges common ancestry as a criterion, whatever extra insight is provided by sociohistorical understanding can be gained only by observing the common impulses and strivings. Reflection suggests, however, that this cannot be true. For what common impulses—whether voluntary or involuntary—do the Romance people share that the Teutons and the English do not?

Du Bois had read the historiography of the Anglo-Saxon school, which accounted for the democratic impulse in America by the racial tradition of the Anglo-Saxon moot. He had read American and British historians in earnest discussion of the "Latin" spirit of Romance peoples; and perhaps he had believed some of it. Here perhaps may be the source of the notion that history and sociology can observe the differing impulses of races.

In all these writings, however, such impulses are allegedly discovered to be the a posteriori of racial and national groups, not criteria of membership in them. It is, indeed, because the claim is a posteriori that historical evidence is relevant to it. And if we ask what common impulses history had detected that allow us to recognize the Negro, we will see that Du Bois's claim to have found a criterion of identity in these impulses is mere bravado. If, without evidence about his or her impulses, we can say who is a Negro, then it cannot be part of what it is to be a Negro that he or she has them; rather, it must be an a posteriori claim that people of a common race, defined by descent and biology, have impulses, for whatever reason, in common. Of course, the common impulses of a biologically defined group may be historically caused by common experiences—common history. But Du Bois's claim can only be that biologically defined races happen to share, for whatever reason, common impulses. The common impulses cannot be a criterion of group membership. And if that is so, we are left with the scientific conception.

How, then, is it possible for Du Bois's criteria to issue in eight groups, while the scientific conception issues in three? The reason is clear from the list. Slavs, Teutons, English, Hindus, and Romance peoples each live in a characteristic geographical region. (American English—and, for that matter, American Teutons, American Slavs, and American Romance people—share recent ancestry with their European "cousins" and thus share a relation to a place and certain languages and traditions.) Semites and Mongolians each inhabit a rather large geographical region also. Du Bois's talk of common history conceals his superaddition of a geographical criterion: group history is, in part, the history of people who have lived in the same place.[13]

The criterion Du Bois actually uses amounts to this: people are members of the same race if they share features in virtue of being descended largely from people of the same region. Those features may be physical—hence African Americans are Negroes—or cultural—hence Anglo-Americans are English. Focusing on one sort of feature—"grosser . . . differences of color, hair and bone"— defines "whites and Negroes, possibly the yellow race" as the "final word of science, so far." Focusing on a different feature— language and shared customs—defines instead Teutons, Slavs, and

Romance peoples. The tension in Du Bois's definition of race reflects the fact that, for the purposes of European historiography (of which his Harvard and University of Berlin training had made him aware), it was the latter that mattered; but for the purposes of American social and political life, it was the former.

The real difference in Du Bois's conception, therefore, is not that his definition of race is at odds with the scientific one. It is, rather, as the classic dialectic requires, that he assigns to race a moral and metaphysical significance different from that of his contemporaries. The distinctive claim is that the Negro race has a positive message, a message not only of difference but of value. And that, it seems to me, is the significance of the sociohistorical dimension: the strivings of a race are, as Du Bois viewed the matter, the stuff of history. "The history of the world is the history, not of individuals, but of groups, not of nations, but of races, and he who ignores or seeks to override the race idea in human history ignores and overrides the central thought of all history."[14] By studying history, we can discern the outlines of the message of each race.

Crisis: **August 1911**

We have seen that, for the purpose that concerned him most—understanding the status of the Negro—Du Bois was thrown back on the scientific definition of race, which he officially rejected. But the scientific definition (Du Bois's uneasiness with which is reflected in his remark that races "perhaps transcend scientific definition") was itself threatened as he spoke at the first meeting of the Negro Academy. In the later nineteenth century most thinking people (like too many even today) believed that what Du Bois called the "grosser differences" were a sign of an inherited racial essence which accounted for the intellectual and moral deficiency of the "lower" races. In "The Conservation of Races" Du Bois elected, in effect, to admit that color was a sign of a racial essence but to deny that the cultural capacities of the black-skinned, curly-haired members of humankind were inferior to those of the white-skinned, straighter-haired ones. But the collapse of the sciences of racial inferiority led Du Bois to deny the connection between cultural capacity and gross morphology—the familiar impulses and strivings of his earlier definition.

We can find evidence of his change of mind in an article in the August 1911 issue of the *Crisis*.

The leading scientists of the world have come forward[15] . . . and laid down in categorical terms a series of propositions which may be summarized as follows:

1. (a) It is not legitimate to argue from differences in physical characteristics to differences in mental characteristics. . . .

2. (b) The civilization of a . . . race at any particular moment of time offers no index to its innate or inherited capacities.[16]

These results have been amply confirmed since then. And we do well, I think, to remind ourselves of the current picture.

Human characteristics are genetically determined, to the extent that they are determined, by sequences of DNA in the chromosomes—in other words, by genes.[17] The region of a chromosome occupied by a gene is called a locus. Some loci are occupied in different members of a population by different genes, each of which is called an allele; and a locus is said to be polymorphic in a population if there is at least one pair of alleles for it. Perhaps as many as half the loci in the human population are polymorphic; the rest, naturally enough, are monomorphic.

Many loci have not just two alleles but several, and each has a frequency in the population. Suppose a particular locus has n alleles, which we can call 1, 2, and so on up to n; then we can call their frequencies x_1, x_2, . . . , to x_n. If we consider two randomly chosen members of a population and look at the same locus on one chromosome of each of them, the probability that they will have the same allele at that locus is just the probability that they will both have the first allele (x_1^2) plus the probability that they will both have the second (x_2^2) plus the probability that they will both have the nth (x_n^2). We can call this number the expected homozygosity at that locus: it is just the proportion of people in the population who would be homozygous at that locus—having identical alleles at that locus on each of the relevant chromosomes—provided the population is mating at random.[18]

Now if we take the average value of the expected homozygosity for all loci, polymorphic and monomorphic (which, for some reason, tends to get labeled J), we have a measure of the chance that two people, taken at random from the population, will share the same allele at a locus on a chromosome taken at random. This is a good measure of how similar in biology a randomly chosen pair of individuals should be expected to be *and* a good (though rough) guide to how closely the populations are genetically related.

I can now express simply one measure of the extent to which

members of the human populations we call races differ more from each other than they do from members of the same race. For example, the value of J for Caucasoids—based largely on samples from the English population—is estimated to be about 0.857, while that for the whole human population is estimated at 0.852.[19] The chances, in other words, that two people taken at random from the human population will have the same characteristic at a locus are about 85.2 percent, while the chances for two (white) people taken from the population of England are about 85.7 percent. And since 85.2 is 100 minus 14.8 and 85.7 is 100 minus 14.3, this is equivalent to what I said earlier: the chances of two people who are both Caucasoid differing in genetic constitution at one site on a given chromosome are about 14.3 percent, while for any two people taken at random from the human population they are about 14.8 percent. The conclusion is obvious: given only a person's race, it is hard to say what his or her biological characteristics will be, except in respect of the "grosser" features of color, hair, and bone (the genetics of which are, in any case, rather poorly understood)—features of "morphological differentiation," as the evolutionary biologist would say. As Nei and Roychoudhury express it, somewhat coyly, "The extent of genic differentiation between human races is not always correlated with the degree of morphological differentiation." [20]

To have established that race is relatively unimportant in explaining biological differences between people, where biological difference is measured in the proportion of differences in loci on the chromosome, is not yet to show that race is unimportant in explaining cultural difference. It could be that large differences in intellectual or moral capacity are caused by differences at very few loci and that at these loci all (or most) black-skinned people differ from all (or most) white-skinned or yellow-skinned ones. As it happens, there is little evidence for any such proposition and much against it. But suppose we had reason to believe it. In the biological conception of the human organism, in which characteristics are determined by the pattern of genes in interaction with environments, it is the presence of the alleles (which give rise to these moral and intellectual capacities) that accounts for the observed differences in those capacities in people in similar environments. So the characteristic racial morphology—skin and hair and bone—could only be a sign of those differences if it were (highly) correlated with those alleles. Furthermore, even if it were so correlated, the causal explanation of the differences would be that they differed in those alleles, not that they differed in race. Since there are no such strong correlations, even those who think that intellectual and moral character are strongly genetically determined must accept that *race* is at best a poor indicator of capacity.

But it was earlier evidence, pointing similarly to the conclusion that "the genic variation within and between the three major races of man . . . is small compared with the intraracial variation"[21] and that differences in morphology were not correlated strongly with intellectual and moral capacity, that led Du Bois in the *Crisis* to an explicit rejection of the claim that biological race mattered for understanding the status of the Negro:

> So far at least as intellectual and moral aptitudes are concerned, we ought to speak of civilizations where we now speak of races. . . . Indeed, even the physical characteristics, excluding the skin color of a people, are to no small extent the direct result of the physical and social environment under which it is living. . . . These physical characteristics are furthermore too indefinite and elusive to serve as a basis for any rigid classification or division of human groups.[22]

This is straightforward enough. Yet it would be too swift a conclusion to suppose that Du Bois here expresses his deepest convictions. After 1911, he went on to advocate Pan-Africanism, as he had advocated Pan-Negroism in 1897, and whatever African Americans and Africans, from Ashanti to Zulu, share, it is not a single civilization.

Du Bois managed to maintain Pan-Africanism while officially rejecting talk of race as anything other than a synonym for color. We can see how he did this by turning to his second autobiography, *Dusk of Dawn*, published in 1940.

Dusk Of Dawn

In *Dusk of Dawn*—the "essay toward an autobiography of a race concept"—Du Bois explicitly allies himself with the claim that race is not a scientific concept.

> It is easy to see that scientific definition of race is impossible; it is easy to prove that physical characteristics are not so inherited as to make it possible to divide the world into races; that ability is the monopoly of no known aristocracy; that the possibilities of human

development cannot be circumscribed by color, nationality, or any conceivable definition of race.[23]

But we need no scientific definition, for

all this has nothing to do with the plain fact that throughout the world today organized groups of men by monopoly of economic and physical power, legal enactment and intellectual training are limiting with determination and unflagging zeal the development of other groups; and that the concentration particularly of economic power today puts the majority of mankind into a slavery to the rest.[24]

Or, as he puts it pithily a little later, "the black man is a person who must ride 'Jim Crow' in Georgia."[25]

Yet, just a few pages earlier, he has explained why he remains a Pan-Africanist, committed to a political program which binds all this indefinable black race together. The passage is worth citing extensively. Du Bois begins with Countée Cullen's question, "What is Africa to me?" and answers,

Once I should have answered the question simply: I should have said "fatherland" or perhaps better "motherland" because I was born in the century when the walls of race were clear and straight; when the world consisted of mut[u]ally exclusive races; and even though the edges might be blurred, there was no question of exact definition and understanding of the meaning of the word. . . .

Since then [the writing of "The Conservation of Races"] the concept of race has so changed and presented so much of contradiction that as I face Africa I ask myself: what is it between us that constitutes a tie which I can feel better than I can explain? Africa is, of course, my fatherland. Yet neither my father nor my father's father ever saw Africa or knew its meaning or cared overmuch for it. My mother's folk were closer and yet their direct connection, in culture and race, became tenuous; still, my tie to Africa is strong. On this vast continent were born and lived a large portion of my direct ancestors going back a thousand years or more. The mark of their heritage is upon me in color and hair. These are obvious things, but of little meaning in themselves; only important as they stand for real and more subtle differences from other men. Whether they do or not, I do not know nor does science know today.

But one thing is sure and that is the fact that since the fifteenth century these ancestors of mine and their other descendants have had a common history; have suffered a common disaster and have one long memory. The actual ties of heritage between the individuals of this group, varying with the ancestors that they have in common [with] many others: Europeans and Semites, perhaps Mongolians, certainly American Indians. But the physical bond is least and the badge of color relatively unimportant save as a badge; the real essence of this kinship is its social heritage of slavery; the discrimination and insult; and this heritage binds together not simply the children of Africa, but extends through yellow Asia and into the South Seas. It is this unity that draws me to Africa.[26]

This passage is affecting, powerfully expressed. We might like to be able to follow it in its conclusions. But we should not; since the passage seduces us into error, we should begin distancing ourselves from the appeal of its argument by noticing how it echoes an earlier text. Color and hair are unimportant save "as they stand for real and more subtle differences," Du Bois says here, and we recall the "subtle forces" that "generally followed the natural cleavage of common blood, descent and physical peculiarities" of "The Conservation of Races." There it was an essential part of the argument that these subtle forces—"impulses" and "strivings"—were the common property of those who shared a "common blood"; here, Du Bois does "not know nor does science" whether this is so. But if it is not so, then, on Du Bois's own admission, these "obvious things" are "of little meaning." If they are of little meaning, then his mention of them marks, on the surface of his argument, the extent to which he cannot quite escape the appeal of the earlier conception of race.

Du Bois's yearning for the earlier conception which he prohibited himself from using accounts for the pathos of the gap between the unconfident certainty that Africa is "of course" his fatherland and the concession that it is not the land of his father or his father's father. What use is such a fatherland? What use is a motherland with which your own mother's connection is "tenuous"? What does it matter that a large portion of his ancestors have lived on that vast continent, if there is no subtler bond with them than brute— that is, culturally unmediated—biological descent and its entailed "badge" of hair and color?

Even in the passage that follows Du Bois's explicit disavowal of the scientific conception of race, the references to "common history"—the "one long memory," the "social heritage of slavery"— only leads us back into the now familiar move of substituting a sociohistorical conception of race for the biological one; but that is simply to bury the biological conception below the surface, not to transcend it. Because he never truly "speaks of civilization," Du Bois cannot ask if there is not in American culture—which undoubtedly *is* his culture—an African residue to take hold of and rejoice in, a subtle connection mediated not by genetics but by intentions, by meaning. Du Bois has no more conceptual resources here for explicating the unity of the Negro race—the Pan-African identity— than he had in "The Conservation of Races" half a century earlier. A glorious non sequitur must be submerged in the depths of the argument. It is easily brought to the surface.

If what Du Bois has in common with Africa is a history of "discrimination and insult," then this binds him, by his own account, to "yellow Asia and . . . the South Seas" also. How can something he shares with the whole nonwhite world bind him to only a part of it? Once we interrogate the argument here, a further suspicion arises that the claim to this bond may be based on a hyperbolic reading of the facts. Du Bois's experience of "discrimination and insult" in his American childhood and as an adult citizen of the industrialized world was different in character from that experienced by, say, Kwame Nkrumah in colonized West Africa; it is absent altogether in large parts of "yellow Asia." What Du Bois shares with the nonwhite world is not insult but the *badge* of insult; and the badge, without the insult, is the very skin and hair and bone which it is impossible to connect with a scientific definition of race.

Concluding Unscientific Postscript

Du Bois died in Nkrumah's Ghana, led there by the dream of Pan-Africanism and the reality of American racism. If he escaped that racism, he never completed the escape from race. The logic of his argument leads naturally to the final repudiation of race as a term of difference and to speaking instead "of civilizations where we now speak of races." The logic is the same logic that has brought us to speak of genders where we spoke of sexes, and a rational assessment of the evidence requires that we should endorse not only the logic but the premises of each argument. I have only sketched the evidence for these premises in the case of race, but it is all there in the scientific journals. Discussing Du Bois has been largely a pretext for adumbrating the argument he never quite managed to complete.

I think the argument is worth making because I believe that we—scholars in the academy—have not done enough to share it with our fellow citizens. One barrier facing those of us in the humanities has been methodological. Under Saussurian hegemony, we have too easily become accustomed to thinking of meaning as constituted by systems of differences purely internal to our endlessly structured *langues*.[27] Race, we all assume, is, like all other concepts, constructed by metaphor and metonymy; it stands in, metonymically, for the Other; it bears the weight, metaphorically, of other kinds of difference.

Yet, in our social lives away from the text-world of the academy, we too easily take reference for granted. Even if the concept of race *is* a structure of oppositions—white opposed to black (but also to yellow), Jew opposed to Gentile (but also to Arab)—it is a structure whose realization is, at best, problematic and, at worst, impossible. If we can now hope to understand the concept embodied in this system of oppositions, we are nowhere near finding referents for it. The truth is that there are no races: there is nothing in the world that can do all we ask "race" to do for us. The evil that is done is done by the concept and by easy—yet impossible—assumptions as to its application. What we miss through our obsession with the structure of relations of concepts is, simply, reality.

Talk of "race" is particularly distressing for those of us who take culture seriously. For, where race works—in places where "gross differences" of morphology are correlated with "subtle differences" of temperament, belief, and intention—it works as an attempt at a metonym for culture; and it does so only at the price of biologizing what *is* culture, or ideology. To call it "biologizing" is not to consign our concept of race to biology. What is present there is not our concept but our word only. Even the biologists who believe in human races use the term "race," as they say, "without any social implication."[28] What exists "out there" in the world—communities of meaning, shading variously into each other in the rich structure of the social world—is the province not of biology but of hermeneutic understanding.

I have examined these issues through the writings of Du Bois, with the burden of his scholarly inheritance, and have tried to transcend the system of oppositions that, had Du Bois accepted it, would have left him opposed to the (white) norm of form and value. In his early work, Du Bois took race for granted and sought to revalue one pole of the opposition of white to black. The received concept is a hierarchy, a vertical structure, and Du Bois wished to rotate the axis, to give race a "horizontal" reading. Challenge the assumption that there can be an axis, however oriented in the space of values, and the project fails for loss of presuppositions. In his later work, Du Bois—whose life's work was, in a sense, an attempt at just this impossible project—was unable to escape the notion of race he had explicitly rejected. We may borrow his own metaphor: though he saw the dawn coming, he never faced the sun. And we must surely admit that he is followed in this by many in our culture today; we too live in the dusk of that dawn.

Notes

1. Masatoshi Nei and Arun K. Roychoudhury, "Genetic Relationship and Evolution of Human Races," *Evolutionary Biology* 14 (1983): 11.
2. Ibid., 1–59.
3. W. E. B. Du Bois, "The Conservation of Races," in *W. E. B. Du Bois Speaks: Speeches and Addresses, 1890–1919*, ed. Philip S. Foner (1897; New York: Pathfinder Press, 1970), 73, 74, 75.
4. Ibid., 75.
5. Ibid., 75–76.
6. Ibid., 76.
7. Ibid., 78.
8. Ibid.
9. Ibid., 78, 79. This talk of racial absorption (and similar talk of racial extinction) reflects the idea that African Americans might disappear because their genetic heritage would be diluted by the white one. This idea might be considered absurd in any view propounding the notion of a racial essence: either a person has it or he/she doesn't. But this way of thinking conceives of racial essences as being like genes, though Mendelian genetics was not yet "rediscovered" when Du Bois wrote this piece. Du Bois is probably thinking of "passing for white"; in views of inheritance as the blending of parental "blood," the more that black "blood" is diluted, the more it is likely that *every* person of African descent in America *could* pass for white. That, of course, would be a kind of extinction of the Negro. It is interesting that those who discuss this issue assume that it would not cause the extinction of the white race also and the creation of a "hybridized" human race. But, as I say, such speculation is ruled out by the rise of Mendelian genetics.
10. Du Bois, "The Conservation of Races," 84.
11. I owe this way of thinking about the distance between social and biological ancestry to chapter 6 of R. B. Le Page and A. Tabouret-Keller's forthcoming book, *Acts of Identity*. I am very grateful to R. B. Le Page for allowing me to see a typescript.
12. Du Bois, "The Conservation of Races," 75.

13. This seems to me the very notion that the biologists have ended up with: a population is a group of people (or, more generally, organisms) occupying a common region (or, more generally, an environmental niche), along with people largely descended from that original group who now live in other regions. See Nei and Roychoudhury, "Genetic Differences between Caucasian, Negro, and Japanese Populations," *Science* 177 (August 1972): 434–35, and "Genetic Relationship," 4.

14. Du Bois, "The Conservation of Races," 75.

15. This claim was prompted by G. Spiller; see *Papers in Inter-Racial Problems Communicated to the First Universal Races Congress Held at the University of London, July 26–29, 1911*, ed. G. Spiller (New York: Arno Press, 1969 [1911].

16. W. E. B. Du Bois, "Races," *Crisis* 2, no. 4 (August 1911): 157–59.

17. Strictly we should say that the character of an organism is fixed by genes, along with sequences of nucleic acid in the cytoplasm and some other features of the cytoplasm of the ovum. But these latter sources of human characteristics are largely swamped by the nucleic DNA and are, in any case, substantially similar in almost all people. It is the latter fact that accounts, I think, for their not being generally mentioned.

18. It follows from these definitions that where a locus is monomorphic, the expected homozygosity is going to be one.

19. These figures come from Nei and Roychoudhury, "Genetic Relationship," and I have used the figures derived from looking at proteins, not blood-groups, since they claim these are likely to be more reliable. I have chosen a measure of "racial" biological difference that makes it look spectacularly small, but I would not wish to imply that it is not the case, as these authors say, that "genetic differentiation is real and generally statistically highly significant" (8, 11, and 41). I would dispute their claim that their work shows the existence of a biological basis for the classification of human races; what it shows is that human populations differ in their distributions of genes. That *is* a biological fact. The objection to using this fact as a basis of a system of classification is that far too many people don't fit into just one category that can be so defined.

20. Nei and Roychoudhury, "Genetic Relationship," 44.

21. Ibid., 40.

22. Du Bois, "Races," 158.

23. W. E. B. Du Bois, *Dusk of Dawn: An Essay toward an Autobiography of a Race Concept* (New York: Schocken, 1968 [1940]), 137.

24. Ibid., 137–38.

25. Ibid., 153.

26. Ibid., 116–17.

27. Post-structuralism is not a step forward here, as Terry Eagleton has observed (see *Literary Theory: An Introduction* [Oxford, 1983], 143–44).

28. Nei and Roychoudhury, "Genetic Relationship," 4.

5

On W. E. B. Du Bois's "The Conservation of Races"

Lucius Outlaw

There is, of course nothing more fascinating than the question of the various types of mankind and their intermixture.

W. E. B. Du Bois[1]

"Race" and Contemporary Politics in the United States of America

Among many problems faced by Americans today are those that in very substantial ways continue to involve troublesome valorizations of "race": that is, value-laden conceptualizations of combinations of inherited biological characteristics, cultural traditions (for example, language, arts and literature, religion, forms of life in general), and histories of origins and continuities associated with specific geographic settings. This is true, as well, for problematic situations in which what is at issue, directly or indirectly, is "ethnicity": value-laden conceptions of cultural factors primarily (practices, traditions, histories, sites of origin and occupancy), not biological features, as the distinguishing and identity-forming factors that define a group of people. In both cases the factors are thought to combine in various ways to make up the distinctive racial or ethnic identity of a group of people and are regarded as being key to the meaningfulness, authenticity, and legitimacy of the lives of the members of the group.

Adding to the complexity of the situation is the fact that any particular racial group is further divided into a number of ethnies (ethnic groups) or nationalities that continue to develop and evolve and among whom conflicts can and do arise. And because the terms "race" and "ethnic group" are often used interchangeably, it is difficult to grasp all of the complexities and nuances of problematic situations in which race and ethnicity are contested matters in order to achieve consensual understandings that are much needed today to facilitate the realization of social peace and harmony on the basis of democratic justice. For much as W. E. B. Du Bois predicted, what he referred to as "the problem of the color line"—that is, problematic relations between races distinguished first by their lighter and darker skin tones—has been one of the major problems of the twentieth century. And while there have been substantial achievements in this nation in recent decades in social relations, in jurisprudence, in political life, and in the formation and application of policies in public and private institutions that have addressed some of the conflicts involving race and ethnicity, we are not yet on the verge of realizing complete social peace and harmony, with justice, as a result of having resolved all problems involving these still complex matters. One of the major reasons for this is the fact that in this nation we are not on the verge of achieving consensus regarding the principles and policies by which justice might be realized in situations in which race and ethnicity are involved as highly charged factors. In fact, we are living through yet another period of heightened tensions and continuing social struggle in which race and ethnicity are central issues as the persons involved identify themselves and/or are identified as members of racial or ethnic groups and claims for justice are framed in terms that valorize race or ethnicity in various ways.

For many persons such valorizations improperly sanction the resurgence of what they regard as anachronistic, divisive, and socially disruptive particularist sentiments and conceptions concerning *groups* which were supposed to have been displaced by the "self-evident" universalist conceptions and principles concerning *individuals* ("all men are created equal") that are the foundation of the political organization of the United States as *the* historically paradigmatic, distinctively modern, democratic, Liberal nation. For these persons neither race nor ethnicity should have any place whatsoever in the formation of ideals and principles of social order and justice or in the conception of what it is to be a human being, even though, in some anthropological sense, there are different races and ethnies. However, for other people the reality of different races and ethnic groups is one of the most obvious features of our social worlds. The factors of racial and ethnic difference are *real* and thus fundamentally constitutive of different groups such that each member of the group shares them, more or less, and is substantially identified by them. Ethnicity and race must therefore be taken into account in important instances when devising social principles and applying them in practice. Moreover, for many people who continue to suffer oppression, invidious discrimination, and diminished life chances and quality of life because of their race and/or ethnicity, their struggles for freedom and justice that involve valorizations of race and ethnicity are the continuation of ongoing and unfinished efforts to achieve justice with dignity. Such struggles are necessitated by a long history of institutionalized failures on the part of empowered persons of one or more of the socially dominant ethnies of the "white" race to apply principles for ordering social, political, and economic life and the administration of justice—that is, to apply them to all persons "without regard for race, creed, color, sex, or national origin." The seeming universal applicability of norms regarding "Man" ostensibly incorporated in the founding principles of this nation as it was being constructed was in fact restricted primarily to a privileged "white" race, allowing many of them to practice formally rationalized and legitimated racism and invidious ethnocentrism: that is, to disparage, oppress, and otherwise subordinate other races and ethnies. From the outset, America was a racialized, hierarchic nation-state structured by white supremacy and further complicated by class and gender hierarchies. Social power was restricted almost exclusively to property-owning males of particular ethnies of people of European descent, that is, to the white race.

Thus, struggles against racism and invidious ethnocentrism (and against sexism as well) are for many persons necessitated by what they regard as serious inadequacies in the very notion of the human being that is at the center of modern Liberal political principles. Many who regard the cluster of factors that together constitute the race or ethnicity of a group of persons as crucial to their very being and identity consider the abstract "Man" at the core of Liberal principles as insufficient for characterizing persons concretely. Moreover, in a nation-state made complex by different racial and ethnic groups and by long and continuing legacies of racism and invidious ethnocentrism, justice, it is thought, cannot be realized without giving due regard to race and ethnicity.

However, even those who are thus committed are also conditioned by—and often committed to—the complex of modern Liberal principles that require, in important respects, in important contexts, and for important purposes that all persons be treated as having a shared *essential* identity as human beings, without regard to a person's race or ethnicity, among other things. Each citizen must have an equal opportunity to acquire resources critical to the realization of life, liberty, and the pursuit of happiness, including equality before the law and the enjoyment of the rights, privileges, and responsibilities of free citizens. Multiple commitments to diverse and seemingly divergent principles thus add to the complexities and tensions of contemporary American social life.

The increased number, widespread appearance, and intensity of struggles in the present era centering around race and ethnicity challenge us to transform the ways in which many of us have come to think of ourselves and of this nation. The two agendas—a politics of identity and recognition which seeks respect and empowerment for racial and ethnic groups, on one hand; on the other, affirmation of the common humanity of all peoples, thus regarding all persons as in essence "the same"—are so difficult to reconcile that they stretch the fabric of contemporary American society and threaten social and political unity, particularly as racial and ethnic demographic changes continue to increase the numbers of "peoples of color" in the population.[2] Recently several of the critical issues involved in this historic demographic shift were raised in poignant fashion in a cover story in *Time* magazine, in which it was noted, "Someday soon, surely much sooner than most people who filled out their Census forms . . . realize, white Americans will become a minority group. Long before that day arrives, the presumption that the 'typical' citizen of the United States is someone who traces his or her descent in a direct line to Europe will be part of the past."[3] This rapidly developing situation is prompting major changes in American society and posing major challenges to social ordering and the administration of justice. Along the way, however, in all areas of social, political, economic, and private life, empowered persons and others hoping to become empowered will continue their organized efforts to maintain or secure and, in either case, rationalize advantages gained for persons in their racial or ethnic groups.

Is it possible to resolve the problems in which race and ethnicity are the bases of tensions and social struggles and thereby substantially reduce—if not completely eliminate—threats to social order and political unity by achieving and maintaining harmony and justice while allowing for the recognition, celebration, and nurturing of racial and ethnic differences? Doing so by conceiving a set of principles and related practices, securing widespread consensus in support of them, and institutionalizing them as a framework that structures social life overall is a daunting task. For this will require substantial revisions of some of the most fundamental conceptions, values, and practices and their intellectual underpinnings that support the partial, but ideologically and politically dominant, consensus with regard to the complex of universalist notions of human being and attendant political ideals that have significantly defined and shaped modern American life. Foremost among them is the principle that race and ethnicity should not be factors in determining or recognizing the fundamental being and worth of a person, individually or as a member of a particular group, nor in deciding who is or can be a citizen in political communities and, thereby, what rights each citizen enjoys. A revision of this commitment such that race and ethnicity become explicit factors in achieving social justice, and in understanding the historical and social being of a person, requires conceptualizations of race and ethnicity that are compatible with likewise revised and enlightened principles of justice, order, and harmony. But doing so while preserving the achievements of social ordering won through modern universalist principles is a major challenge. And part of this challenge is a consideration of race on the way to a rethinking of the philosophical anthropology of Liberalism.

Toward a (Re-)conception of "Race"

What is to be achieved by a rethinking of "race"?[4] It would be a contribution to the fulfillment of the revised agenda of modern critical thought: that is, enlightened, mediating understanding that guides the way to possible resolutions of difficulties involving race by the promotion of (and practical effort to realize) "progressive" or "emancipatory" social evolution. What I have in mind is the development of new forms of shared self-understanding—and corresponding forms of social practice—devoid of the conflicts resting on inappropriate valorizations and rationalizations of race, for the "emancipatory project"[5] that was at the center of the modern Enlightenment has, in numerous instances, foundered on the crucible of race (and those of ethnic, gender, and class groupings of persons). The persistence of struggles around matters involving race present those of us informed by and committed to traditions of critical thought and practice with unresolved problems. Among them is the need for a critical review of these traditions that will reveal the extent to which they have failed to accommodate race appropriately: that is, to provide understandings that are sufficiently enlightening as to be compelling for understanding ourselves, individually and collectively, and for understanding social reality at large. Such understandings are needed to assist efforts to mobilize persons and groups to effect social reconstructions that realize emancipatory promises and possibilities in situations in which problems of race are involved. It may well be that we will need to review what we think will constitute "emancipation" and determine whether our notions coincide with struggles to realize aspirations to liberation and self-realization that are part of the traditions of various racial groups in our nation.

An effort to rethink race must be sensitive to several matters. First, there is the lack of stability and precision in the very idea of race. A close review of the history of efforts by natural philosophers and their subsequent replacements, natural and social scientists, to identify various "races," for example, leads one to the decisive conclusion that race is only partially a function of biology. Even then biology alone does not *determine* race, but in complex interplay with environmental, cultural, and social factors provides not yet fully understood boundary conditions and possibilities that affect "raciation" (that is, the development of the relatively distinctive gene pools of various groups which, along with social and cultural factors, determine the relative frequencies of "statistically covarying properties" shared by group members, but certainly not by them alone) and the development of "geographical races."[6] Race is thus to be understood as a cluster concept that brings together biological, cultural, and geographical properties in "indefinitely long disjunctive definitions" in which the properties do not define a race by each property being "severally necessary and the entire set of necessary properties . . . jointly sufficient."[7] Further, I am convinced that any definition of race, to a great extent, is a function of prevailing norms and strategies (on the first level, those constitutive of the everyday life-world in which ideas, attitudes, and valuations of race are elements of common sense; on the second level, those constituted by the discursive rules of communities of "experts") that are always subject to challenge and change. "Racial" categories, though they refer, in part, to biological characteristics, are in large part socially determined rather than simply reflecting "natural kinds" or a population of individuals who are what they are necessarily by virtue of intrinsic properties that are "severally necessary and jointly sufficient" to constitute their defining nature or essence.[8] To this extent both the concept of race and that of racial categories refer to heterogeneous complexes of socially normed biological and cultural factors. The biological features in racial distinctions are conscripted into projects of cultural, political, and social construction.

A review of the career of race in America makes this clear. One such review is Howard Winant and Michael Omi's *Racial Formation in the United States*.[9] A central feature of their analysis is the notion of "racial formation," a concept intended to displace race as an "essence" ("as something fixed, concrete and objective . . .") or, alternatively, as a "mere illusion, which an ideal social order would eliminate." For Winant and Omi, the meaning of race is socially constructed and changes as a consequence of social struggle, hence is irreducibly political. Thus, race should be understood as

> *an unstable and 'decentered' complex of social meanings constantly being transformed by political struggle*. . . . The crucial task . . . is to suggest how the widely disparate circumstances of individual and group racial identities, and of the racial institutions and social practices with which these identities are intertwined, are formed and transformed over time. This takes place . . . through *political contestation over racial meanings*.[10]

Part of the strength of Winant and Omi's view lies in the conceptionalization of race as a "formation," an approach that makes possible an appreciation of the politics involved in any construction of notions of race and does so within the context of a theory of social evolution where learning is a central feature.[11] This places at our disposal the prospects of an understanding of race in keeping with the original promises of critical thought: enlightenment leading to emancipation. Social learning regarding race, steered by critical social thought, might help us to move beyond racism, without socially unnecessary reductionism that promotes an amorphous universalism, to a socially productive pluralist democracy.

Lest we move too quickly here, however, the other side of race must still be explored: that is, the lived experiences of those who are part of identified and self-identified racial groups, particularly those that have been subordinated in the American racialized social hierarchy. That the notion of race cannot be constructed and secured by the authority of biological or other sciences as an unvarying *essence* determinable and constitutive of "natural kinds" does *not* mean, thereby, that there is no real referent for the term and that "race" is void of positive social value. The exploration of race through the lived experiences of groups of people whose subordination has been rationalized via strategies of racialization is required before we can have an adequate understanding that truly contributes to enlightenment and emancipation. What must be provided for is the possibility of appreciating the integrity of those who see themselves through the prism of race. In so doing, however, we need not hypostatize race as a fixed and heritable essence shared equally by all members of a given group. On the other hand, we need not err yet again in thinking that "race thinking" must be completely eliminated on the way to enlightened thought that will lead the way to fuller social emancipation for oppressed peoples.

That elimination is, I think, unlikely—and unnecessary. Certainly the invidious, socially unnecessary, divisive forms and consequences of thought and practice associated with race ought to be eliminated, to whatever extent possible. For, in the United States in particular, yet another compelling conjuncture has been reached in a long historical saga: the need to achieve further democratization in a multiethnic and multiracial society where "group thinking" is a decisive and increasingly highly valorized feature of intellectual, social, cultural, economic, and political life. Critical understandings of race and ethnicity that contribute to the learning and social evolution that secure democratic emancipation in the context of racial and ethnic diversity would be of no small consequence. Such understandings are needed as many of us struggle to find ways through the maze of "the politics of difference." W. E. B. Du Bois's 1897 essay "The Conservation of Races" is an important example of how one might work toward an understanding of race that is appropriate for a democratic society composed of a plurality of races and ethnies.[12] I shall review Du Bois's approach while defending it against the recently advanced strong criticisms of Kwame Anthony Appiah.[13]

"The Conservation of Races": Du Bois and Appiah

"The Conservation of Races" has long been a particularly rich resource of strategic insight for me. I was prompted recently to return to it once again as a result of my dissatisfaction with a discussion by Anthony Appiah of Du Bois's notion of "race" as set out in "The Conservation of Races" and in another essay by Du Bois published in the August 1911 issue of *Crisis* magazine. According to Appiah, the strategy in Du Bois's argument is the "antithesis" of what Appiah calls the "classic dialectic of reaction to prejudice," namely, a denial of difference. Rather, Du Bois's strategy involves "the acceptance of difference, along with a claim that each group has its part to play; that the white race and its racial Other are related not as superior to inferior but as complementaries; that the Negro message is, with the white one, part of the message of humankind."[14] And this strategy is predicated on Du Bois's understanding that "race" cannot be defined on the basis of biological factors alone:

> Although the wonderful developments of human history teach that the grosser physical differences of color, hair and bone go but a short way toward explaining the different roles which groups of men have played in Human Progress, yet there are differences— subtle, delicate and elusive, though they may be—which have silently but definitely separated men into groups. While these subtle forces have generally followed the natural cleavage of common blood, descent and physical peculiarities, they have at other times swept across and ignored these. At all times, however, they have divided human beings into races, which, while they perhaps transcend scientific definition, nevertheless, are clearly defined to the eye of the Historian and Sociologist.
>
> . . . *What, then, is a race? It is a vast family of human beings, generally of common blood and language, always of common history, traditions and impulses, who are both voluntarily and involuntarily striving together for the accomplishment of certain more or less vividly conceived ideals of life.*[15]

According to Appiah, though Du Bois attempts to transcend the nineteenth-century biology-based scientific conception of race, he does not succeed and, in Appiah's reading, relies on it while, following the "requirement" of the dialectic, engaging in "a revaluation of the Negro race in the face of the sciences of racial inferiority." The evidence for this reading? Du Bois's reference to "common blood" in his definition: "for this, dressed up with fancy craniometry, a dose of melanin, and some measure for hair-curl, is what the scientific notion amounts to. If he has fully transcended the scientific notion, what is the role of this talk about 'blood'? . . . If Du Bois's notion is purely sociohistorical, then the issue is common history and traditions; otherwise, the issue is, at least in part, a common biology."[16]

However, as I read him, Du Bois has *not* offered a definition of race that is intended as "purely sociohistorical." Rather, he seeks to have the concept of *race* include both sociohistorical or cultural factors (language, history, traditions, "impulses," ideals of life) and biological factors (a *family* of "common blood"). A crucial question is how Du Bois's definition is to be understood. Stated differently, we should interrogate the strategizing, as well as the sociohistorical goal and objectives that it serves, that is part of the structuring project in which Du Bois's defining effort should, I think be properly situated. I will return to this subject later in the discussion.

Appiah goes on to isolate, analyze, and evaluate *individually* each of the elements in Du Bois's definition (a strategy of critique that is, I think, key to what I regard as Appiah's misreading of Du Bois). While Du Bois includes in his conception of race the idea that members of a racial group "generally" share a common language, Appiah regards this as "plainly inessential."[17] Where Du Bois speaks of a race as a "vast family," Appiah takes this as evidence that Du Bois did not transcend the nineteenth-century scientific notion "which presupposes common features in virtue of a common biology derived from a common descent. . . ." Continuing, Appiah argues that "A family can . . . have adopted children, kin by social rather than biological law. By analogy . . . a vast human family might contain people joined not by biology but by an act of choice. But it is plain that Du Bois cannot have been contemplating this possibility: like all of his contemporaries, he would have taken for granted that race is a matter of birth."[18] This is an odd claim, for in the second paragraph following Appiah notes that Du Bois was a descendant of Dutch (as well as of African) ancestors yet identified himself as a member of the Negro race. Was there no choice involved in his doing so? It is not "plain" to me that there was not. Rather, I read Du Bois as following social conventions in appropriating in his own way a socially imposed racial identity linked to a particular line of his ancestry.

As for whether a common history "can be a criterion that distinguishes one group of human beings—extended in time—from another . . . ," Appiah claims "[t]he answer is no. . . ." He continues,

[I]n order to recognize two events at different times as part of the history of a single individual, we have to have a criterion for identity of the individual at each of those times, independent of his or her participation in the two events . . . sharing a common group history cannot be a criterion for being members of the same group, for we would have to be able to identify the group in order to identify *its* history. Someone in the fourteenth century could share a common history with me through our membership in a historically extended race only if something accounts both for his or her membership in the race in the fourteenth century and for mine in the twentieth. That something cannot, on pain of circularity, be the history of the race. Whatever holds Du Bois's races together conceptually cannot be a common history; it is only because they are bound together that members of a race at different times can share a history at all.[19]

Consequently, says Appiah, common history and traditions, along with language, "must go too" as criteria. Here, I think, Appiah is wrong: the strategy would be circular (and viciously so) only if common history were the *only* criterion. As one criterion among others taken severally, however, its use is not circular.

This seems to Appiah to leave Du Bois's common descent and common impulses and strivings as the remaining criteria that must do the work of providing a sociohistorical definition of race. Since common descent is tied to biology and, on Appiah's reading, Du Bois wanted a "purely sociohistorical" definition, common descent, according to Appiah, cannot be used as a criterion. That would leave common impulses. However, he says, these cannot be criteria of membership in a racial group but, if detected, can only be what he terms "a posteriori properties":

If, without evidence about his or her impulses, we can say who is a Negro, then it cannot be part of what it is to be a Negro that he or she has them; rather, it must be an a posteriori claim that people of a common race, defined by descent and biology, have impulses, for whatever reason, in common. Of course, the common impulses of a biologically defined group may be historically caused by common experiences, common history. But Du Bois's claim can only be that biologically defined races happen to share, for whatever reason, common impulses. The common impulses cannot be a criterion of group membership. And if that is so, we are left with the scientific conception.[20]

After his critical, eliminative analysis Appiah concludes that what remains of Du Bois' criteria will not support the effort to define race in a purely sociohistorical way. Further, the notion of a common group history, he argues, conceals a "superadded geographical criterion": "group history is, in part, the history of people who have lived in the same place."[21] Consequently, Du Bois's criterion "actually . . . amounts to this: people are members of the same race if they share features in virtue of being descended largely from people of the same region. Those features may be physical . . . or cultural. . . ." Du Bois's definition of race, Appiah claims, thus founders on a tension that "reflects the fact that, for the purposes of European historiography . . . , it was the latter [cultural features] that mattered; but for the purposes of American social and political life, it was the former [shared physical features of a geographical population]."[22]

Appiah is right: Du Bois's effort to give an account of race does harbor a tension. He is wrong, however, to think that the tension resulted from conflicts between agendas from Europe (historiography) and America (social and political life). Rather, Europe and America shared an agenda: the enslavement of Africans. The histories of racism in Europe and America provide abundant evidence that invidious notions of African peoples *as a race* covered both physical features and culture-making. In point of fact, this transatlantic, two-continent racism made a point of making putative causal linkages between biology and culture: black cultural achievements were deemed unequal to those of peoples of the white race, hence not worthy of admiration, *because* of the biologically determined, "natural" limitations of the African race. Rather, the tension in Du Bois's conception is a function of the effort to capture in the same term reference to changeable cultural (historical and social) factors and to physical features during an era when the long-standing notions of species-specific and race-specific biologically determined fixed "natures" had not yet been falsified.

Appiah goes on to examine Du Bois's approach to race in Du Bois's 1911 *Crisis* essay and his 1940 *Dusk of Dawn*. The gist of Appiah's review is that Du Bois was involved in what Appiah regards as an "impossible project": Du Bois "took race for granted" and attempted to "revalue one pole of the opposition of white to black" ensconced in the "vertical hierarchy" of the received concept of race by "rotating the axis" through a "'horizontal' reading" of race. Such effort, says Appiah, keeps one contained within the "space of values" the notion of race inscribes. The way out? "Challenge the assumption that there can be an axis, however oriented in the space of values, and the project fails for loss of presuppositions."[23] For Appiah, as I read him, this is where Du Bois should have ended up, because the logic of Du Bois's argument

> leads naturally to the final repudiation of race as a term of difference and to speaking instead "of civilizations where we now speak of races." The logic is the same logic that has brought us to speak of genders where we spoke of sexes, and a rational assessment of the evidence requires that we should endorse not only the logic but the premises of each argument. . . . One barrier facing those of us in the humanities has been methodological. Under Saussurian hegemony, we have too easily become accustomed to thinking of meaning as constituted by systems of differences purely internal to our endlessly structured *langues*. . . . Race, we all assume, is, like all other concepts, constructed by metaphor and metonymy; it stands in, metonymically, for the Other; it bears the weight, metaphorically, of other kinds of difference.
>
> Yet, in our social lives away from the text-world of the academy, we take reference for granted too easily. Even if the concept of race *is* a structure of oppositions . . . it is a structure whose realization is, at best, problematic and, at worst, impossible. If we can now hope to understand the concept embodied in this system of oppositions, we are nowhere near finding referents for it. The truth is that there are no races: there is nothing in the world that can do all we ask "race" to do for us. The evil that is done is done by the concept and by easy—yet impossible—assumptions as to its application. What we miss through our obsession with the structure of relations of concepts is, simply, reality.[24]

But what is the "reality" for Appiah that is missed by the notion of race? It is, he says, "culture": "Talk of 'race' is particularly distressing for those of us who take culture seriously. . . . What exists 'out there' in the world—communities of meaning, shading variously into each other in the rich structure of the social world—is the province not of biology but of hermeneutic understanding."[25]

I agree with Appiah that hermeneutic understanding is central. Adherence to the most rigorous standards for confirming or falsifying hypotheses leads us to the conclusion that there are no fixed and invariant biological connections to particular cultures that would support a purely biological definition of race as the ultimate carrier of culture. But none of this was lost on Du Bois.

As I read Du Bois, he *was* committed to "taking culture seriously." He was, indeed, concerned to "rotate the axis" defining the
"scale of values" in the concept of race from vertical hierarchic to
horizontal egalitarian, democratic racial and ethnic pluralism, and
to do so by proposing that each race had a "message" to offer to
civilization. The "messages," for Du Bois, are manifested in achievements the forms and meanings of which are relative to cultural life-
worlds that are "generally" populated by persons who, historically
and sociologically, tend to share, more or less, certain physical
characteristics that become valorized as partially constitutive of the
race. His was an effort to make room in the "space of values" for
a positive valorization and appreciation of the cultural achievements
of peoples of African descent, and of other groups: "Manifestly
some of the great races of today—particularly the Negro race—
have not as yet given to civilization the full spiritual message which
they are capable of giving."[26]

In defining race, however, Du Bois was sufficiently insightful
not to regard the relationship between physical characteristics and
moral and cultural factors as necessary such that the former determined the latter. More subtle still, Du Bois, as I read him, did not
define race by making the elements in the definition (physical characteristics, geography, cultural practices and traditions) *essential*
and invariant in terms of being severally necessary, connected con-
junctively, and jointly sufficient.[27] Appiah, it seems clear, reads Du
Bois as though Du Bois considered races as natural kinds, each of
which was constituted and distinguished by an abiding "heritable
racial essence"[28] that was to be kept "pure" by limiting interracial
breeding (as notable proponents of supposed scientific accounts of
races advanced during the nineteenth century believed), and as though
the point of Du Bois's defining race was to capture this supposed
"reality" of human groupings. This way of reading Du Bois seems
to miss the fact that his notion of race is best read as a *cluster*
concept: that is, race refers to a group of persons who share and
are distinguished by several properties taken *dis*junctively such that
"each property is severally sufficient and the possession of at least
one of the properties is necessary."[29] Otherwise, reading Du Bois's
effort as though he were struggling to work out a definition for
natural kinds with fixed "heritable racial essences" disregards his
explicit concern to situate a discussion of race squarely within an
understanding conditioned by attention to history and sociology, and,
as well, to the work of Charles Darwin:

[S]o far as purely physical characteristics are concerned, the differences between men do not explain all the differences of their history. It declares, as Darwin himself said, that great as is the physical unlikeness of the various races of men their likenesses are greater, and upon this rests the whole scientific doctrine of Human Brotherhood.[30]

Appiah's analysis and conclusions are particularly disturbing because he does not take up what he describes as Du Bois's effort to "rotate the axis" of the "space of values" within which groups of persons are defined as comprising races that are opposed to one another except to say that Du Bois's project to define race can be shown to be "impossible" simply by challenging its presuppositions. Appiah, I think, misconstrues Du Bois's project. It is *not* simply or even primarily an effort devoted to definition and taxonomy. Rather, it is a decidedly *political* project, as Winant and Omi argue that definitions of race tend to be. Du Bois's project involves prescribing norms for the social reconstruction of identity and for self-appropriation by a particular people suffering racialized subordination to the end of mobilizing and guiding them in efforts of emancipatory social transformation. For Du Bois, "the history of the world is the history, not of individuals, but of groups, not of nations, but of races. . . ." In posing the question of how peoples of African descent, the African race, would contribute their message to world history, Du Bois answered:

The answer is plain. . . . For the development of Negro genius, of Negro literature and art, of Negro spirit, only Negroes bound and welded together, Negroes inspired by one vast ideal, can work out in its fullness the great message we have for humanity.[31]

I take this to be one of the grounding assumptions of "The Conservation of Races," which was prepared and delivered as the second of the Occasional Papers of the newly formed American Negro Academy, which was devoted to encouraging intellectual activity among black folk and defending them against racist attacks.[32] While the purposes to be served by a definitional project in no way secure its adequacy as an account, in this case having a sense of Du Bois's overall project is crucial to an understanding of just what his effort to define race involves. It is not accurate to say, as Appiah does, that Du Bois "took race for granted" since he goes to such lengths to define it—except to the extent that he presupposed what

he set out to define. And while his effort to define race does involve a tension, I do not agree with Appiah's judgment regarding
the source of the tension. It is to be found, I think, in Du Bois's
desire to have "the unit of classification . . . be the unit of identification."[33] His is an effort to mobilize and galvanize black folk,
whose oppression was rationalized using oppositions that had been
inscribed in the notion of race. Crucial to this mobilization, for Du
Bois, would be a shared sense of identity growing out of a recognition and appropriation of commonalities of a geographic race,
including those of history, language, and culture more generally.
And it was Du Bois's sense that people of African descent in America
were too quickly accepting American ideals of human brotherhood
and forgetting "the hard limits of natural law" governing human
associations, namely, that groups make history:

> Turning to real history, there can be no doubt, first, as to the wide-
> spread, nay, universal, prevalence of the race idea, the race spirit,
> the race ideal, and as to its efficiency as the vastest and most in-
> genious invention for human progress. We, who have been reared
> and trained under the individualistic philosophy of the Declaration
> of Independence and the laisser-faire philosophy of Adam Smith,
> are loath to see and loath to acknowledge this patent fact of human
> history. . . . We are apt to think in our American impatience, that
> while it may have been true in the past that closed race groups
> made history, that here in conglomerate America *nous avons changer*
> [sic] *tout cela*—we have changed all that, and have no need of this
> ancient instrument of progress. This assumption of which the Ne-
> gro people are especially fond, can not be established by a careful
> consideration of history.[34]

In his turning to "real history" Du Bois, nonetheless, was not
unmindful of the deeply troubling tensions involved in the effort to
forge an identity in racial terms in the context of a nation-state
that called for its own socially constructed identity as "American":

> Here, then, is the dilemma, and it is a puzzling one, I admit. No
> Negro who has given earnest thought to the situation of his people
> in America has failed, at some time in life, to find himself at these
> cross-roads; has failed to ask himself at some time: What, after all,
> am I? Am I an American or am I a Negro? Can I be both? Or is it
> my duty to cease to be a Negro as soon as possible and be an
> American? If I strive as a Negro, am I not perpetuating the very
> cleft that threatens and separates Black and White America? Is not

my only possible practical aim the subduction of all that is Negro in me to the American? Does my black blood place upon me any more obligation to assert my nationality than German, or Irish or Italian blood would?[35]

The oscillating questioning that this dilemma gave rise to, in Du Bois's judgment, was having devastating effects on persons of African descent, collectively and individually:

> It is such incessant self-questioning and the hesitation that arises from it, that is making the present period a time of vacillation and contradiction for the American Negro; combined race action is stifled, race responsibility is shirked, race enterprises languish, and the best blood, the best talent, the best energy of the Negro people cannot be marshaled to do the bidding of the race.

Du Bois next answers whether this situation is right, rational, or good policy, whether black folks in America have a different and distinct *mission* as a race, or whether "self-obliteration [is] the highest end to which Negro blood dare aspire?" [36]

The import of these questions is such that the appropriateness of answers cannot be determined solely by criteria of logical rigor. Rather, it is the end-in-view—the overall project including the means proposed for completing it—that is at issue. In Du Bois's case the project was devoted to the historical development and well-being of a relatively distinct group of people who suffered oppression at the hands of persons of various ethnies of another race. For him that development and well-being require a strategically crucial form of self-understanding.

> Here, it seems to me, is the reading of the riddle that puzzles so many of us. We are Americans, not only by birth and by citizenship, but by our political ideals, our language, our religion. Farther than that, our Americanism does not go. At that point, we are Negroes, members of a vast historic race that from the very dawn of creation has slept, but half awakening in the dark forests of its African fatherland.[37]

It also requires concerted and coordinated efforts *on the part of black people themselves:*

> [A]s a race we must strive by race organization, by race solidarity, by race unity to the realization of that broader humanity which freely

recognizes differences in men, but sternly deprecates inequality in
their opportunities of development.

For the accomplishment of these ends we need race organizations. . . . Let us not deceive ourselves at our situation in this country.
. . . [O]ur one haven of refuge is ourselves, and but one means of
advance, our own belief in our great destiny, our own implicit trust
in our ability and worth.[38]

Thus must the race be mobilized and organized. The unit of focus, for Du Bois, if one is to understand human history and attempt to structure the making of the future through organized effort, is the racial group, the "vast family" of related individuals.
Individuals are necessary, but they are neither sufficient nor self-
sufficing, the political philosophy of modern Liberalism notwithstanding. Survival is tied to the well-being of the group; and the
well-being of the group requires concerted action predicated on self-
valorization, but not chauvinism, with reference to racial (or ethnic) identity. Further, the racial/ethnic life-world provides the resources and nurturing required for the development of individual
talent and accomplishment such that distinctive contributions by
particular persons can be made to human civilization. Thus must
the African race and its ethnies—and by extension of the argument
all races and ethnies—be "conserved."

In a very important sense Appiah is right: what is at the heart of
the matter, "What exists 'out there' in the world—communities of
meaning, shading variously into each other in the rich structure of
the social world—is the province not of biology but of hermeneutic
understanding."[39] But what are the sociohistorical, anthropological
bases of "communities of meaning"? How do such communities come
to be? How do they cohere and persist? Of whom are they composed? If on some relevant occasions we cannot use race and/or
ethnicity to identify the persons constituting such a community,
particularly when the members of the community *do* share physical as well as historical and cultural characteristics, how ought we
to describe the sociohistorical world in *sociological* terms? Since
there are various groups composed of persons who are more or less
distinct physiologically, culturally, and geographically who seem
appropriate candidates for being designated races and ethnies, how
are they to be identified?

A key to understanding Appiah's strenuous effort to eliminate
race as a candidate for this characterizing work is to be found, I
think, in an important footnote in his "The Uncompleted Argument."

Referring to an essay on which he draws in which the authors, apparently, discuss genetic relationships and the evolution of human races, he argues: "I would dispute their claim that their work shows the existence of a biological basis for the classification of human races; what it shows is that human populations differ in their distributions of genes. That *is* a biological fact. The objection to using this fact as a basis of a system of classification is that far too many people don't fit into just one category that can be so defined."[40] Since "too many people" don't fit into just one racial category, does that show that racial classification is thereby inappropriate? I think not. It might well just mean that another way of characterizing such people is needed. However, the problem that Appiah is concerned with here is not, I think, simply that of racial classification or taxonomy. Rather, it is the troubling question of the politics of *identity*: with which race does a person identify himself or herself when his or her parents are persons of *different* races? For Appiah, and for "many people," as it is even for those of us who have parents of the same race, this is more than an issue of semantics in racially hierarchic societies in which white supremacy continues as norm and practice. Racial categories thus come with the valorizations of the hierarchy and thereby affect the formation and appropriation of identities as well as life chances.

So it was for Du Bois as well. Yet he *chose* his racial identity— at least he consciously embraced an identity that was partly proscribed for him by prevailing conventions regarding the race of a person if any ancestor, unto several generations, possessed African "blood." Many people of mixed racial parentage have done likewise without, at the same time, underrepresenting their ancestry. That is, they have made the choice of an identity defined in terms of one line of parental ancestry while acknowledging the other line as a constitutive aspect of who they are. The choice, depending on the person and circumstances, may be more or less difficult. Such choices are often made more difficult by racist or chauvinist proscriptions tied to commitments to the erroneous notion that a heritable racial essence determines the character, personality, and capacities of individuals of a given race and thereby determines the culture-making of the race as a whole. The formation and appropriation of subjective and social identities *always* involve socially conditioned choice as well as social imposition. Our identities are never a result of simply acknowledging an identity-determining heritable raciality. Rather, identities are ongoing projects involving configurations of meanings and values in which our bodies, in racialized societies especially, are made the sites at which the meanings and values cohere and skin color, for example, is made both their self-evident sign and symbol.

Further, Appiah is certainly right in noting: "Few candidates for laws of nature can be stated by reference to the colors, tastes, smells, or touches of objects. It is hard for us to accept that the colors of objects, which play so important a role in our visual experience and our recognition of everyday objects, turn out neither to play an important part in the behavior of matter nor to be correlated with properties that do."[41] However, the truth of this metaphysical insight underappreciates a crucial fact noted: the colors of objects are very important *to us* and to our valuation and utilization of things in everyday life, to the routine, meaningful organization of everyday life. It is crucial that we uncouple any notion of race as a term that refers to biological *and* sociohistorical cultural groupings from any presumed grounding in a purported race-defining, unchanging heritable biological essence. Still, we must be mindful of the ways in which group-based phenotypes (and, in important instances, genotypes, as well, as when two persons who are considering a sexual relationship are mindful of the potential for problematic genetic consequences in offspring) do figure in the normed aesthetics and somatic imaging of social life, even as we continue to work to revise the politics assisted by ontologies and aesthetics of invidious, essentialist, biologized notions of race. The "laws of nature" cannot themselves settle questions regarding what import and value, if any, phenotype and morphology ought to have for humans.

However, there are many more people for whom a racial identity is not such a complicated matter, for whom the issue is not the purity of a definition of race in terms of clear lines of biological descent evidenced in a compelling set of physical criteria. It is, rather, the important and still pressing business of getting on within and among racially and ethnically complex societies that make for a world with many "communities of meaning." For many persons, myself included, the continued existence of discernible racial/ethnic communities of meaning is highly desirable *even if, in the very next instant, racism and invidious ethnocentrism in every form and manifestation were to disappear forever.* I am certain they will not.

But that is not really the issue. Like Du Bois, I am convinced that *both* the struggle against racism and invidious ethnocentrism and the struggles on the part of persons of various races and ethnicities to create, preserve, refine, and, of particular importance, share their "messages"—that is to say, their cultural meanings—with human civilization at large, require that the constantly evolving groups we refer to as races—too often in our ugliest pasts and presents in erroneous and invidious ways with horrific consequences—nonetheless be "conserved" in democratic polities. As many of us in America continue to struggle to consolidate the realization of racial justice with harmony in some areas of our collective life and work to extend justice and harmony to new areas of our shared lives or new forms of justice to both new and old areas of life, I remain unconvinced that we must do away with the notion of race, the difficulties of definition and ugly legacies of racism notwithstanding. The challenge, as I view the historical moment, is to find ways to conserve a revised notion of race that is both socially useful and consistent with a revised notion of democratic justice.

Du Bois, in my judgment, was one of the foremost thinkers in modern history to have wrestled in a promising way with the seemingly intractable and *always* potentially divisive and destructive "problem of the color line." His offerings, I think, are particularly worthy and reward a close and careful reading and consideration. They are a valuable aid to efforts to achieve understanding and to guide social praxis that would steer us clear of difficulties, focused through the prisms of race and ethnicity, that, for example, even as I write, are being played out in projects of genocide and mass destruction in the former nation-state of Yugoslavia and Rwanda, as just two among other examples. These living lessons, in all of their horror, are not the inevitable fate of the conservation of ethnic groups and races. There are other examples of successful multiracial, multiethnic unity in diversity—in communities, institutions, and organizations throughout this nation and others—that validate hope. Learning from these examples, I think, provides resources that can assist us in rescuing ourselves from a much too probable distorted fate, of our own making, that otherwise might well be our undoing.

Notes

This paper was originally prepared for and presented during the Symposium on Racism and Sexism: Differences and Connections hosted by the Department of Philosophy of Georgia State University, Atlanta, Georgia, on May 3–4, 1991. A revised version was read at St. John's College, Annapolis, Maryland, on September 20, 1991; was the basis of a public lecture at Hartwick College, Oneonta, New York, on February 27, 1992; was read at Pennsylvania State University during a conference on "The Thought of W. E. B. Du Bois" on March 21, 1992; and subsequently was circulated in the *SAPINA Newsletter* (Bulletin of the Society for African Philosophy in North America) IV, no. 1 (January–July 1992): 13–28. Portions of an earlier draft are included in Lucius Outlaw, "Against the Grain of Modernity: The Politics of Difference and the Conservation of 'Race,'" *Man and World* 25: 1992 (443–68): 460–66. The present version is a revision of that read at the Pennsylvania State University conference. Special thanks to Bernard Bell, Emily Grosholz, and James Stewart for their careful reading of that draft and for their especially helpful comments and suggested improvements.

1. W. E. B. Du Bois, "The Concept of Race," in *Dusk of Dawn: An Essay Toward an Autobiography of a Race Concept* (1940; New York: Schocken, 1968), 103.

2. For provocative discussions of some of the challenges see Arthur M. Schlesinger, Jr., *The Disuniting of America: Reflections on a Multicultural Society* (New York: W. W. Norton, 1992), and Charles Taylor and Amy Gutman, ed., *Multiculturalism and "The Politics of Recognition"* (Princeton, N.J.: Princeton University Press, 1992).

3. William A. Henry, III, "Beyond the Melting Pot," *Time* 135, no. 15 (April 9, 1990): 28–31.

4. For the rest of this discussion I shall focus almost wholly on race though much, if not all, of what I shall say applies equally to ethnicity.

5. This project anticipates "a release of emancipatory reflection and a transformed social praxis" that emerges as a result of the restoration, via critical reflection, of "missing parts of the historical self-formation process to man and, in this way, to release a self-positing comprehension which enables him to see through socially unnecessary authority and control systems." Trent Schroyer, *The Critique of Domination: The Origins and Development of Critical Theory* (Boston: Beacon Press, 1973), 31.

6. "When we refer to races we have in mind their geographically defined categories which are sometimes called 'geographical races,' to indicate that while they have some distinctive biological characteristics they are not pure types." Michael Banton and Jonathan Harwood, *The Race Concept* (New York: Praeger, 1975), 62.

7. David L. Hull, "The Effect of Essentialism on Taxonomy—Two Thousand Years of Stasis (I)," *British Journal for Philosophy of Science* 15 (1965): 314–26.

8. See T. E. Wilkerson, "Natural Kinds," *Philosophy* 63 (1988): 29–42; John Dupré, "Wilkerson on Natural Kinds," *Philosophy* 64 (1989): 248–51; Leroy N. Meyer, "Science, Reduction and Natural Kinds," *Philosophy* 64

(1989): 535–46; and John Dupré, "Natural Kinds and Biological Taxa," *The Philosophical Review* XC, no. 1 (January 1981): 66–90.

9. Howard Winant and Michael Omi, *Racial Formation in the United States* (New York: Routledge & Kegan Paul, 1986). Other especially helpful texts are Michael Banton's *The Idea of Race* (Boulder, Colo.: Westview Press, 1977) and Michael Banton and Jonathan Harwood's *The Race Concept.*

10. Winant and Omi, 68–69.

11. The notion of social evolution I have in mind is that of Jürgen Habermas. See, in particular, his "Historical Materialism and the Development of Normative Structures" and "Toward a Reconstruction of Historical Materialism," in Jürgen Habermas, *Communication and the Evolution of Society*, trans. Thomas McCarthy (Boston: Beacon Press, 1979), 95–177.

12. W. E. B. Du Bois, "The Conservation of Races." The text used for this discussion is reprinted in *African-American Social and Political Thought, 1850–1920*, ed. Howard Brotz (New Brunswick, N.J.: Transaction Publishers, 1992), 483–92.

13. Anthony Appiah, "The Uncompleted Argument: Du Bois and the Illusion of Race," in *"Race" Writing, and Difference*, ed. Henry Louis Gates, Jr. (Chicago: University of Chicago Press, 1986), 21–37. Appiah revised and extended his argument against Du Bois as "Illusions of Race" in his *In My Father's House: Africa in the Philosophy of Culture* (New York: Oxford University Press, 1992), 28–46.

14. Appiah, "The Uncompleted Argument," 25.

15. Du Bois, "The Conservation of Races," 485; emphasis added.

16. Appiah, "The Uncompleted Argument," 25–26.

17. Ibid., 26.

18. Ibid., 26.

19. Ibid., 27.

20. Ibid., 28.

21. Ibid., 29.

22. Ibid., 29.

23. Ibid., 36.

24. Ibid., 35–36.

25. Ibid., 36.

26. Du Bois, "The Conservation of Races," 487.

27. Hull, "The Effect of Essentialism on Taxonomy," 318.

28. See Appiah, *In My Father's House*, 39.

29. Hull, "The Effect of Essentialism on Taxonomy," 323. For example, given several groups of features A (heritable physical features), B (shared cultural practices by way of), C (linked if not quite common histories and traditions, which have their beginnings in), and D (a common site of origin which accounts, in significant part, for the shared physical features), which are shared by members of a group in a limited number of patterned combinations, necessarily one feature—any one (say B)—plus several others (C *or* A *or* D) would be sufficient to identify a person as a member of a particular race.

30. Du Bois, "The Conservation of Races," 484–85.

31. Ibid., 487.

32. "On March 5, 1897, the one hundred twenty-seventh anniversary of the Boston Massacre where Crispus Attucks, who was believed to have been a mulatto, was the first to die, eighteen black men assembled in the District of Columbia's Lincoln Memorial Church to formally inaugurate the American Negro Academy. This date was chosen because it recalled 'an event especially sacred to the Negro.' To the men who planned the meeting, Attucks' death in 1770 was a symbol of the patriotic and heroic role black Americans played in the creation of the United States. Consequently, they felt it appropriate that a black society formed to encourage intellectual activity among blacks, and to defend them from 'vicious assaults' should begin its public life on this day." Alfred A. Moss, Jr., *The American Negro Academy: Voice of the Talented Tenth* (Baton Rouge: Louisiana State University Press, 1981), 35. Du Bois was one of the eighteen founding members of the Academy.

33. Hull, "The Effect of Essentialism on Taxonomy," 322.

34. Du Bois, "The Conservation of Races," 485.

35. Ibid., 488.

36. Ibid., 488.

37. Ibid., 488–89.

38. Ibid., 489.

39. Appiah, "The Uncompleted Argument," 36.

40. Ibid., 37, note 10.

41. Appiah, *In My Father's House*, 39.3

6

Conjuring Race

Stephen Prothero

The problems in W. E. B. Du Bois's "The Conservation of Races" (1897), Anthony Appiah's "The Uncompleted Argument: Du Bois and the Illusion of Race" (1985), and Lucius Outlaw's essay under consideration here all seem at first glance to reduce to an ontological question: whether races really exist; whether "the race concept," as Du Bois describes it, points to something true and thereby merits "conservation."[1] Lurking behind this question in all three essays is a political concern, since to affirm the reality of "race" in the name of "difference" would seem to imply the denial of liberalism's beloved "universal human being" and all the tolerance that construct purportedly secures, while to deny the reality of "race" in the name of "commonality" would seem to imply the denial of the existence and thus the importance of African American community and culture.

Du Bois begins his essay (delivered, by the way, just two years after Booker T. Washington's notorious "Atlanta Compromise" address of 1895) by rejecting certain racist constructions of race— ostensibly "scientific" constructions of nineteenth-century thinkers like Arthur Gobineau that began by linking biological traits with intellectual and moral capacities and ended by calling for a cessation of the intermixing of "higher" (read, for example, English and Teutons) and "lower" (read, for example, Negroes and Mongolians) races.[2] But Du Bois also rejects in the essay the typical liberal response to this racist argument, which would deny in the name of the "universal human being" and for the sake of "commonality" the reality of race. Du Bois then devotes the remainder of the article to a sociohistorical reconstruction of race and the races, each of which, he claims, has a unique "Ideal" to contribute to our common humanity. In this way Du Bois's reconstruction retains elements of the arguments he rejects, since he simultaneously affirms both racial particularism (there are many races—eight, in fact) and pan-racial universalism (there is one humanity to which the many races are contributing).

Anthony Appiah's "Uncompleted Argument" is a sophisticated piece of work. Here I can deal only with what I understand to be its two main theses: first, its denial of the biological reality of race ("The truth is that there are no races," Appiah contends), and second, its rejection of Du Bois's sociohistorical reconstruction of "the race concept" ("there is nothing in the world," Appiah concludes, "that can do all we ask 'race' to do for us").[3]

I concede the first part of Appiah's conclusion: at least from the perspective of science, the truth *is* that there are no races. But even if race *is*, from the scientific perspective, a fiction, is it entirely unreal? I think not. Over the past two decades, many scholars in the humanities and social sciences have come to see that categories we previously interpreted as given "essences" (for example, motherhood, self, memory, tradition) ought to be understood as contingent historical and social constructions.[4] Among these categories is race, which in my view is as historically and socially real as it is scientifically ephemeral.

Given this double-sidedness of the race concept itself, we would seem to be left with two options: either to go with the scientists and give race up, or, waxing historical and sociological, to reconstruct (or, if you will, "reinvent") it. The former is Appiah's choice. The latter is mine and, I argue, that of Du Bois.

Although Du Bois was born too early to be said to be fully versed in arguments for "the social construction of reality,"[5] I don't think it is anachronistic to attribute to him something akin to a recognition of the constructedness of race. It is true that Du Bois states rather unequivocally in his essay that "human beings are divided into races."[6] But I do not understand him to mean by this that races are a biological reality. What Du Bois was doing—and here we should remember that he was a social scientist with a Harvard Ph.D. in sociology—was telling us something about how social groups construct reality. Humans, according to Du Bois, are social animals who perceive themselves as members of racial groups and thus divide the human family into races. No matter how Appiah and other modern-day philosophers might rage, ordinary folk are going to see themselves as belonging to collectives substantially smaller than the human community. To retreat to the terminology of Mahayana Buddhists, who affirm the coexistence of both absolute and conventional truths (even when those truths are apparently contradictory), Du Bois was denying the absolute ontological reality of race even as he was affirming its conventional or sociohistorical inescapability.[7] Hence his preference for referring to the race concept (as a human construct) rather than to race (as a biological reality) itself.

Du Bois thus disagrees with Appiah on two substantive points. First, while he affirms, along with Appiah, that the race concept is scientifically empty, he is convinced, contrary to Appiah, that any hope of its disappearance from ordinary language and thought is naive, at least for the time being. "There can be no doubt," he writes, "as to the widespread, nay, universal, prevalence of the race idea."[8] Races are firmly rooted in the human imagination; current attempts to eradicate racial consciousness are futile.

Du Bois thus shifts the debate over "the race question" from ontological to hermeneutical grounds—from the question of whether races really exist to the question of how the race concept is to be interpreted. "The question, then, that we must seriously consider is this: "Du Bois writes, "What is the meaning of race?"[9] And the answer is that the meaning of race, like all words in Lewis Carroll's *Alice in Wonderland*, is malleable. It will mean whatever we tell it to mean, neither more nor less.

Given this starting point, I must dispute Appiah's claim that the argument of Du Bois's "The Conservation of Races" ought to be understood as a typical antithesis in what Appiah refers to as "the classic dialectic of reaction to prejudice."[10] According to Appiah, the thesis in this dialectic (which, as he correctly reports, can also be found in discussions of gender) is the universalist's denial of difference while the antithesis is the particularist's affirmation of difference.

There are, of course, problems with both this thesis and this antithesis, and it may be helpful to single out at least some of those problems here. The thesis seeks in the name of commonality to eliminate racism by eliminating race. While laudable in aim, this argument fails to make sense of the sociohistorical reality of race and may serve to undermine the one American community that is most vociferous in its denunciations of racism, namely the community of African Americans. The antithesis, on the other hand, seeks in the name of difference to eliminate racism by fostering pride in African American culture. This argument bolsters the African American community but risks fueling both racism and inequality.

Where Appiah errs, in my view, is in his reading of Du Bois's argument as an instance, or at least a typical instance, of the classical antithesis. Du Bois distinguished himself from most thinkers committed to racial difference, in my view, by his sophisticated awareness that race is not a given biological essence but a contingent social construct. Since he is both theoretically committed to a nonracial theory of commonality (Appiah's thesis) and practically committed to a racial theory of difference (Appiah's antithesis), his position should be understood either as an alternative antithesis or, perhaps, a new synthesis.

It may be useful here to recall Ruth Frankenberg, who argues in *White Women, Race Matters: The Social Construction of White Women* (1993) that Americans have recourse to three "discursive repertoires" when it comes to discussing race. The first is "essentialist racism," which affirms the ontological reality of race in order to bolster an argument for white superiority. The second, "color and power evasion," denies the ontological reality of race in an assimilative effort to undercut racism. This popular liberal strategy fails, according to Frankenberg, to recognize the sociohistorical reality of race difference and is blind to the privileges that this discursive repertoire grants to dominant whites, whose differentness becomes, according to the logic of this discursive repertoire, normative even as their racialness becomes hidden. Frankenberg thus commends to her readers a third strategy, "race cognizance," which affirms the sociohistorical reality of race difference but denies the racism inherent in theories of white superiority.[11]

To return to Du Bois, I contend that Du Bois was "race cognizant" in a way that differs from Appiah's classic antithesis to the "classic dialectic of reaction to prejudice." His was, in short, a theory of racial difference informed by a critique of the race concept itself and an awareness of the social construction of race. Only from this purview can we make sense both of Du Bois's racial particularism and of his universalistic view that "the duty of the Americans of Negro descent, as a body, to maintain their race identity" will obtain only until "this mission of the Negro people is accomplished, and the ideal of human brotherhood has become a practical possibility."[12]

How, then, are we to judge Du Bois's effort to reinvent the invention of race—his determination to invest the race concept with positive rather than negative import? At first glance—and here I am glancing as a historian—Du Bois's investment would seem to be a rather poor one indeed. Though the notion of race was invented in sixteenth-century Europe, it matured in the nineteenth century, when it was conflated with two complementary (and equally problematic) discourses.[13] The first was evolutionary discourse, including early theories on "the nature and origin" of religion that either stated or implied that species, races, and religions progressed from "lower" to "higher" forms, from aborigines to Europeans, from idol-worshippers to Christians, from apes to British gentlemen.[14] The second discourse was colonial. It included missionary reports and travelogues of explorers like David Livingstone and Sir Richard F. Burton,[15] genres which sought to maximize the difference between the subjects of colonialism (the Europeans) and its objects (Africans, Indians, and the like) through symbolic constructions of the "primitive" and the "civilized," the "Christian" and the "heathen."[16]

The discourse about race was, like these evolutionary and colonial discourses, explicitly hierarchical and therefore toxic to Africans, African Americans, and other "lesser breeds" assigned by the grammar of that discourse to the bottom of the racial heap. Such a discourse does not, on the face of it, seem to be a good place to start if one is attempting to deconstruct racism and work toward more equitable and humane social and political arrangements.

But to stop here (as I take it Appiah wishes to do) is to grant too much interpretive leverage to the racists. There is not, in my view, anything essentially racist about the concept of race—unless of course racists are to be that concept's only legitimate interpreters. Just because the idea of racism was invented by antiracists—the word first appeared in English in 1936 as a reaction to Hitler and Nazism[17]—doesn't mean the idea cannot be manipulated for racist purposes. And just because race has been most fiercely manipulated by racists doesn't mean that nonracists can't reconstruct it, and invest it with positive import.

I read Du Bois's essay as just such a reconstruction: a protest against the racist's monopoly on interpreting the concept as well as a determination not merely to buy but also to sell interpretations of race. More than a social scientific discourse on the objective reality (or nonreality) of race, "The Conservation of Races" is, as Appiah himself recognizes, a hermeneutical and political act—an attempt to seize some interpretive control and to wield the power that seizure entails.

To use language that emerges from West Africa itself, Du Bois is not only "conserving" but also "conjuring" race—adopting the concept from Europe in order to adapt it in accordance with his own therapeutic purposes. Not unlike the conjure woman or root doctor from western Nigeria or Benin who uses otherwise dangerous herbs or roots to heal, Du Bois is using his substantial transformative powers to convert race from something that is toxic into something that is tonic—from something that can injure to something that can heal. Through his creative imagination, the seemingly fixed and given "thing" of race dissolves, as does its seemingly "natural" racist message. In the interpretive void that results from this dissolution, Du Bois ventures to manufacture something wholly new.[18]

When a client presents herself with aches and chills at the home of the conjure woman, the conjure woman doesn't care whether that client has been visited with a cold or a hex or a psychosomatic disorder. What is important is that the client be healed. Similarly, Du Bois's "The Conservation of Races" is more concerned with the physical than the metaphysical. It is addressed to "the practical difficulties of every day." Du Bois's concern is not so much to diagnose the race concept as to manipulate it—to transform it into something that has the power to heal, the leverage to tilt a unified nation of distinct peoples toward freedom.

Thus Du Bois does for race what other African Americans have done for centuries with the Bible or with the Declaration of Independence—conjure a potentially toxic text for tonic effect. Just as black preachers in slavery turned the slavemaster's Bible ("slaves obey your masters") into the free black's scripture ("there is in Christ Jesus neither slave nor free") and as black politicians converted the slavemaster's Declaration of Independence ("all white men are created equal") into the African American's freedom song ("all people are created equal"), so does Du Bois reconstruct race to deconstruct racism.

In conclusion, I am reminded of Mark Twain's response to a skeptic who inquired of him whether he believed in baptism. "Believe in it?" Twain is said to have replied, "I've seen it!" Whether we believe in races—or sexes for that matter—seems to be irrelevant. The fact is that we have all seen both and will probably continue to see them, despite Appiah's protestations, at least for a century or so. The crucial matter, then, is not whether races really do exist, but which notions of race serve to buttress and which to demolish racism.

It is interesting to note that one aspect of Du Bois's answer to this latter question was that any positive notion of race must incorporate not only an affirmation of any particular race's need for some separate development, but also a requirement that that separate development serve to advance the human community as a whole. No positive concept of race, in short, would deny the kind of paradoxical "twoness" Du Bois discerned in himself (as both American and African, white and black). Races, too, should exhibit a sort of "double-consciousness." They should strive not merely for themselves but also for humanity; they should struggle to preserve and develop their unique features not simply for their own sakes but also for the sake of the world.

Here Du Bois is working interpretive turf that will be familiar to contemporary feminists who reject both the sexist argument (that women are inferior to men) and the liberal, universalistic response (that women are not essentially different from men and are therefore deserving of equal rights) in favor of an alternative, particularist response (of Carol Gilligan and most nineteenth-century American feminists) that women and men are different but complementary, that women have something uniquely female to offer American society and the world.[19] Du Bois is, by the way, simultaneously rejecting a stronger response, analogous to the feminism of Mary Daly and Andrea Dworkin (invoked by Laurence Thomas in this volume), that asserts that women and men are different but not complementary—that women ought to understand and conduct their lives largely in relationship with one another.[20] It was Du Bois's rejection of this sort of separatist alternative that led later thinkers such as Marcus Garvey to label him an accommodating "Uncle Tom."

Let me conclude with two additional comments. First, I must say that I remain skeptical about the direction in which Outlaw seems to be moving with his reconstruction of race on the basis of critical theory. If the race concept is to be reinvented on a nonracist basis, perhaps it ought to be reconstructed on a non-Eurocentric basis as well. The European critical theory to which Outlaw appeals remains, at least in my view, a dubious starting point both for reinventing race and for reinterpreting people like Du Bois. Du Bois was no doubt conjuring race for freedom. But was he involved in an "emancipatory project" or (to quote Outlaw citing Trent

Schroyer) in the anticipation of "a release of emancipatory reflection and a transformed social praxis" that emerges as a result of the restoration, via critical reflection, of "the missing parts of the historical self-formation process to man and, in this way, to release a self-positing comprehension which enables him to see through socially unnecessary authority and control systems"?

My approach to African American texts, both in my research and in the classroom, is to attempt to interpret those texts, at least in part, through West African and African American models rather than through Eurocentric models alone. If we study Du Bois and other recent additions to the ever-changing academic canon solely through European theories—critical or otherwise—how multicultural will our study really be? I, for one, think the war on Eurocentrism is better fought (and won) by reading Plato through the eyes of the conjure woman than by reading Spike Lee through the eyes of Marx or Habermas.

My second and final comment is really a reflection. While it may be true that men and women do not "exist" as natural, eternal realities any more or less than do blacks and whites, feminists seem not to have burdened themselves unduly with the question of the reality of gender. Rather than laboring to eradicate the category of "woman," they have worked to revalorize her, to drain her of toxic connotations and infuse her with properties that can heal (not the least of which is the exquisitely connotative womyn's "y"). This re-creative project seems analogous to the project of Du Bois. It also seems, at least to me, to be the profitable path to follow, both with regard to gender and with regard to race.

Notes

1. Lucius Outlaw has invited me to consider Du Bois's article in light of Appiah's critique. My response is directed, therefore, more to Du Bois and Appiah than to Outlaw himself.

The Du Bois article, which first appeared in *American Negro Academy Occasional Papers* 2 (1897), has been reprinted frequently. My references are to "The Conservation of Races" in *W. E. B Du Bois Speaks: Speeches and Addresses, 1890–1919*, ed. Philip S. Foner (New York: Pathfinder Press, 1970), 73–85. Appiah's "The Uncompleted Argument: Du Bois and the Illusion of Race" has also been reprinted—in *"Race" Writing, and Difference*, ed. Henry Louis Gates, Jr. (Chicago: University of Chicago Press, 1986), 21–37—but my references are to its original appearance in *Critical Inquiry* 12 (Autumn 1985) 21–37.

2. See, for example, Arthur Gobineau, *The Moral and Intellectual Diversity of Races* (1856; New York: Garland Publishing, 1984).

3. Appiah, "The Uncompleted Argument," 75.

4. I am borrowing here from Werner Sollors's introduction to *The Invention of Ethnicity*, ed. Werner Sollors (New York: Oxford University Press, 1989), ix–xx. In an exhaustive footnote (238–39), Sollors lists a myriad of recent titles, including Roy W. Wagner, *The Invention of Culture* (Chicago: University of Chicago Press, 1981); Ann Dally, *Inventing Motherhood: The Consequences of an Ideal* (New York: Schocken, 1985); and John O. Lyons, *The Invention of the Self: The Hinge of Consciousness in the Eighteenth Century* (Carbondale, Ill.: Southern Illinois University Press, 1978). In the few years that have passed since Sollors compiled his list, a spate of parallel books has appeared. Among them are Adam Kuper, *The Invention of Primitive Society: Transformations of an Illusion* (New York: Routledge, 1988); Israel Rosenfield, *The Invention of Memory: A New View of the Brain* (New York: Basic Books, 1988); Peter J. Bowler, *The Invention of Progress: The Victorians and the Past* (Cambridge, Mass.: Basil Blackwell, 1989); Allen W. Batteau, *The Invention of Appalachia* (Tucson: University of Arizona Press, 1990); and, most recently and provocatively, Marta Morazzoni, *The Invention of Truth*, trans. M. J. Fitzgerald (New York: A. A. Knopf, 1993). Another influential book, which Sollors lists elsewhere (240), is Eric Hobsbawm and Terence Ranger, eds., *The Invention of Tradition* (Cambridge: Cambridge University Press, 1983).

5. I am thinking of Peter L. Berger and Thomas Luckmann, *The Social Construction of Reality: A Treatise in the Sociology of Knowledge* (New York: Doubleday, 1966).

6. Du Bois, "The Conservation of Races," 73.

7. Here I am contending that Du Bois would have agreed with Howard Winant and Michael Omi who, as Outlaw notes, contend in *Racial Formation in the United States* (New York: Routledge, 1986) that just because "race" is not an "essence" does not mean that it is a "mere illusion" (68–69). Race is real, in short, insofar as it is believed by social groups to be real and thus has real sociohistorical effects.

8. Du Bois, "The Conservation of Races," 76.

9. Ibid., 74.

10. Appiah, "The Uncompleted Argument," 63.

11. Ruth Frankenberg, *White Women, Race Matters: The Social Construction of Whiteness* (Minneapolis: University of Minnesota Press, 1993), esp. 13–15, 137–90. Frankenberg acknowledges her indebtedness to Omi and Winant, *Racial Formation*, in a note on page 268.

12. Du Bois, "The Conservation of Races," 84.

13. See *Oxford English Dictionary*, ed., J. A. Simpson and E. S. C. Weiner (Oxford: Clarendon Press, 1989) vol. XIII, 67–71.

14. An early and influential such evolutionary scheme can be found in E. B. Tylor's *Primitive Culture* (1871; New York: Harper & Row, 1958). Tylor contended that religion originated in "animism" and then developed into

"polytheism" and, finally, "monotheism." For a useful overview of the development of the discipline of the study of religion from its origins in missionary and evolutionary thinking, see Eric J. Sharpe, *Comparative Religion: A History* (La Salle, Ill.: Open Court, 1986).

15. See, for example, Burton's *Personal Narrative of a Pilgrimage to al-Madinah and Meccah* (1893; New York: Dover, 1964) and Livingstone's *Missionary Travels and Researches in South Africa* (New York: Harper, 1858).

16. The most influential early critique of this colonial discourse can be found in Edward Said, *Orientalism* (New York: Pantheon, 1978). For a more recent treatment, see Robert Young, *White Mythologies: Writing History and the West* (London: Routledge, 1990).

17. *Oxford English Dictionary*, vol. XIII, 75.

18. I am influenced here by conversations with Theophus H. Smith of Emory University. See his *Conjuring Culture: Biblical Formations of Black America* (New York: Oxford University Press, 1994) and his "The Spirituality of Afro-American Traditions," in *Christian Spirituality: Post-Reformation and Modern*, ed. Louis Dupré and Don E. Saliers (New York: Crossroad, 1989), 377–413.

19. I am thinking of Carol Gilligan's *In A Different Voice: Psychological Theory and Women's Development* (Cambridge: Harvard University Press, 1982). See also Carol Gilligan et. al., eds., *Mapping the Moral Domain: A Contribution of Women's Thinking to Psychological Theory and Education* (Cambridge: Harvard University Press, 1988). Du Bois's position on race differs importantly from that of Gilligan on gender, however, insofar as Du Bois wants to deny the scientific reality of race.

20. I am most familiar with the theological instances of this argument. See, for example, Mary Daly, *Beyond God the Father: Toward a Philosophy of Women's Liberation* (Boston: Beacon Press, 1973), and her more recent *Outercourse: the Be-Dazzling Voyage: Containing Recollections from my Logbook of a Radical Feminist Philosopher (Being an Account of my Time/Space Travels and Ideas—Then, Again, Now, and How)* (San Francisco: HarperSanFrancisco, 1992).

7

White Woman Feminist

Marilyn Frye

This essay is the latest version of something I have been (re-)writing ever since my essay "On Being White" was published in *The Politics of Reality*. In a way, this *is* that first essay, emerging after several metamorphoses.

"On Being White" grew out of experiences I had in my home lesbian community in which I was discovering some of what it means for a woman, a feminist, to be white. These were very frustrating experiences: they played out and revealed the ways in which the fact that I am white gave unbidden and unwanted meanings to my thought and my actions and poisoned them all with privilege.

An intermediate version of this work, delivered at various colleges and universities around 1984–86, began with the following account of my attempts to come to grips with the fact of being white in a white-supremacist racist state, and with some of the criticism my first effort had drawn.[1]

Many white feminists, myself included, have tried to identify and change the attitudes and behaviors that blocked our friendly and effective comradeship with women of color and limited our ability to act against institutional racism. I assumed at first that these revisions would begin with analysis and decision: I had to understand the problems and then do whatever would effect the changes dictated by this understanding. But as I entered this work, I almost immediately learned that my competence to do it was questionable.

The idea was put to me by several women of color (and was stated in writings by women of color) that a white woman is not in a good position to analyze institutional or personal racism and a white woman's decisions about what to do about racism cannot be authentic. About consciousness-raising groups for white women, Sharon Keller said to me in a letter,

> I think that there are things which white women working together can accomplish but I do not think that white women are in the best positions usually to know what those things are or when it is the right time to do them. It would go a long way . . . for white women to take seriously their [relative] helplessness in this matter.

White women's analysis of their own racism has also often been heard by women of color as "mere psychologizing." To be rid of racism, a white woman may indeed have to do some introspecting, remembering, and verbalizing feelings, but the self-knowledge that she might achieve by this work would necessarily produce profound change, and there are many reasons why many white women may not want to change. White women's efforts to gain self-knowledge are easily undermined by the desire not to live out the consequences of getting it; their/our projects of consciousness raising and self-analysis are very susceptible to the slide from "working on your-self" to "playing with yourself." Apparently the white woman her-self is ill-situated for telling which is which.

All of my ways of knowing seemed to have failed me—my per-ception, my common sense, my goodwill, my anger, honor, and affection, my intelligence and insight. Just as walking requires something fairly sturdy and firm underfoot, so being an actor in the world requires a foundation of ordinary moral and intellectual confidence. Without that, we don't know how to be or how to act; we become strangely stupid; the commitment against racism be-comes itself immobilizing. Even obvious and easy acts either do not occur to us or threaten to be racist by presumptuous assump-tions or misjudged timing, wording, or circumstances. Simple things like courtesy or giving money, attending a trial, working on a project initiated by women of color, or dissenting from racist views ex-pressed in white company become fraught with possibilities of er-ror and offense. If you want to do good, and you don't know good from bad, you can't move.[2] Thus stranded, we also learned that it was exploitive and oppressive to ask for the help of women of color in extricating ourselves from this ignorance, confusion, incompe-tence, and moral failure. Our racism is our problem, not theirs.[3]

Some white women report that the great enemy of their efforts to combat their own racism is their feelings of guilt. That is not my own experience, or that is not my word for it. The great enemies in my heart have been the despair and the resentment that come with being required (by others and by my own integrity) to repair something apparently irreparable, to take responsibility for something apparently beyond my powers to effect. Both confounded and angry, my own temptation is to collapse—to admit defeat and retire from the field. What counteracts that temptation, for me, seems to be little more than willfulness and lust: I *will* not be broken, and my appetite for woman's touch is not, thank goodness, thoroughly civilized to the established categories. But if I cannot give up and I cannot act, what do Will and Lust recommend? The obvious way out of the relentless logic of my situation is to cease being white.

The Contingency of Racedness

I was brought up with a concept of race according to which you cannot stop being the race you are: your race is an irreversible physical, indeed, ontological fact about you. But when the criteria for membership in a race came up as an issue among white people I knew, considerations of skin color and biological lineage were not definitive or decisive, or rather, they were so only when white people decided they should be, and were not when white people wanted them not to be.[4] As I argued in "On Being White,"[5] white people actively legislate matters of race membership, and if asserting their right to do so requires making decisions that override physical criteria, they ignore physical criteria (without, of course, ever abandoning the ideological strategy of insisting that the categories are given in nature). This sort of behavior clearly demonstrates that people construct race actively, and that people who think they are unquestionably white generally think the criteria of what it is to be of this race or that are theirs to manipulate.[6]

Being white is not a biological condition. It is being a member of a certain social/political category, a category that is persistently maintained by those people who are, in their own and each other's perception, unquestionably in it. It is like being a member of a political party or a club or a fraternity—or being a Methodist or a Mormon. If one is white, one is a member of a continuously and politically constituted group that holds itself together by rituals of unity and exclusion, that develops in its members certain styles and attitudes useful in the exploitation of others, that demands and rewards fraternal loyalty, that defines itself as the paradigm of humanity, and that rationalizes (and naturalizes) its existence and its practices of exclusion, colonization, slavery, and genocide (when it bothers to) in terms of a mythology of blood and skin. If you were born to people who are members of that club, you are socialized and inducted into that club. Your membership in it is, in a way or to a degree, compulsory—nobody gave you any choice in the matter—but it is contingent and, in the Aristotelian sense, accidental. If you don't like being a member of that club, you might think of resigning your membership or of figuring out how to get yourself kicked out of the club, how to get yourself excommunicated.

But this strategy of "separation" is vulnerable to a variety of criticisms. A white woman cannot cease having the history she has by some sort of divorce ritual. Furthermore, the renunciation of whiteness may be an act of self-loathing rather than an act of liberation.[7] And disassociation from the race-group one was born into might seem to be an option for white folks, but it seems either not possible or not politically desirable to most members of the other groups from which whites set themselves off.[8] This criticism suggests that my thinking of disassociating from membership in the white fraternity is just another exercise (hence, another reinforcement) of that white privilege that I was finding so onerous and attempting to escape. All these criticisms sound right (and I will circle back to them at the end of the essay), but there is something very wrong here. This closure has the distinctive finality of a trap.

In academic circles where I now circulate, it has become a commonplace that race is a "social construction" and not a naturally given and naturally maintained grouping of human individuals with naturally determined sets of traits. And the recognition of race as nonnatural is presumed, in those circles, to be liberatory. Pursuing the idea of disassociating from the race category in which I am placed and from the perquisites attached to it is a way of pursuing the question of what freedom can be made of this, and for whom. But it seems to me that race (together with racism and race privilege) is *constructed as* something inescapable. And it makes sense that it would be, since such a construction would best serve those served by race and racism. *Of course* race and racism are impossible to escape; of course a white person is always in a sticky web of privilege that permits only acts that reinforce ("reinscribe") racism. This just means that some exit must be forced. That will require conceptual creativity, and perhaps conceptual violence.

The "being white" that has presented itself to me as a burden and an insuperable block to my growth out of racism is not essentially about the color of my skin or any other inherited bodily trait, even though doctrines of color are bound up with this status in some ways. The problem, then, is to find a way to think clearly about some kind of whiteness that is *not essentially* tied to color and yet has some significant relation to color. The distinction feminists have made between maleness and masculinity provides a clue and an analogy. Maleness we have construed as something a human animal can be born with; masculinity we have construed as something a human animal can be trained to—and it is an empirical fact that most male human animals are trained to it in one or another of its cultural varieties.[9] Masculinity is not a blossoming consequence of genetic constitution, as lush growths of facial hair seem to be in the males of many human groups. But the masculinity of an adult male is far from superficial or incidental, and we know it is not something an individual could shuck off like a coat or snap out of like an actor stepping out of his character. The masculinity of an adult male human in any particular culture is also profoundly connected with the local perceptions and conceptions of maleness (as "biological"), its causes and its consequences. So it may be with being white, but we need some revision of our vocabulary to say it rightly. We need a term in the realm of race and racism whose grammar is analogous to the grammar of the term "masculinity." I am tempted to recommend the neologism "albosity" for this honor, but I am afraid it is too strange to catch on. So I will introduce "whitely" and "whiteliness" as terms whose grammar is analogous to that of "masculine" and "masculinity." Being white-skinned (like being male) is a matter of physical traits presumed to be physically determined; being whitely (like being masculine) I conceive as a deeply ingrained way of being in the world. Following the analogy with masculinity, I assume that the connection between whiteliness and light-colored skin is a *contingent* connection: whiteliness can be manifested by persons who are *not* "white"; it can be absent in persons who *are*.

In the next section, I talk about whiteliness in a free and speculative way, exploring what it may be. This work is raw preliminary sketching; it moves against no such background of research and attentive observation as there is to guide accounts of masculinity. There is of course a large literature on racism, but I think that what I am after here is not one and the same thing as racism, either institutional or personal. Whiteliness is connected to institutional

racism (as this discussion will show) by the fact that individuals
with this sort of character are well suited to the social roles of agents
of institutional racism, but it is a character of persons, not of institutions. Whiteliness is also related to individual or personal racism, but I think it is not one and the same thing as racism, at least
in the sense where "racism" means bigotry/hate/ignorance/indiffer-
ence. As I understand masculinity, it is not the same thing as
misogyny; similarly, whiteliness is not the same thing as race-
hatred. One can be whitely even if one's beliefs and feelings are
relatively well informed, humane, and goodwilled. So I approach
whiteliness freshly, as itself, as something which is both familiar
and unknown.

Whiteliness

To begin to get a picture of what whiteliness is, we need to invoke a certain candid and thoughtful reflection on the part of white
people, who of course in some ways know themselves best; we also
need to consider how people of color perceive white people, since
in some ways they know white people best. For purposes of this
preliminary exploration, I draw on material from three books for
documentation of how white people are, as presented in the experience of people of color. The three are *This Bridge Called My Back*,[10]
which is a collection of writings by radical women of color, *Feminist Theory: From Margin to Center*,[11] by black theorist bell hooks,
and *Drylongso*,[12] which is a collection of narratives of members of
what its editor calls the "core black community."[13] For white voices,
I draw on my own and those I have heard as a participant/observer
of white culture, and on Minnie Bruce Pratt.

Minnie Bruce Pratt, a feminist and a white southerner, has spelled
out some of what I call the whitely way of dealing with issues of
morality and change.[14] She said she had been taught to be a *judge*—
a judge of responsibility and of punishment, according to an ethical system that countenances no rival; she had been taught to be a
preacher—to point out wrongs and tell others what to do; she had
been taught to be a *martyr*—to take all responsibility and all glory;
and she had been taught to be a *peacemaker*—because she could
see all sides and see how it all ought to be. I too was taught something like this, growing up in a small town south of the Mason-
Dixon line, in a self-consciously Christian and white family. I learned
that I, and "we," knew right from wrong and had the responsibility

to see to it that right was done, that there were others who did not know right from wrong and should be advised, instructed, helped, and directed by us. I was taught that *because* one knows what is right, it is morally appropriate to have and exercise what I now call race privilege and class privilege. Not "might is right," but "right is might," as Carolyn Shafer puts the point.[15] In any matter in which we did not know what is right, through youth or inexpertise of some sort, we would await the judgment or instruction of another (white) person who did.

Drylongso: White people are bolder because they think they are supposed to know everything anyhow. (97)

White men look up to their leaders more than we do and they are not much good without their leaders. (99)

White people don't really know how they feel about anything until they consult their leaders or a book or other things outside themselves. (99)

White people are not supposed to be stupid, so they tend to think they are intelligent, no matter how stupidly they are behaving. (96)

Margin: The possibility [they] were not the best spokes-people for all women made [them] fear for [their] self-worth. (13)

Whitely people generally consider themselves to be benevolent and goodwilled, fair, honest, and ethical. The judge, preacher, peace-maker, martyr, socialist, professional, moral majority, liberal, radical, conservative, working men and women—nobody admits to being prejudiced, everybody has earned every cent they ever had, doesn't take sides, doesn't hate anybody, and always votes for the person they think best qualified for the job, regardless of the candidate's race, sex, religion, or national origin, maybe even regardless of their sexual preferences. The professional version of this person is always profoundly insulted by the suggestion that s/he might have permitted some personal feeling about a client to affect the quality of services rendered. S/he believes with perfect confidence that s/he is not prejudiced, not a bigot, not spiteful, jealous, or rude, does not engage in favoritism or discrimination. When there is a

serious and legitimate challenge, a negotiator has to find a resolution that enables the professional person to save face, to avoid simply
agreeing that s/he made an unfair or unjust judgment, discriminated against someone, or otherwise behaved badly. Whitely people
have a staggering faith in their own rightness and goodness, and
that of other whitely people. We are not crooks.

Drylongso: Every reasonable black person thinks that most
                    white people do not mean him well. (7)

                    They figure, if nobody blows the whistle, then
                    Nothing wrong has gone down. (21)

                    White people are very interested in seeming to be
                    of service. . . . (4)

                    Whitefolks *can't* do right, even if there was one
                    who wanted to. . . . They are so damn greedy and
                    cheap that it even hurts them to *try* to do right.
                    (59)

Bridge: A child is trick-or-treating with her friends. At one
                    house the woman, after realizing the child was an
                    Indian, "quite crudely told me so, refusing to give
                    me treats my friends had received." (47)

Drylongso: I used to be a waitress, and I can still remember
                    how white people would leave a tip and then
                    someone at the table, generally some white woman,
                    would take some of the money. (8)

Bridge: The lies, pretensions, the snobbery and cliquish-
                    ness. (69)

                    We experience white feminists and their organiza-
                    tions as elitist, crudely insensitive, and conde-
                    scending. (86)

                    White people are so rarely loyal. (59)

Whitely people do have a sense of right and wrong, and are ethical. Their ethics is in great part an ethics of forms, procedures,
and due process. As Minnie Bruce Pratt said, their morality is a

matter of "ought-to," not "want to" or "passionately desire to." And
the "oughts" tend to factor out into propriety or good manners and
abiding by the rules. Change cannot be initiated unless the moves
are made in appropriate ways. The rules are often-rehearsed. I have
participated in whitely women's affirming to each other that some
uncomfortable disruption caused by someone objecting to some
injustice or offense could have been avoided: had she brought "her"
problem forth in the correct way, it could have been correctly pro-
cessed. We say:

> She should have brought it up in the business meeting.

> She should have just taken the other woman aside and explained
> that the remark had offended her.

> She should not have personally attacked me; she should have just
> told me that my behavior made her uncomfortable, and I would
> have stopped doing it.

> She should take this through the grievance procedure.

By believing in rules, by being arbiters of rules, by understanding
agency in terms of the applications of principles to particular situations, whitely people think they preserve their detachment from
prejudice, bias, meanness, and so on. Whitely people tend to believe that one preserves one's goodness by being principled, by acting
according to rules instead of according to feeling.

> *Drylongso*:   We think white people are the most unprincipled
> folks in the world. . . . (8)

> White people are some writing folks! They will
> write! They write everything. Now they do that
> because they don't trust each other. Also, they are
> the kind of people who think that you can think
> about everything, about whether you are going to
> do, before you do that thing. Now, that's bad for
> them because you can't do that without wings. . . .
> All you can do is do what you know has got to be
> done as right as you know how to do that thing.
> White people don't seem to know that. (88)

> . . . he keeps changing the rules. . . . Now, Chahlie
> will rule you to death. (16)

Authority seems to be central to whiteliness, as you might expect from a people who are raised to run things, or to aspire to that: belief in one's authority in matters practical, moral, and intellectual exists in tension with the insecurity and hypocrisy that are essentially connected with the pretense of infallibility. This pretentiousness makes a whitely person simultaneously rude, condescending, overbearing, and patronizing on the one hand, and on the other, weak, helpless, insecure, and seeking validation of their goodness.

Drylongso: White people have got to bluff it out as rulers . . . [they] are always unsure of themselves. (99)

No matter what Chahlie do, he want his mama to pat him on the head and tell him how cute he is. (19)

[I]n a very real sense white men never grow up. (100)

Hard on the outside, soft on the inside. (99)

Bridge: Socially . . . juvenile and tasteless. (99)

No responsibility to others. (70)

The dogmatic belief in whitely authority and rightness is also at odds with any commitment to truth.

Drylongso: They won't tell each other the truth, and the lies they tell each other sound better to them than the truth from our mouths. (29)

As long as they can make someone say rough is smooth, they are happy. . . . Like I told you, whitefolks don't care about what the truth is. . . . It's like when you lie but so much, you don't know what the truth is. (21)

You simply cannot be honest with white people. (45)

Bridge: White feminists have a serious problem with truth and "accountability." (85)

And finally, whitely people make it clear to people of other races that the last thing those people are supposed to do is to challenge whitely people's authority.

Bridge: [W]e are expected [by white women] to move, charm or entertain, but not to educate in ways that are threatening to our audiences. (71)

Margin: Though they expected us to provide first hand accounts of black experience, they felt it was their role to decide if these experiences were authentic. (11)

Often in situations where white feminists aggressively attacked individual black women, they saw themselves as the ones who were under attack, who were the victims. (13)

Drylongso: Most white people—anyways all the white people I know—are people you wouldn't want to explain Anything to. (67)

No wonder whitely people have so much trouble learning, so much trouble receiving, understanding, and acting on moral or political criticism and demands for change. How can you be a preacher who does not know right from wrong, a judge who is an incompetent observer, a martyr who victimizes others, a peacemaker who is the problem, an authority without authority, a grownup who is a child? How can those who are supposed to be running the world acknowledge their relative powerlessness in some matters in any politically constructive way? Any serious moral or political challenge to a whitely person must be a direct threat to her or his very being.

Whiteliness and Class

What I have been exploring here, and calling whiteliness, may sound to some like it is a character of middle-class white people, or perhaps of middle-class people whatever their race; it may sound like a class phenomenon, not a race phenomenon. Before addressing this question more deeply, I should register that it is my impression, just looking around at the world, that white self-righteousness is not exclusive to the middle class. Many poor and working-class white people are perfectly confident that they are more intelligent, know more, have better judgment, and are more moral than black people or Chicanos or Puerto Ricans or Indians or anyone else they view as not white, and believe that they would be perfectly competent to run the country and to rule others justly and righteously if given the opportunity.

But this issue of the relationship of whiteliness to class deserves further attention.

Though I think that what I am talking about *is* a phenomenon of race, I want to acknowledge a close interweaving and double determination of manifestations and outcomes of race and of class, and to consider some of the things that give rise to the impression that what I am calling whiteliness may really be just "middle-class-liness." One thing that has happened here is that the person who contributed to the observations assembled in the preceding section as a "participant observer" among white people (that is, the author of this analysis) is herself a lifelong member of the middle class. The whiteliness in which she has participated and about which she can write most vividly and authentically is that of her own kin, associates, and larger social group. This might, to a certain extent, bias that description of whiteliness toward a middle-class version of it.

Another reason that what I am calling whiteliness might appear to be a class character rather than a race one is that even if it is not peculiar to whites of the middle classes, it is nonetheless peculiarly suitable to them: it suits them to their jobs and social roles of managing, policing, training, disciplining, legislating, and administering, in a capitalist bureaucratic social order.

Another interesting point in this connection is that the definition of a dominant race tends to fasten on and project an image of a dominant group within that race as *paradigmatic* of the race.[16] The ways in which individual members of that elite group enact and manifest their racedness and dominance would constitute a sort of norm of enacting and manifesting this racedness to which nonelite members of the race would generally tend to assimilate themselves. Those ways of enacting and manifesting racedness would also carry marks of the class position of the paradigmatic elite within the race, and these marks too would appear in the enactments of race by the nonelite. In short, the ways in which members of the race generally enact and stylistically manifest membership in the race would tend to bear marks of the class status of the elite paradigmatic members of the race.

I do not think whiteliness is just middle-class-liness misnamed. I think of whiteliness as a way of being that extends across ethnic, cultural, and class categories and occurs in ethnic, cultural, and class varieties—varieties that may tend to blend toward a norm set by the elite groups within the race. Whatever class and ethnic variety there is among white people, though, such niceties seem often to have no particular salience in the experience that people of other races have with white people. It is very significant that the people of color from whose writings and narratives I have quoted in the preceding section often characterize the white people they talk about in part by class status, but they do not make anything of it. They do not generally indicate that class differences among white people make much difference to how people of color experience white people.

Speaking of the oppression of women, Gayle Rubin noted its "endless variety and monotonous similarity."[17] There is great variety among the men of all the nationalities, races, religions, and positions in various economies and polities, and women do take into account the particulars of the men they must deal with. But when our understanding of the world is conditioned by consciousness of sexism and misogyny, we see *also*, very clearly, the impressive and monotonous *lack* of variety among "masculinities." With my notion of whiteliness, I am reaching for the monotonous similarity, not the endless variety, in white folks' ways of being in the world. For various reasons, that monotonous similarity may have a middle-class cast to it, or my own perception of it may give it a middle-class cast, but I think that what I am calling "whiteliness" is a phenomenon of race. It is integral to what constructs and what is constructed by race, and only indirectly related to class.

Feminism and Whiteliness

Being whitely, like being anything else in a sexist culture, is not the same thing in the lives of white women as it is in the lives of white men. The political significance of one's whiteliness interacts with the political significance of one's status as female or male in a male-supremacist culture. For white men, a whitely way of being in the world is very harmonious with masculinity and their social and political situation. For white women it is, of course, much more complicated.

Femininity in white women is praised and encouraged but is nonetheless contemptible as weakness, dependence, feather-brainedness, vulnerability, and so on, but whiteliness in white women is unambivalently taken among white people as an appropriate enactment of a positive status. Because of this, for white women whiteliness works more consistently than femininity does to disguise and conceal their negative value and low status as women, and at the same time to appear to compensate for it or to offset it.

Those of us who are born female and white are born into the status created by white men's hatred and contempt for women, but white girls aspire to Being and integrity, like anyone else. Racism translates this into an aspiration to whiteliness. The white girl learns that whiteliness is dignity and respectability; she learns that whiteliness is her aptitude for partnership with white men; she learns that partnership with white men is her salvation from the original position of Woman in patriarchy. Adopting and cultivating whiteliness as an individual character seems to put it in the woman's own power to lever herself up out of a kind of nonbeing (the status of woman in a male-supremacist social order) over into a kind of Being (the status of white in white-supremacist social order). But whiteliness does not save white women from the condition of *woman*. Quite the contrary. A white woman's whiteliness is deeply involved in her oppression as a woman and works against her liberation.

White women are deceived, deceive ourselves, and will deceive others about ourselves, if we believe that by being whitely we can escape the fate of being the women of the white men. Being rational, righteous, and ruly (rule-abiding and rule-enforcing) does for some of us some of the time buy a ticket to a higher level of material well-being than we might otherwise be permitted (though it is not dependable). But the reason, right, and rules are not of our own making. White men may welcome our whiteliness as endorsement of their own values and as an expression of our loyalty to them (that is, as proof of their power over us) and because it makes us good helpmates to them. But if our whiteliness commands any respect, it is only in the sense that a woman who is chaste and obedient is called (by classic patriarchal reversal) "respectable."

It is commonly claimed that the women's movement in the United States, during the past couple of decades, is a white women's movement. This claim is grossly disrespectful to the many feminists whom the label "white" does not fit. But it is indeed the case that millions of white women have been drawn to and engaged in feminist action and theorizing, and this creative engagement did *not* arise from those women's being respected for their nice whitely ways by white men: it arose from the rape, battery, powerlessness, poverty or material dependence, spiritual depletion, degradation, harassment, servitude, insanity, drug addiction, botched abortions, and murder of those very women, those women who are white.[18]

As doris davenport put it in her analysis of white feminists' racism:

> A few of us [third world women] . . . see beyond the so-called privilege of being white, and perceive white wimmin as very oppressed, and ironically, invisible. . . . [I]t would seem that some white feminists could [see this] too. Instead, they cling to their myth of being privileged, powerful, and less oppressed . . . than black wimmin. . . . Somewhere deep down (denied and almost killed) in the psyche of racist white feminists there is some perception of their real position: powerless, spineless, and invisible. Rather than examine it, they run from it. Rather than seek solidarity with wimmin of color, they pull rank within themselves.[19]

For many reasons it is difficult for women (of any intersection of demographic groups) to grasp the enormity, the full depth and breadth, of their oppression and of men's hatred and contempt for them. One reason is simply that the facts are so ugly and the image of that oppressed, despised, and degraded woman so horrible that recognizing her as oneself seems to be accepting utter defeat. Some women, at some times, I am sure, must deny it to survive. But in the larger picture, denial (at least deep and sustained denial) of one's own oppression cuts one off from the appreciation of the oppression of others that is necessary for the alliances one needs. This is what I think Cherríe Moraga is pointing out when she says: "Without an emotional, heartfelt grappling with the source of our own oppression, without naming the enemy within ourselves and outside of us, no authentic, non-hierarchical connection among oppressed groups can take place."[20] If white women are not able to ally with women of other races in the construction of another world, we will indeed remain defeated, in this one.

White women's whiteliness does not deliver the deliverance we were taught it would. Our whiteliness interferes with our ability to form necessary alliances both by inhibiting and muddling our understanding of our own oppression as women and by making us personally obnoxious and insufferable to many other women much of the time; it also is directly opposed to our liberation because it joins and binds us to our oppressors. By our whitely ways of being we enact partnership and racial solidarity with white men, we animate a social (if not also sexual) heterosexual union with white men, and we embody and express our possession by white men.

A feminism that boldly names the oppression and degraded condition of white women and recognizes white men as its primary agents and primary beneficiaries—such a feminism can make it obvious to white women that the various forms of mating and racial bonding with white men do not and will not ever save us from that condition. Such a feminist understanding might free us from the awful confusion of thinking that our whiteliness is dignity, and might make it possible for us to know that it is a dreadful mistake to think that our whiteliness earns us our personhood. Such knowledge can open up the possibility of practical understanding of whiteliness as a learned character (as we have already understood masculinity and femininity), a character by which we facilitate our own containment under the "protection" of white men, a character that interferes constantly and often conclusively with our ability to be friends with women of other races, a character by which we station ourselves as lieutenants and stenographers of white male power, a character that is not desirable in itself and neither manifests nor merits the full Being to which we aspire. A character by which, in fact, we both participate in and cover up our own defeat. We might then include among our strategies for change a practice of unlearning whiteliness, and as we proceed in this, we can only become less and less well-assimilated members of that racial group called "white." (I must state as clearly as possible that I do not claim that unbecoming whitely is the only thing white women need to do to combat racism. I have said that whiteliness is not the same thing as racism. I have no thought whatever that I am offering a panacea for the eradication of racism. I *do* think that *being* whitely interferes enormously with white women's attempts in general to be antiracist.)

Disaffiliation, Deconstruction, Demolition

To deconstruct a concept is to analyze it in a way that reveals its construction—both in the temporal sense of its birth and development over time and in a certain cultural and political matrix, and in the sense of its own present structure, its meaning, and its relation to other concepts.[21] One of the most impressive aspects of such an analysis is the revelation of the "contingency" of the concept, that is, the fact that it is only the accidental collaboration of various historical events and circumstances that brought that concept into being, and the fact that there could be a world of sense without that concept in it. The other impressive thing about such analyses is what they reveal of the complex and intense interplay of construction of concepts and construction of concrete realities. This interplay is what I take to be that phenomenon called the "social construction of reality."

In combination, the revelation of the historical contingency of a concept and the revelation of the intricacy of interplay between concept and concrete lived reality gives rise to a strong sense that "deconstruction" of a concept simultaneously dismantles the reality in whose social construction the evolution of the concept is so closely involved. But things do not work that way. In the first place, analyzing a concept and circulating the analysis among a few interested colleagues does not make the concept go away, does not dislodge it from the matrix of concepts in the active conceptual repertoire even of those few people, much less of people in general. In the second place, even if the deconstructive analysis so drains the concept of power for those few individuals that they can no longer use it, and perhaps their participation in the social constructions of which that concept is a part becomes awkward and halting (like tying your shoelaces while thinking directly about what you are doing), it still leaves those social constructions fully intact. Once constructed and assimilated, a social construct may be a fairly sturdy thing, not very vulnerable to erosion, decay, or demolition.[22] It is one thing to "deconstruct" a concept, another to dismantle a well-established, well-entrenched social construct. For example, Foucault's revelations about the arbitrariness and coerciveness of classifications of sexualities did not put an end to queer-bashing or to the fears lesbians and gay men have of being victims of a witch-hunt.

I am interested, as I suggested earlier, in the matter of how to translate the recognition of the social-constructedness of races into some practice of the freedom these contingencies seem to promise, some way to proceed by which people can be liberated from the concrete reality of races as determined by racism. But the social-constructedness of race and races in the racist state has very different meanings for groups differently placed with respect to these categories. The ontological freedom of categorical reconstruction may be generic, but what is politically possible differs for those differently positioned, and not all the political possibilities for every group are desirable. Attempts by any group to act in this ontological freedom need to be informed by understanding of how the action is related to the possibilities and needs of the others.

I have some hope that if I can manage to refuse to enact, embody, animate this category—the white race—as I am supposed to, I can free my energies and actions from a range of disabling confinements and burdens, and align my will with the forces that eventually will dissolve or dismantle that race as such. If it is objected that it is an exercise of white privilege to dissociate myself from the white race this way, I would say that in fact this project is strictly forbidden by the rules of white solidarity and white supremacy, and is *not* one of the privileges of white power. It may also be objected that my adoption or recommendation of this strategy implies that the right thing to do, in general, for everyone, is to dissolve, dismantle, and bring an end to races; and if this indeed is the implication, it can sound very threatening to some of the people whose races are thus to be erased. This point is well made by Franz Fanon in a response to Jean-Paul Sartre, described by Henry Louis Gates, Jr., "Reading Sartre's account of Négritude (as an antithesis preparatory to a 'society without races,' hence 'a transition and not a conclusion'), Fanon reports: 'I felt I had been robbed of my last chance . . . Sartre, in this work, has destroyed black zeal. . . .'"[23] The dynamic creative claiming of racial identities (and gender identity), identities that were first imposed as devices of people's oppression, has been a politically powerful and life-enhancing response of oppressed people in modern and contemporary times. For members of oppressor groups to suddenly turn around and decide to abolish races would be, it seems, genocide, not liberation. (I have a parallel unease about the project of dismantling the category of women, which some feminists seem to favor.)

But I am not suggesting that if white women should try to abandon the white race and contribute to its demolition, then women of other races should take the same approach to their racial categorization and their races. Quite the contrary. Approaches to the matter of dismantling a dominance-subordinance structure surely should be asymmetrical—they should differ according to whether one has been molded into its category of dominance or its category of subordination. My hope is that it may contribute to the demise of *rac-ism* if we upset the logical symmetry of race—if black women, for instance, cultivate a racial identity and a distinctive (sexually egali-tarian) black community (and other women of racialized groups, likewise), while white women are undermining white racial iden-tity and cultivating communities and agency among women along lines of affinity not defined by race. Such an approach would work toward a genuine redistribution of power.

Growing Room

The experiences of feminists' unlearning femininity and our readi-ness to require men to unlearn masculinity show that it is thinkable to unlearn whiteliness. If I am right about all this, then, indeed, we even know a good deal about how to do it.

We know we have to inform ourselves exhaustively of its poli-tics. We know we have to avoid, or be extremely alert in, environ-ments in which whiteliness is particularly required or rewarded (for example, academia). We know we have to *practice* new ways of being in environments that nurture different habits of feeling, per-ception, and thought, and that we will have to make these environ-ments for ourselves since the world will not offer them to us. We know that the process will be collective and that this collectivity does not mean we will blend seamlessly with the others into a colorless mass; women unlearning femininity together have not become clones of each other or of those who have been valuable models. As feminists we have learned that we have to resist the temptation to encourage femininity in other women when, in mo-ments of exhaustion and need, we longed for another's sacrificial mothering or wifing. Similarly, white women have to resist the temptation to encourage whiteliness in each other when, in moments of cowardice or insecurity, we long for the comfort of "solidarity in superiority," or when we wish someone would relieve our pain-ful uncertainty with a timely application of judgments and rules.

Seasoned feminists (white feminists along with feminists of other races) know how to transform consciousness. The first breakthrough is in the moment of knowing that another way of being is possible. In the matter of a white woman's racedness, the possibility in question is the possibility of disengaging (on some levels, at least) one's own energies and wits from the continuing project of the social creation and maintenance of the white race, the possibility of being disloyal to that project by stopping constantly making oneself whitely. And this project should be very attractive to white women once we grasp that it is the possibility of *not being whitely*, rather than the possibility of *being whitely*, that holds some promise of our rescuing ourselves from the degraded condition of women in a white men's world.

Notes

1. The working title during that period was "Ritual Libations and Points of Explosion," which referred to a remark made by Helene Wenzel in a review of my *Politics of Reality* which appeared in *The Women's Review of Books* 1, no. 1 (October 1983). Wenzel said, "Even when white women call third world women our friends, and they us, we still agonize over 'the issue.' The result is that when we write or teach about race, racism and feminism we tend either to condense everything we have to say to the point of explosion, or, fearing just that explosion, we sprinkle our material with ritual libations which evaporate without altering our own, or anyone else's consciousness." And, coming down to cases, she continued, "Frye has fallen into both of these traps."

2. For critical reflection on "wanting to do good" and on "not knowing how to act," see "A Response to *Lesbian Ethics*: Why Ethics?" in *Willful Virgin: Essays in Feminism*, ed. Marilyn Frye (Freedom, Calif.: The Crossing Press, 1992), 138–46.

3. Actually, what I think women of color have communicated in this matter is not so harsh as that. The point is that no one can do someone else's growing for her, that white women must not expect women of color to be *on call* to help, and that there is a great deal of knowledge to be gained by reading, interacting, and paying attention, which white women need not ask women of color to supply. Some women of color have helped me a great deal (sometimes in spite of me).

4. Tamara Buffalo, mixed-race Chippewa, writes: "My white husband said, 'Don't think that you have any Indian-ness, that was taken from you years ago. You speak English don't you? The way you think is white, how you dress, your ambitions, how you raise your daughter, all this is white. I know what is white and what is not white!' I told the group word for word, everything he said. Repeating it in the same flat tone he used. I was bearing witness. I was testifying against him." Tamara Buffalo, "Adopted Daughter," in *Hurricane Alice: A Feminist Quarterly* 10, no. 2 (Spring 1994). Thanks to Carolyn Shafer for bringing this statement to my attention.

5. Marilyn Frye, *The Politics of Reality* (Freedom, Calif.: The Crossing Press, 1983), 115–16.

6. It is easy for a white person who is trying to understand white privilege and white power in white supremacist states to make the mistake of

(self-servingly) exaggerating that power and privilege, assuming it is total. In this case, I was making the mistake earlier of thinking that white domination means that white people totally control the definition of race and the races. Reading bell hooks's *Yearning* (Boston: South End Press, 1990), I awoke to the fact that Afro-Americans (and other racialized people) are also engaged in the definition of black (and other "race" categories); white people have the power to enforce their own definitions in many (but not all) situations, but they are not the only people determining the meanings of race categories and race words, and what they determine for themselves (and enforce) is not necessarily congruent with what others are determining for *them*selves.

7. I want to thank María Lugones, whose palpably loving anger on this point made me take it seriously. See María Lugones, "Hablando cara a cara/ Speaking Face to Face: An Exploration of Ethnocentric Racism," in *Making Face, Making Soul: Haciendo Caras: Critical and Creative Perspectives by Women of Color*, ed. Gloria Anzaldúa (San Francisco: aunt lute foundation press, 1990).

8. Carrie Jane Singleton, "Race and Gender in Feminist Theory," *Sage* VI, no. 1 (Summer 1989): 15.

9. I am not unmindful here of the anxiety some readers may have about my reliance on a distinction between that which is physically given and that which is socially acquired. I could complicate this passage immensely by shifting from the material mode of talking about maleness and skin colors to the formal mode of talking about conceptions or constructions of maleness and skin colors. But it would not make anything clearer. It is perfectly meaningful to use the term "male" and the term "white" (as a pigment word), while understanding that sex categories and color categories are "constructed" as the kinds of categories they are, that is, physical categories as opposed to social categories like "lawyer" or arithmetic categories like "ordinals."

10. Cherríe Moraga and Gloria Anzaldúa, eds., *This Bridge Called My Back: Writing By Radical Women of Color* (Brooklyn, N.Y.: Kitchen Table: Women of Color Press, 1981). I quote from writings by Barbara Cameron, Chrystos, doris davenport, and Mitsuye Yamada.

11. bell hooks, *Feminist Theory: From Margin to Center* (Boston: South End Press, 1985).

12. John Langston Gewaltney, *Drylongso: A Self-Portrait of Black America* (New York: Random House, 1983). I quote from statements by Jackson Jordan, Jr., Hannah Nelson, John Oliver, Howard Roundtree, Rosa Wakefield, and Mabel Lincoln.

13. The people speaking in *Drylongso* were responding to questions put by an interviewer. The narratives as published do not include the questions, but the people clearly were asked in some manner to say something about how they see white people or what they think white people generally are like. Most of them, but not every one, prefaced or appended their comments with remarks to the effect that they did not think white people were "like that" by birth or blood, but by being brought up a certain way in certain circumstances.

14. Minnie Bruce Pratt, "Identity: Skin Blood Heart," in *Yours in Struggle*, ed. Elly Bulkin, Minnie Bruce Pratt, and Barbara Smith (Brooklyn: Long Haul Press, 1984).

15. For more exploration of some of the meanings of this, see Frye, "A Response to *Lesbian Ethics*: Why Ethics?"

16. Cf. Etienne Balibar, "Paradoxes of Universality," trans. Michael Edwards, in *Anatomy of Racism*, ed. David Theo Goldberg (Minneapolis: University of Minnesota Press, 1990), 284–85, extracted from "Racisme et nationalism," in *Race, Nation, Classe*, Etienne Balibar and Immanuel Wallerstein (Paris: Editions La Decouverte, 1988).

17. Gayle Rubin, "The Traffic in Women," in *Toward An Anthropology of Woman*, ed. Rayna R. Reiter (New York: Monthly Review Press, 1975), 160.

18. Carolyn Shafer is the one who brought to my attention the fact that there is a certain contradiction in claiming *both* that this stage of the women's movement was created by and belongs to white women *and* (on the grounds of the generally better material welfare of white women, compared to women of other races in the United States) that white women are not all that badly off and don't really know what suffering is about. If white women were as generally comfortable, secure, and healthy as they might appear to some observers, they would not have participated as they have in an enormous movement the first and most enduring issues of which are bodily integrity and economic self-sufficiency.

19. doris davenport, "The Pathology of Racism: A Conversation with Third World Wimmin," in *This Bridge Called My Back*, ed. Moraga and Anzaldda, 89–90.

20. Moraga, *This Bridge Called My Back*, 21.

21. It will be clear to those who learned the word "deconstruction" from the writings of Jacques Derrida that I have wandered off with it in pursuit of interests other than his. They will agree, though, that he gave it up the moment he first wrote it down or uttered it.

22. My lover Carolyn was explaining what I do for a living to our coheart Keyosha, and included an account of "deconstruction." Keyosha, a welder and pipefitter in the construction trades, said that it wasn't a real word and offered "demolition" as the real word for this. Carolyn then had to admit (on my behalf) that all this deconstructing did not add up to any demolition, and a made-up abstract word was probably suitable to this abstract activity.

23. Henry Louis Gates, Jr., "Critical Remarks," in *Anatomy of Racism*, ed. David Theo Goldberg (Minneapolis: University of Minnesota Press, 1990), 325.

8

Reflections on the Meaning of White

Victoria Davion

Marilyn Frye is right to insist that the link between promoting white supremacy and being white skinned is contingent. Certainly white people do not have to act in ways that promote white supremacy. Acting in these ways is not a matter of genetic coding; it is a matter of social training. Frye is also right to point out that although there is only a contingent link between promoting a system based on white supremacy and having white skin, ceasing to promote white supremacy requires more than simply believing in racial equality, and even more than consciously trying to promote racial equality. It requires close examination of and changes in behaviors that may not appear on the surface to promote white supremacy but in fact keep a white supremist system in place. Frye's strategy of searching for these behaviors and attitudes in both her own experiences and experiences that people of color have of white people is a good one. Thus, I want to add to this project by looking at how ethnic differences fit into this kind of analysis.

Frye's description of whiteliness is very familiar to me. It also seems very Protestant, and I am Jewish. I don't deny that white Jews and other ethnic groups engage in the kinds of behaviors she describes, but I want to make clear that many different worldviews can produce these behaviors. Whiteliness is not a particular worldview. Frye focuses on the monotonous similarity of whitely oppression, and I think she is right to do this. If, however, her analysis implies that in order to stop being whitely we must disaffiliate from our ethnic backgrounds, as a Jew I cannot accept it. I don't in fact think that ceasing to be whitely requires this, and I think it is important that this be made clear.

Frye states that whitely people trust each other. One of the quotations she cites from *Drylongso* claims just the opposite: "White people are some writing folks! They will write. They write everything. Now they do that because they don't trust each other."[1] Interestingly, I think both perceptions are right. My upbringing as a white Jew in America included education about anti-Semitism. I was raised not to trust non-Jews because they can turn on you at any time. I will return to this point shortly.

As Frye characterizes some of the other values and beliefs involved in whiteliness, these are not the values I was taught. She states: "I learned that I, and 'we,' knew right from wrong and had the responsibility to see to it right was done, that there were others who did not know what is right and wrong and should be advised, instructed, helped, and directed by us. . . . Not 'might is right,' but 'right is might.'"[2] As a Jew, I was taught that being right doesn't insure one any power whatsoever, and that the majority doesn't know right from wrong. Yet, because might makes right in reality, I was taught to leave the Christian majority alone to do its own thing. I was certainly not encouraged at all to spread the truth of Judaism. Rather, I was warned to shut up about all of this if I wanted to be safe.

It is in the ways that I learned how to be careful around non-Jews that I recognize much of what Frye calls whitely behavior in myself. I learned how to tone down behaviors that might be considered stereotypically Jewish around those who might find me too loud or pushy. Although I was taught to trust and favor Jews and to hate certain groups of whites, I know how to behave as if I hate no one, trust other white people, and don't discriminate.

Why do I know how to behave in these ways? I was taught this as a survival mechanism. Although this was never stated explicitly, I now realize that I was given the message that white skin alone wouldn't guarantee me certain privileges. In addition to having white skin, I needed to be or pretend to be Christian. Often, passing for a white Christian doesn't involve doing anything. However, I learned to be sure not to call attention to the fact that I wasn't really Christian. The message was that insofar as I am white, it is safe to trust other whites in seeking white privileges. However, insofar as I am Jewish in a primarily Christian society, this isn't the case.

What does this imply about whiteliness in general and about me as a white Jew? Whiteliness is not, in my opinion, a particular worldview. Whitely behavior can be the result of a variety of worldviews. The motivation for being whitely, and also for stopping being whitely, will therefore come from a variety of sources depending on who one is. I have come to realize that in my own case, to promote the particular white-supremacist system in which we now live is at the same time to promote a system that is anti-Semitic to its roots. This is why it is so important to learn the dominant behaviors and practices and to avoid acting too Jewish in public. In supporting the myth that all white people are basically the same in certain respects, which is what a white-supremacist system must do, I contribute to the fracturing of my being by being whitely. I cannot be whole in such a system.

I want to make a few things clear before going any further. I am not saying that white Jews are any less whitely or even any less racist than other whites. In fact, we may be more whitely in that the behaviors are learned as a survival mechanism. Nor am I saying that white Jews should be excused for being whitely while others should not. Supporting a white-supremacist system is wrong no matter who does it. I don't want to try to rank blame for whitely behavior. What I am saying is that as a white Jew, I have a particular motive for ceasing to be whitely. In being whitely I contribute to the erasure of myself as Jewish, and the fracturing of my identity.

If whitely behaviors are behaviors that whites from various backgrounds engage in, then getting rid of them need not mean getting rid of one's ethnicity. Rather, it will mean looking at behaviors and attitudes and rooting out the whitely ones, the ones that promote white supremacy. This brings me to a final point with regard to Frye's analysis of whiteliness. Many of the characteristics Frye names seem as if they might not be bad in themselves, but only in certain contexts. If this is true, then nobody's ethnic background is polluted to the point where it must be discarded. Instead, the strategy will be to look at the way one engages in various behaviors. Following rules is one example. Rule-following has its place. However, it is oppressive to insist that everyone follow the rules when not everyone thinks rules are appropriate for that situation to begin with, or not everyone has had the opportunity to help construct the rules. Voting for the person one thinks is best qualified for the job doesn't seem like a bad behavior in itself. It depends on what is meant by most qualified. Therefore, it is not the behaviors them-selves that are the problem; it is the way that we engage in them.

Some of the other attitudes and behaviors Frye mentions are always unfortunate regardless of the context. She says:

> Many poor and working class white people are perfectly confident that they are more intelligent, know more, have better judgment, and are more moral than Black people or Chicanos or Puerto Ricans or Indians or anyone else they view as not white, and believe that they would be perfectly competent to run the country and to rule others justly and righteously if given the opportunity.[3]

The version of whiteliness described above sounds like racism. One of the things I find very important in Frye's project is her insis-tence that whitely behaviors can be manifested in people who be-lieve in racial equality. That is, even those of us who do not think that whites are more intelligent, know more, and so on, can act in ways that promote white supremacy. This description does not seem to capture that.

I conclude that Frye is exactly right to seek something analo-gous to masculinity that white people are socialized into but that we can learn to stop being and doing. She is also right to listen to people of color describe the endless monotony and similarity in their experiences of race oppression. I think it is a mistake, how-ever, to conclude that this monotony is due to any common worldview in those who behave in whitely ways (I am not saying that she does this). Many systems are at work. In addition, while I think Frye is right to look for whiteliness as she describes it abstractly, I am still not sure exactly what it is. I am not sure because some of the be-haviors she mentions do not seem necessarily bad in themselves, and others seem blatantly racist. Nevertheless, her analysis has started me thinking about when and why I behave in whitely ways. It has helped me to realize that acting whitely involves affirming a frame-work in which behavior stereotyped as ethnically Jewish is looked down upon. Thus, in acting whitely I erase my ethnicity. Perhaps if more white people celebrated our differences publicly, the myth that whites are basically the same, a myth that is necessary for upholding a white-supremacist system, would be impossible to maintain. Thus, I regard this essay as a call for the celebration of ethnic diversity as well as a call for whites to stop acting whitely. I hope I have shown that these projects are compatible.

Notes

1. John Langston Gewaltney, *Drylongso: A Self-Portrait of Black America* (New York: Random House, 1983), 88.
2. Marilyn Frye, "White Woman Feminist," 118–19 in this volume.
3. Ibid., 123–24.

9

On Race, Racism, and Ethnicity

Claudia Card

These reflections explore strands of thought suggested primarily in essays by three thinkers whose work has been helpful to me for thinking about race, racism, ethnicity, and ethnocentrism.[1] I do not develop a thesis so much as raise questions and explore some interrelated themes and considerations surrounding these concepts.

The thinkers to whom I refer are W. E. B. Du Bois, Marilyn Frye, and María Lugones.[2] W. E. B. Du Bois, in his 1897 essay "The Conservation of Races," offers a positive outlook on race from an internal point of view, that is, from the point of view of those who have been racialized.[3] He offers a positive view of the potentialities of identifying as members of a race, however negatively the concept of race may have originated in the unfriendly projects of others. In doing so he seems to suggest the possibility of nonracist uses of the concept of race, other than simply to acknowledge or address its racist uses by others. In contrast, in her essays on being white and being gendered, Marilyn Frye offers a negative picture of race, treating the concept as external, as imposed upon a people by outsiders whose interests were to mark them for domination, to set them apart as inferior, to prohibit intermarriage, and so on.[4] María Lugones suggests yet another dimension, that of interaction, in her essays "Pedagogy and Racism," "Hablando cara a cara/Speaking Face to Face: An Exploration of Ethnocentric Racism," and other essays that address issues arising from cultural confrontations and interpenetrations.[5] She stresses the interactive nature of rac*ism*, which suggests the possibility that the concept of race may also develop interactively, regardless of how it originated. These views are not necessarily alternatives. Each of these thinkers has had his or her purposes for stressing different aspects of race. Yet they might fit together as complementary elements of a more comprehensive view.

If "race" may have internal, external, and interactive aspects, "racism" suggests first and foremost a negative external view, that is, a negative view held toward members of another group. Like "sexism," "rac*ism*" refers to oppressive behaviors, policies, and attitudes ranging from institutionalized murder to unwitting support of insensitive practices by the well-intentioned.[6] In analyses of racism, the very concept of race is often problematized in ways analogous to the problematizing of gender in analyses of sexism. Worlds seem imaginable in which neither concept structures social relations. Neither races nor genders appear to be natural kinds.[7] In 1945 Ashley Montagu argued that there are no races, on the ground that behaviors cannot be meaningfully correlated with biological ancestry.[8] However, social construction does not make races unreal, even if it makes them arbitrary and unnatural. I say "if" because Du Bois's essay raises the possibility that races need not continue to be totally arbitrarily delineated, even if they are cultural constructions and were initially arbitrary.

"Racism" appears to be a contraction of the earlier "racialism," suggesting the verb "to racialize" which, in turn, suggests social construction and for that reason may be a preferable term.[9] Being race-conscious, however, is not necessarily racializing: it is one thing to *make* something a matter of race and another to *acknowledge* that this has been done. After five centuries of Euro-American racializing of Africans, Asians, and Native Americans, it would seem as irresponsible for white people suddenly to act as though races did not matter as it would be for men suddenly to act as though gender did not matter. For Du Bois, however, race consciousness was not only about oppression. He took issue with the integrationists regarding possible sources of pride and what might be of value in the preservation of races for African Americans and for humanity in general. He was not thinking first of all of holding whites accountable for black oppression. He was concerned here with the development of black talent and genius.

The American Heritage Dictionary speculates that the word "race" may come from the Latin, *ratio*, meaning "a reckoning, account." What "accounts"? What "reckonings"? Rendered by whom to whom? One answer is that the "reckonings" or "accounts" of the conquered were produced by the conquerors, thus embedding their own biases in the concept of race. This interpretation supports the view of race as a construction externally imposed, as in Marilyn Frye's understanding of the concept, that is, applied first to others. Another possible answer, however, is that the "reckoning" or "account" refers to one's own record of one's ancestors, handed on to one's descendants, documenting their heritage. This interpretation suggests an internal view of race, that is, a conception applied first of all to oneself. The latter interpretation is also compatible with a negative view, however, insofar as it may be combined with insider chauvinism and hostility regarding outsiders.

"Race," as sometimes used in the late-nineteenth century by Charlotte Perkins Gilman in *Women and Economics*, refers to a people who share a lineage (a biological ancestry) and a social history.[10] This might be an interesting idea conceived as applying to oneself if individual races were not defined too broadly—if they were not, say, reduced to four or five in the world. Neither she nor Du Bois does so. They usually identify races not by color but by nationality or geographic origin. When races are defined so broadly that one can list them on the fingers of one hand, intraracial differences become more significant than interracial differences, and it is difficult to claim that racial groups so conceived share a social history.

Among social critics, *ethnicity* is often embraced as something positive, while *race* more often arouses suspicion and skepticism. Yet the differences are not always clear or obvious.[11] Both suggest birthplaces and birthrights. Both races and ethnicities may become dispersed through the homelands of others. Like "national," "ethnic" may suggest geographic origins.[12] Like "race," it suggests heritage. However, "race," unlike "ethnicity," suggests the biological as well as the sociopolitical. Thus, Pierre L. van den Berghe defines "race" as "a group that is *socially* defined but on the basis of *physical* criteria" and ethnic groups as "socially defined but on the basis of *cultural* criteria."[13] Because the social heritage of race is commonly one of oppression or privilege, it is plausible that races are products of conquest, a way of maintaining social hierarchy and of preventing intermarriages that would entail property dispersals and consequent power dispersals.

"Race" suggests color more readily than does "ethnicity." "Ethnic" can be used as a euphemism for "racial" where it is thought impolite (or impolitic) to refer to color (as "erotic" in "erotic art" can be a euphemism for "pornographic" where it is thought impolite or impolitic to refer directly to sex). Today in the United States, "ethnic" is popularly used (misused) to refer to anything that isn't white Anglo-Saxon Protestant (WASP), as in the "ethnic" section of the library, "ethnic" restaurants, and the like, as though WASP were not itself an ethnic concept. If one accepts van den Berghe's distinction between race and ethnicity, WASP appears to be a hybrid of race (white) and ethnicity, with ethnicity identified in two ways: by linguistic origin (Anglo) and by religious connection (Protestant). When "ethnic" is used to refer to groups other than WASP, it can refer both to nonwhite races and to non-Anglo ethnicities. Thus, Thomas Sowell's *Ethnic America* offers chapters on Germans, Jews, Italians, Chinese, Japanese, Puerto Ricans, Mexicans, and blacks, identifying only blacks by color.[14]

"Ethnicity," as distinct from "race," suggests culture, especially folk culture, produced by people who share a history that is usually tied to a geographical territory. In the case of Jewish ethnicity, the shared history is tied to a religion or, at least, a body of texts. Either way leaves it open whether co-ethnics share *biological* ancestry. Ethnic groups sometimes fall within racial groups and in other cases cut across them. Ethnicity seems to cut across race in the case of Jewish blacks and whites and to fall under it in the case of whites who may be Italian or German. W. E. B. Du Bois treats Slavic as a race within which there are Russian and Hungarian ethnicities. But is Slavic a racial identification? Or an ethnic one? Like "Anglo" and "Semitic," "Slavic" names a language group, which suggests ethnicity. Yet according to Amoja Three Rivers, the term "slave" comes from "Slavic."[15] If slavery is a racializing practice, perhaps the Slavs were thereby racialized at a certain time in history.

There appears a certain asymmetry between race and ethnicity. No noun "ethnicism" corresponds to "racism." Instead, there is "ethnocentrism," referring to one's attitude regarding one's *own* ethnicity and only by implication, if at all, to one's attitudes toward others. "Racism" (or "racialism"), on the other hand, refers first to one's (usually hostile) attitudes toward *other* races, only by implication suggesting arrogance regarding one's own. Their structures thus seem opposite. There are, of course, terms such as "ethnic prejudice" (and more specific terms, such as "anti-Semitism") and "race supremacist" for attitudes running the other direction in each case.

María Lugones once argued that ethnocentrism need not be racist, meaning that it need not involve a negative attitude toward others.

In her early essay "Pedagogy and Racism," she used the analogy of a mother saying that her child is "the most beautiful in the world," meaning simply that the child is the center of the mother's attention but not intending objectively the comparative value judgment that the words seem to imply. If ethnocentrism could be the analogue of this, it suggests a healthy pride and joy. However, in "Hablando cara a cara/Speaking Face to Face" María Lugones presents a revised conception of ethnocentrism as basically arrogant, arguing that an *absorption in one's own culture* (like a mother's absorption in her child) is *not necessarily ethnocentric*. Yet she retains the idea that ethnocentrism—although arrogant—is not necessarily racist. Ethnocentrism becomes racist, she argues, when it involves the idea of the racial state.[16] Racist ethnocentrism combines the orientations of racism and ethnocentrism.

Because histories and ancestries crisscross and their boundaries are arbitrary and vague, race identifications are bound to be arbitrary, regardless of their motivations. They may be *more* arbitrary than ethnic ones if one's ethnicity—enculturation—is less liable to multiplicity than one's genealogy. It may seem as though one's ethnicity *is* liable to serious multiplicity, in that biculturalism is common, especially among the oppressed in ethnocentrically racist societies. However, biculturalism need not involve *identifying with* or *identifying oneself as a member of* both cultures. It may simply be a matter of facility in negotiating one's way in another culture. One who is bicultural might think of oneself as a "'world'-traveler," in María Lugones's sense of that term, without necessarily identifying oneself as *belonging* to "worlds" in which one travels well.[17]

Neither one's race nor one's ethnicity seems reducible to one's loyalties. An interesting question, however, is what significance, if any, one's self-identification has for one's racial or ethnic identity, perhaps especially if one's ancestry or one's cultural heritage is evidently mixed.[18] Identifying someone as a member of a certain race may suggest either that they *do* identify with a certain ancestry and history or that the speaker thinks they *should* identify with it, perhaps for political reasons. From a political point of view, the latter sort of view need not be arbitrary, even if the relevant biological ancestry were evidently mixed. Further, whether one chooses to identify with a race may not be decisive for how others identify one, and how others identify one may come to have implications for what the racial category means. There is also such a thing as refusing to face up to one's identity; there is such a thing as "passing." Yet, there is also such a thing as justifiably disowning a heritage, although the resulting implications for one's identity may be unclear. If I disown my Protestant heritage, I may have changed my identity *somewhat*, but I do not cease thereby to be WASP.

I have been told that I hail from a line of Scots. Should I identify with that? I do not voluntarily identify with Scottish ethnicity. I love music but have a low tolerance for bagpipes. I like plaids but do not wear skirts, not even kilts. And I seem not to have inherited proverbial Scottish attitudes toward money. Yet, such things may not be decisive for who I am. My sensibilities and dispositions may be inherited from Gaelic ancestors with whom I have no particular higher-order desire to identify. Even my attitudes and values may be influenced by a more palpable Presbyterianism which I do not willingly embrace. Such characteristics may have enabled me throughout my life to hook into advantageous social networks and to develop what assets I have that others value in me (and that I value in myself). If such influences are transmitted through the parenting process, and if they construct me ethnically, my ethnicity may have little to do with my choices or voluntary identifications. Being an ethnic Scot may be part of my moral luck, something to be taken into account if I am to appreciate the political meanings of my relationships and interactions with others and avoid the arrogance that María Lugones identifies as ethnocentric. To regard as *simply human* the attitudes, values, sensibilities, and dispositions that define *one's ethnicity* is a form of arrogance that might justifiably be regarded as ethnocentric, however unwittingly it is done.

Just as combating ethnocentrism may require developing a consciousness that many of one's values, attitudes, and so forth have roots in one's ethnic heritage, antiracism may require—as it has, in my case—developing a higher-order race consciousness: becoming conscious, for instance, of how one has learned to process perceptions of racial difference (in order to deny them, for example). Such consciousness goes against the grain of my upbringing. Terms like "color conscious," in my corner of Anglo culture, conjure up such thoughts as that if people are classified by readily visible physical characteristics such as color, these characteristics will not be treated as value-neutral and then masses of people will be instantly targetable by each other for friendship (as in elitist cliques) or hostility (as in people of color being tracked by white security guards in predominantly white department stores), independently of who they are as individuals.[19] "Racial" thinking blocks getting to know people. Hasty generalization is not the worst danger. Generalizing at all in terms of race about highly undesirable or highly desirable characteristics (such as intelligence) is readily enlisted in the service of oppression. Yet among those who are in fact targets of racism, instant recognition of potential friends or potential enemies can be necessary for survival. Instant recognition of contexts in which racism is a potential danger can be necessary for effective resistance by anyone. In the context of what María Lugones calls "the racial state," color consciousness facilitates positive contacts among the oppressed as well as oppressive contacts of dominant with subordinate. It facilitates political separatism of the oppressed as well as segregation and oppressive avoidance by the dominant.[20] The segregationist potentialities are terrifying: capture, concentration of peoples, imprisonment, enslavement. Yet they are hardly a reason to reject color consciousness in a society that is *already* racist—rather the opposite: such dangers can hardly be combatted without it. This creates a challenge for white people in a society such as the United States: how to be race or color conscious without being racist or in other ways oppressive. As Pat Parker put it in her poem "For the white person who wants to know how to be my friend":

> The first thing you do is to forget that i'm Black.
> Second, you must never forget that i'm Black.[21]

One may ask, must color consciousness, or race consciousness, be at best only a necessary evil? Can good purposes, other than resistance to oppression, be served by race consciousness? Good for whom? I want to say good for those on both sides, or at least on the oppressed or subordinated side, of a given racial distinction. W. E. B. Du Bois was interested in the good of affirming racial identity for African Americans. But he also spoke of its value to humanity. His idea was that different cultural developments distinguish racial groups and that it takes many generations to produce these cultural developments. He feared that if races were not conserved—if, for example and in particular, African Americans assimilated to European Americans—valuable cultural developments would be lost. The focus on culture by Du Bois may suggest a concern more with ethnicity than with race. And yet, how separable are they, if he is also right that significant cultural developments require many generations? Du Bois, in his essay on conserving races, seems to think of race as having internal aspects, which he identifies as cultural potentialities that may require generations to realize, as well as whatever external aspects may be defined by practices of others. Neither seems originally the object of individual choice, although individuals can affirm or deny them.

In my liberal Anglo upbringing, race was supposed to be morally irrelevant at least partly because individuals have no *control* over their racial identity, and individuals were supposed to have control over who they *really are*. One can adopt or reject many aspects of an ethnicity—as I do with the Scots. Perhaps for this reason, Anglo liberals have not worried historically about the importance of ethnicity as they have about that of race. Race has been thought totally involuntary—except for the choice whether to procreate (which can, of course, affect the race of one's offspring although it does not affect one's own racial identity).

Marilyn Frye's essay, "On Being White," challenges the assumption that one has no control with respect to one's race by arguing that one can at least choose where to place one's loyalties. This approach preserves the idea that the individual, morally speaking, is basically revealed by her choices. At any rate, it does not challenge that idea. I have come to question, however, such historically liberal reasons for regarding race as morally irrelevant. Although who I am is importantly affected—and revealed—by my choices, I do not choose everything that is important to my identity, nor even all of it that matters morally. I am a relational being, and my choices alone are not decisive for all my relations. A heritage that has given me privileges or liabilities from birth, whether I affirm it or reject it, is important to who I am and who I can become. Even whether I have a heritage to which to be loyal or disloyal is not the product of my choices.

"Heritage" is a slippery term. If one thinks of it as whatever led up to one's existence, it seems that everyone has a heritage. But what makes a past *one's own* is not just causal precedence. When a heritage is a cultural legacy, one can be disinherited or alienated from it. One can be robbed of one's culture. Cultures of one's ancestors may have been annihilated. They may have been appropriated by others and assimilated into their cultures.[22] Thus, not all have the privilege of being able to *claim* a heritage. Nor do all want to claim as their heritage some of the pasts that produced them (rape and slavery, for example). Amoja Three Rivers writes: "One of the most effective and insidious aspects of racism is cultural genocide. Not only have African Americans been cut off from our African tribal roots, but . . . we have been cut off from our Native American roots as well. Consequently most African Native Americans no longer . . . even know for certain what people they are from."[23] If "race" in its internal aspect refers to certain aspects of cultural heritage—as is suggested in Du Bois's usage in "The Conservation of Race"—an insidious aspect of racism seems to be the *destruction* of races. (This is compatible, of course, with its also *con*structing races). Laurence Thomas points out in his discussions of the evils of American slavery that it takes only seven generations to complete cultural genocide, to erase the memories. For some whose Native American ancestors succumbed to European diseases, it may have been faster.[24]

Perhaps race and ethnicity come together, to some extent, in the notion of a heritage. Cultural genocide may be less complete than it appears if what is primarily destroyed are the means of *identifying* cultural developments but not necessarily those developments themselves. Further, in pondering the question of what significance, if any, one's *biological* heritage has for one's social identity, I want to ask: what counts as "biological"? Marilyn Frye once wrote, in thinking about gender: "Enculturation and socialization are misunderstood . . . if one pictures them as processes which apply layers of cultural gloss over a biological substratum. It is with that picture in mind that one asks whether this or that aspect of behavior is due to 'nature' or 'nurture.'"[25] She went on to develop a very bodily picture of gender, concluding that if that makes it "biological," then "biological" means only "of the animal." Likewise, much of what is "biological" in race may not be genetic and what is "cultural" in ethnicity may not be chosen. Thus, it may be more significant for self-understanding to know one's earliest unchosen caretakers and the often also unchosen social contexts of their lives, and *their* early caretakers and the social contexts of *their* lives (and so on), than to know the sources of one's genes. This distinction is obscured when childrearing is done by biological kin. Yet either sort of history might be considered a "genealogy." I conclude with three examples of genealogies where what is of interest are the histories of parenting:

1. An issue of *Lilith* a few years ago contained an article on Indian Catholic Jews of New Mexico, descendants of sixteenth century "conversos" (Jews forced to convert to Christianity) who fled the Inquisition in Mexico.[26] These descendants are reported to be prac-

ticing Catholics who still also practice Jewish customs privately at home without knowing what they mean or even that the customs are Jewish.[27] Some, having accidentally discovered the Jewish meanings, are now, apparently, talking about *discovering their Jewish heritage*. And what customs do they likewise practice without knowing their Native American meanings?

2. Enslaved Africans in the Americas were often separated from biological kin at early ages and raised by others who were enslaved from totally different regions of Africa. Such foster parents may have borne little resemblance to the children's biological kin and may not even have spoken a related language. If a common African American heritage has been developing in this country, undocumentable generations of such parenting under conditions of slavery may be a more significant factor in its unification than the genetic impositions of white rapists who claimed to own African slaves and their descendants.

3. And what is the heritage of white people in the United States who were raised by black servants or slaves? Or, for that matter, of white people generally in the United States today? The culture of white people in the United States is at least as mixed in its genealogy as the genealogy of the Indian Catholic *conversos* of New Mexico, as a result of generations of enforced interracial caretaking and forms of cultural appropriation.[28]

Notes

1. The May 1991 conference "Racism and Sexism: Differences and Connections," sponsored by the Georgia State University Department of Philosophy, was a major stimulus to these reflections, which I first set down in response to a call for essays on race and racism by the Midwest Society of Women in Philosophy later that same year. For comments on that early draft I am grateful to Jeffner Allen, Howard McGary, and Joann Pritchett.

2. These three thinkers were represented on the program of the Georgia State conference: W. E. B. Du Bois in the presentation by Lucius Outlaw, Marilyn Frye in her presentation reflecting on her own earlier essays on the topic, and María Lugones in her presentation on anger.

3. *W. E. B. Du Bois Speaks: Speeches and Addresses 1890–1919*, ed. Philip S. Foner (New York: Pathfinder, 1970), 73–85. This essay was the subject of Lucius Outlaw's presentation at the 1991 Georgia State conference.

4. Marilyn Frye, *The Politics of Reality: Essays in Feminist Theory* (Trumansburg, N.Y.: The Crossing Press, 1983) and *Willful Virgin: Essays in Feminism 1976–1992* (Freedom, Calif.: The Crossing Press, 1992).

5. "Pedagogy and Racism" was presented in Minneapolis at a conference of the Midwest Society of Women in Philosophy in 1984 and printed in Carleton College's *Breaking Ground* 6 (Spring 1984), 38–43. It was later revised and expanded as "Hablando cara a cara/Speaking Face to Face: An Exploration of Ethnocentric Racism," in Gloria Anzaldúa, ed., *Making Face, Making Soul: Haciendo Caras* (San Francisco: Aunt Lute, 1990), 46–54. See also María Lugones, "Playfulness, 'World'-Travelling, and Loving Perception," *Hypatia* 2, no. 2 (Summer 1987): 3–10, and "Hispaneando y lesbiando: On Sarah Hoagland's *Lesbian Ethics*," *Hypatia* 5, no. 3 (Fall 1990): 138–46.

6. See, for examples of the latter, Amoja Three Rivers, *Cultural Etiquette: A Guide for the Well-Intentioned*, 1990 (distributed by Market Wimmin, Box 28, Indian Valley, VA 24105).

7. Although sexual differentiation into *female* and *male* is natural for human beings (however ambiguous it may turn out in particular instances), it does not follow, as a matter of logic, that *femininity* and *masculinity* are also natural, where these concepts are understood to refer not to gross anatomical structure or chromosomal composition but to psychological dispositions or traits and social expectations.

8. Ashley Montagu, "'Ethnic Group' and 'Race,'" *Psychiatry* 8 (1945): 27–33, reprinted in Montagu, *Race, Science and Humanity* (New York: Van Nostrand, 1963). See also Ashley Montagu, *Man's Most Dangerous Myth: The Fallacy of Race* (Cleveland: Meridian, 1964).

9. An essay by Marcus G. Singer first called my attention to this history, "Some Thoughts on *Race* and *Racism*," *Philosophia* (Philosophical Quarterly of Israel) 8, nos. 2–3 (Nov. 1978): 153–183.

10. Charlotte Perkins Gilman, *Women and Economics* (New York: Harper Torchbooks, 1966). This work was first published in 1898. Sometimes the author used "race" in referring to the human species, and at other times, to refer to more specific human groups.

11. In *Racist Culture: Philosophy and the Politics of Meaning* (Cambridge, Mass.: Blackwell, 1993), 74–78, David Theo Goldberg presents "ethnorace" as one of the masks of race.

12. See also Goldberg, *Racist Culture*, 78–80, on "race as nation."

13. Pierre L. van den Berghe, *Race and Racism: A Comparative Perspective*, 2d ed. (New York: Wiley, 1967, 1978), 9–10.

14. Thomas Sowell, *Ethnic America* (New York: Basic Books, 1981).

15. Three Rivers, *Cultural Etiquette*, 9.

16. On the idea of the racial state, see Michael Omi and Howard Winant, *Racial Formation in the United States from the 1960s to the 1980s* (New York: Routledge, 1986), 57–69.

17. In "Playfulness, 'World'-Travelling, and Loving Perception," María Lugones introduced a conception of "world"-travel as the willful exercise of an acquired flexibility, developed spontaneously out of necessity by members of a minority in an oppressive society, in shifting from a construction of life in which one is at home although others are outsiders, to other constructions of life in which some of these former outsiders are at home, or more nearly at home and in which one may figure oneself as an outsider. To

illustrate, she elaborated on what it meant for her to travel to the "world" of her mother, explaining that she was unable to love her mother well until she could do this. Such "world"–travel has the potentiality to develop new aspects of oneself, even new "selves." It seems not, however, to create new ethnic *identities*, perhaps because one's ethnicity has a historical element that remains unchanged by "world"-travel.

18. For a critique of the concept of race based on problems presented by mixed race, see Naomi Zack, *Race and Mixed Race* (Philadelphia: Temple University Press, 1993).

19. For another example of invidious tracking, see Cornel West's account of what occurred when he tried to hail a taxi on the corner of 60th Street and Park Avenue in Manhattan, in *Race Matters* (Boston: Beacon, 1993), x.

20. I here follow Malcolm X and Marilyn Frye in using "separatism" to refer to the voluntary separation from an oppressor by the oppressed, in the interests of the oppressed, and "segregation" to refer to separations from the oppressed imposed by an oppressor, in the interests of the oppressor. See *The Autobiography of Malcolm X*, with the assistance of Alex Haley (New York: Grove, 1964), 246, and Frye, *Politics of Reality*, 96.

21. Pat Parker, *Movement in Black* (Oakland, Calif.: Diana Press, 1978), 68.

22. Regarding cultural death and cultural appropriation, see Laurence Mordekhai Thomas, *Vessels of Evil: American Slavery and the Holocaust* (Philadelphia: Temple University Press, 1993), on the "natal alienation" of descendants in the Americas of enslaved Africans.

23. Three Rivers, *Cultural Etiquette,* 8.

24. This is not to deny the survival of any Native American cultures but only to acknowledge that some have undoubtedly been killed.

25. Frye, *Politics of Reality*, 35.

26. They have also been called "marranos," which means "pigs" in Spanish.

27. Maria Steiglitz, "New Mexico's Secret Jews," *Lilith* (Winter 1991), 8–12. Cf. La Escondida, "Journal Toward Wholeness: Reflections of a Lesbian Rabbi" (also on contemporary descendants of conversos in New Mexico) in *Twice Blessed: On Being Lesbian, Gay, and Jewish*, ed. Christie Balka and Andy Rose (Boston: Beacon Press, 1989).

28. For an example of cultural appropriation, see Alice Walker's story of Joel Chandler Harris, who wrote down and published the Uncle Remus tales, in *Living by the Word* (New York: Harcourt, Brace, Jovanovich, 1988), 25–32.

10

Power, Trust, and Evil

Laurence Mordekhai Thomas

It is undoubtedly true that to have power over others is to be able to get them to do what one would like them to do, whenever one should want them to, and on one's own terms. Even so, abusive power arrangements over others may differ not only in degree, but also in kind. The Holocaust and American slavery were two of the worlds' most dramatic and painful instances of brutal power arrangements. But surely these two evil institutions differ in kind as power arrangements, though there may be similarities between them. Sexism is another power arrangement, and it is one that is reducible neither to the power arrangement of the Holocaust nor to that of American slavery, whatever similarities sexism may have to either or both. I want to discuss the role of power in the context of both trust and evil. I want also to bring out an important way in which trust can be pressed into the service of immorality. It is often supposed that trust is incompatible with abusive power arrangements. But I argue that this is false. And we better understand the nature of evil when we see how trust can be an indispensable part of an evil power arrangement.

At the outset, though, two caveats are in order. First, not all power arrangements are inherently abusive. Presumably, the power arrangement between parent and child is not. Nor is the power arrangement between government and citizen. Second, although being a victim has come to be somewhat fashionable of late, it goes without saying that Jews, blacks, and women are not the only groups of people in the world to have suffered at the hands of others. Native Americans, Asians, Hispanics, and lesbian and gay people have all seen their share of suffering. And while the suffering of women belonging to different ethnic or racial groups has much in common, there have been fundamentally important differences in their suffering.[1] A morally decent and upright person could easily focus on the suffering of the obviously oppressed groups to the exclusion of the groups whose suffering I shall discuss. By broadening the discussion I hope to show how all of us can partake of the good of learning from one another.

Abusive Power Arrangements

It is useful, I believe, to distinguish between two kinds of power arrangements: capricious power arrangements and expectations-generating power arrangements. With the former, the exercise of power over others in terms of threats is simply for the purpose of manipulating or controlling their behavior. There is no desire that those whom one threatens believe that one rightly exercises power over them. Thus, capricious power arrangements lack what I shall call a normative component. In expectations-generating power arrangements, a normative component is present: the nature of group A and the nature of group B are such that, insofar as there are relations between the two groups, group A should have power over group B; hence, the members of group A believe themselves to have justified authority over the members of group B. If group A has authority over group B, then (1) there are norms of behavior for B and, moreover, (2) the members of A are justified in forcing the members of B to comply with those norms. As these two conditions, especially (1), make clear, group A does not have authority over group B simply in virtue of being justified in killing B. This accords with our intuition that killing as an instance of justified self-defense is not tantamount to a manifestation of authority over the one killed.

Most important, although in a capricious power arrangement the subjects usually comply with the commands of the agents out of fear of being harmed, the subjects generally do not have reason to believe that their compliance constitutes any assurance against their being made worse off by the agents. Nor are the agents generally concerned to secure this belief on the part of the subjects. The point here is to be understood in terms of stability. A subject might have reason to believe that a single instance of compliance behavior will make a difference, but the subject has no reason to believe that compliance behavior will, over the long run, yield a floor as to how much worse off she or he will be made by the agent; for in a capricious power arrangement the agents have no desire that the subjects should have trust in them. But if there were a floor to the harm that agents would do to the subjects, then we would have conditions conducive to the agents being trusted by the subjects, as we shall see with expectations-generating power arrangements.

Capricious power arrangements masterfully exploit two features of human psychology: the deep desire to avoid being harmed and the extraordinary fear to which the threat of great harm gives rise. Together, this desire and fear can motivate a subject to comply with an agent's demands although the subject has no reason to believe that compliance will in fact prevent her or him from being harmed. A person is motivated to act out of desperation. Persons act out of desperation when they act with the hope of avoiding, or even forestalling, major harm to themselves or their loved ones, but have no good reason to believe that their actions will yield the desired results.

A capricious power arrangement is to be contrasted with an expectations-generating power arrangement. Of course, as with a capricious power arrangement, the agent in an expectations-generating power arrangement threatens to cause the subjects great harm if they fail to comply with the agent's wishes. However, although the agent has the power to cause the subjects great harm, the agent very much wants the subjects to believe that if they comply with the agent's wishes, then the agent will voluntarily refrain from harming them. This brings us to the normative component of this sort of power arrangement.

As I have said, we have a normative component in a power arrangement, where group A has power over group B, when (1) group A believes that there are norms of behavior for B and (2) that the members of A are justified in forcing the members of B to comply with those norms. In an expectations-generating power arrangement, there is a third component: (3) the agent wants the subjects to believe that given their compliance behavior, the agent will voluntarily refrain from harming them, where the explanation for this restraint does not reduce to mere self-interest. On the contrary, the agent wants the subjects to believe that her or his behavior toward them is modulated by a conception of the good to which the agent subscribes.

It may be tempting to think that whenever compliance behavior requires subservience, then self-interest can be the only explanation for why an agent voluntarily restrains herself or himself, given the compliance of the subjects. The reasoning here is familiar enough: an agent is much more likely to obtain the desired subservient behavior by exercising restraint than by treating the subjects ruthlessly, since ruthless treatment renders the subjects physically less able to perform the behavior that the agent desires of them. While this, of course, is true, it does not follow that self-interest must be the motivation for the agent's exercise of self-restraint. And I do not mean to be making simply a logical point.

There are all sorts of things that it might be in a person's self-interest to do, although it is not out of self-interest that the person actually performs the behavior in question. Self-interest is served when persons show affection toward their children, since children who are the object of affection are less worrisome than those who are not. But clearly this is not, in fact, generally the motivation out of which parents show affection toward their children. Again, I may know that I will get a handsome reward if I save the life of the person drowning right before my eyes; yet this need not be in the least why I am motivated to save the person's life. Finally, it might be in a student's self-interest to impress the professor. Yet, it is certainly possible for a student to do so without being motivated by self-interest. Teaching could not be nearly as rewarding if this possibility were ruled out of court.

So, where compliance calls for subservience, it is perfectly possible that the agents believe that when their subjects exhibit compliance behavior, then it is appropriate to exhibit self-restraint with respect to harming them. In fact, exercising self-restraint could be part and parcel of the agents' conception of what it means to be a good agent with respect to the subjects, given their compliance behavior. Thus, agents could believe that they are following God's will by exercising self-restraint toward compliant subjects, and be deeply motivated by this belief, though exercising self-restraint nonetheless serves their self-interest.

What I draw attention to here is that with the third condition, an expectations-generating power arrangement is a power arrangement involving trust between agent and subjects. Specifically, the agent wishes to be seen by the subjects as trustworthy, in that the agent wishes the subjects to believe that he will not harm them, given their compliance behavior, although he has the power to do so. For trust, after all, is not an all-or-nothing matter. It is false that a person can be trustworthy with respect to a particular piece of behavior only if the individual is completely trustworthy. There can be pockets of trust even in the context of immoral behavior. Thus, there was a time in the United States when the immoral act of thievery was thought to involve a modicum of moral decency, and so victims of robbery could trust the thief not to harm them or take their lives. Today, we lament the fact that the thief shows little, if any, respect for human life. Either we are being rather loose with the language here or there was a time when we thought that being a thief was compatible with the moral restraints that are constitutive of respecting human life. If the latter, then we believe that even in the context of immorality pockets of trust are possible. With expectations-generating power arrangements, we have a pocket of trust, or at least the aim to have such. The existence of threats as a means of ensuring compliance should not blind us to this truth. For we present ourselves as trustworthy to another when we give that person reason to believe that we see ourselves as having a reason, not born of self-interest, to voluntarily refrain from harming the individual. And this may be true, though we are rightly convinced that compliance behavior will not be forthcoming from the other in the absence of threats from us.

My reason for drawing attention to the existence of trust in expectations-generating power arrangements is to bring out the point that such arrangements constitute a moral relationship between the agent and the subjects, unlike capricious power arrangements; for trust is very much a moral phenomenon. Whenever we desire that another believe that she or he can trust us, then, given compliance behavior on the person's part which is recognized as such, we acknowledge that person as a moral agent, if only minimally. It is not just that only moral agents are presumed to be capable of such a complex constellation of beliefs and intentional behavior, though that is true enough, but when we give a person reason to believe that she or he can trust us, then we indicate to the person that our interactions with her or him are guided by a conception of the good.

Although I have distinguished between two kinds of power arrangements, I do not claim that all the manifestations of power in an institution must be one or the other, or that it is always clear whether we have one or the other. Nor do I wish to deny that we can start with one and end up with the other. Finally, I think that one should resist the temptation to suppose that one of the two power arrangements that I have identified must be morally worse than the other.

I now apply the analysis offered to the Holocaust, American slavery, and sexism.

The Logic of Rightful Subservience

In my view the Holocaust was a capricious power arrangement, whereas American slavery was an expectations-generating power arrangement. Although the institution of slavery involved the oppression of black people, that oppression cannot be given a full articulation in the absence of the role that sexism played in that oppression. Part of the horror of slavery is inextricably tied to the ways in which sexism was visited upon black women. Indeed, there is a sense in which American slavery draws some of its inspiration from sexism. For sexism is the view that it is natural for women to be subservient to men. This view, needless to say, has deep roots in various religious traditions, the Judeo-Christian tradition being the most relevant one here. The traditional religious male Jew thanks God that he is not a woman; the traditional Christian believes that as Christ is head of the church so is the man the head of the household. Though American slavery and sexism hardly amount to the same thing, the parallel between them is striking. And this was not always lost on white females. Mary Chesnut, for instance, asserted, "There is no slave, after all, like a wife."[2]

Sexism

As just stated, this is the view that it is natural for some people, namely women, to play a subservient role in the lives of others. In the context of a sexist moral climate, then, American slavery could readily be seen as simply a variation on a very venerable theme. After all, some of the slaves were black women, and in a sexist moral climate it was, of course, natural for them to be subservient to men, in any event. Extending the subservience of black women to include subservience to white women hardly requires much by way of mental gymnastics. On the contrary, I suggest that human psychology is such that if intimate relations between groups A and B is the norm, where B is subservient to A and there is a group C that is subservient to A, then B will likewise regard C as subservient to itself as well. In any case, slaveowners clearly wanted blacks to believe, first, in the inferiority of blacks to whites and, second, that on account of this inferiority blacks were rightfully subservient to whites. A good black in the eyes of whites was one whose behavior embodied these beliefs. Slave owners wanted slavery to be a stable institution, and we have stability in a relationship of subservience precisely when the subservient believe in their own subservience and thus engage in subservient behavior in the absence of coercive threats.

A particularly important point at this juncture is that it is not possible to persuade others that it would be right for them to be subservient to one without their believing, first, that their subservience warrants restraints on one's own behavior and, second, that one will voluntarily restrain one's behavior, where the explanation for this restraint is not pure self-interest. This is the logic of rightful subservient relations. And it applies with equal force to both sexism and slavery. There are formal restraints on what one may do in order for one's actions to be conducive to others, believing that it is right for them to be subservient to one. Otherwise, getting the other to comply with one's demands would simply be tantamount to a command backed up by threats. Individuals may very well have a good self-interested reason to comply with a command of this nature, but as H. L. A. Hart[3] demonstrated in his criticism of John Austin, the individuals will have no reason whatsoever to believe that they rightfully comply, and so are justified in complying, with such commands. Lest there be any misunderstanding, I have hardly claimed that, aside from self-interested reasons, there are in fact good reasons for one group of adults to be generally subservient to another. My point is simply that in order to persuade others that they are rightfully subservient, self-interested reasons alone simply will not do. And it is significant that arguments for the subservience of both women and blacks were not cast simply in self-interested reasons pertaining to the man or the slaveowner, respectively. Instead, an appeal to a conception of the good, however indefensible, has always been made.

In order for a group of people to believe that they are rightfully subservient to someone, they must believe that the one to whom they are subservient will voluntarily refrain from making coercive threats, given their compliance. But this is just to say that they must be able to trust that person to refrain from such behavior, given their compliance. This gives us an insight into what is so painful about the evil of sexism and American slavery.

Normally, trust is an affirming moral phenomenon. We are affirmed by those whom we can trust because we see them as individuals who take our good to heart, in that we believe that they will not harm us in any important way, although they could do so without detection and although it would actually be in their self-interest to do so. Trust does not amount to prediction: if I put everything under lock and key and invite you into my home, I can quite confidently predict that you will not steal anything, yet nothing is clearer than that I do not trust you. I trust you only if I do not hide my valuables when I invite you. Obviously, it can be unreasonable to trust another. My only claim is that trust is an affirming notion, because we believe that those whom we trust will not harm us in important ways.

In my view, one of the deep features of the evil of sexism and American slavery lies in precisely the fact that the moral affirmation of trust is pressed into the service of immorality. Trust is affirming and we want to be affirmed by others. That is, we want to be able to trust others to the extent that we can, at least when it comes to being harmed by them. Ideally, we would like to trust that no one would harm us, for it is in such a context that human flourishing is at its best. Obviously, we have to settle for considerably less than that. American slavery and sexism exploit the deep desire of persons to want to be able to have basic trust in others, for both evils attach inappropriate conditions whereby the victims of these institutions can trust the agents of these institutions not to harm them in basic ways and/or to allow them to enjoy certain privileges and goods, some of which are basic. Submission to the will of another is an inappropriate condition to have to satisfy in order not to be harmed by another or to be able to enjoy basic human freedoms. All human beings should be able to trust others with respect to these matters in the absence of such submission. With slavery and sexism, the conditions for two groups of human beings being able to trust another group of human beings have been radically altered. Had there not been trust involved, neither sexism nor American slavery could have taken the form that it did. The parallel between the two ends here.

A society can be sexist but not necessarily heterosexually oriented. Presumably ancient Greece is a case in point. Aristotle thought it natural that women should be inferior to men, but he did not think that the gender identity of men was tied to sexual relations with women. In Aristotle's day, a good-looking woman did not a real man make via the route of sexual intercourse. Not so in a heterosexually oriented society, where the gender identity of a great many males is inextricably tied to the act of sexual intercourse with women. In a sexist, heterosexually oriented society a woman can take a frail biological male, which is something that is rarely a matter of dispute, and turn him into a "real" man, which can indeed be disputed. That is power! And neither men nor women are unmindful of that power.

Sexism is deeply tied to the desire of men to assure that women affirm the gender identity of men.[4] A good women accepts this as her role in the life of her man. Ideally, to speak rather loosely in the context of a sexist world, she can trust her man to do his part if he can trust her to do her part in affirming his gender identity. Obviously, in a heterosexually oriented world, men play a role in affirming the gender identity of women as well: women want their gender identity affirmed by men. But, generally speaking, women can bear children. (That some women cannot no more militates against the point being made than does the fact that some handicapped people are stunningly successful militate against the truth that being handicapped generally puts one at a substantial disadvantage.) And while there is no reason to suppose that this suffices, in the context of sexism, to affirm entirely the gender identity of women, it need only be observed that there just is no parallel and equally powerful biological capacity possessed by men that plays a role in affirming their gender identity. To be sure, men can impregnate women, but it is too obvious for words this is not an ostensible affirmation of a man's gender identity. One cannot just look at a man and see that he has recently impregnated a woman.

In a heterosexually oriented world, as long as there is gender identity and it can be affirmed only by a member of the other gender, and as long there is an asymmetry in the biological capacities of women and men to affirm their gender identities, sexism is here to stay. If so, then men will always have an interest in women believing that they should be subordinate to men.[5]

American Slavery and Racism

I once thought that slavery lacked a moral floor,[6] meaning that slaves could have been just about any form of animal. The language of chattel slavery suggests that this is so. If, however, I am

right that to some extent the slaveowner wanted there to be a significant trusting relationship between the slaveowner and the slave
(as I discuss later), then I was wrong in thinking that the slave
could have been just about any form of animal. For we do not suppose
that the moral relationship of trust is possible between human beings and animals, though with some animals we think or at least
act as if things can come quite close to that. But history has no
record of humans beings engaging in the practice of having their
children cared for by nonhuman beings. And there can be no surer
sign that the moral relationship of trust exists between two individuals than that the one entrusts the care of her or his children to
the other. So slaveowners simply could not have supposed that the
slaves were mere animals. It is, of course, true that not all slaveowners
had slaves playing this role in their lives, and it is equally true that
coercive threats on the part of slaveowners were at times a factor
in slaves caring for the children of slaveowners. But, first of all, it
is false that it is only because of such threats that slaveowners could
have any confidence that slaves would perform this task well. Second, slaveowners wanted slaves to perform this task well, whether
or not the slaves always did. Hence, slaveowners wanted to be able
to trust slaves in this regard, whether or not, given the behavior of
slaves, the slaveowners always could. So, slaveowners certainly
viewed slaves as belonging to the category of beings capable of at
least some form of deep moral trust.

All the same, slaves clearly did not play the affirming role in
the lives of whites that women have played in the lives of men.
There was not a form of affirmation essential to being a white that
whites could get only from blacks, although slaveowners often insisted that caring for slaves was their Christian duty. They did not,
and could not have meant, that whites who did not care for slaves
were being less Christian. And this fact helps bring out the significance of a heterosexually oriented society.

I began my remarks about sexism with the observation that during Aristotle's time a good-looking woman did not a real man make.
I suggested that in a sexist but non-heterosexually oriented society,
there is no substantial difference between slavery and sexism. To
be sure, even in a sexist but non-heterosexually oriented society
women bear children, yet in such a society gender identity would
not be tied to affirmation from the other gender. In a non-heterosexually oriented society that is sexist (as with the ancient Greeks),
the difference between women and slaves turns more upon the kinds

of goods that the subordinates provide rather than the role they play in the self-identity of (white) men. In a sexist, heterosexually oriented society, by contrast, the difference turns precisely upon the role they play in the self-identity of men. Only women can affirm the gender identity of men, and men the gender identity of women, though as I have indicated the child-bearing capacity of women gives them a considerable advantage over men with respect to gender identity affirmation. This raises the interesting question of whether or not a heterosexually oriented society can be a nonsexist one. The answer is obvious: No, so long as gender identity is defined in the way that it presently is.[7]

The Moral Sentiments

Before turning to the Holocaust, a final comment is in order. It is tempting to think that oppressive power arrangements are such that by their very nature there can be no genuine trust between the victims and the oppressor—that compliance behavior can be explained, without remainder, simply in terms of self-interest on the part of the victim and that the oppressor is simply concerned to see to it that it is in the self-interest of the victim to comply. I do not deny that the behavior of victims and oppressors can be grafted upon a matrix of purely self-interested reasons. I merely note that even the victims of oppression do not always understand their own compliance behavior in terms of sheer self-interest, and it is implausible and inappropriate to insist that in all such cases the victims are self-deceived about their own motivations. Frederick Douglass wrote the following: "If any one thing in my experience, more than another, served to deepen my conviction of the infernal character of slavery, and to fill me with unutterable loathing of slaveholders, it was their base ingratitude to my poor old grandmother. She had served my old master faithfully from youth to old age. . . ."[8]

Assuming that sheer self-interest and serving faithfully are at odds with one another, was Douglass deceived regarding the motivations with which his grandmother served her master? I want to resist such a view of Douglass, of all people. Suffice it to note that his outrage is tied to the belief that his grandmother had served her master faithfully—not that she grudgingly did what she had to do. Note, also, that given the assumption of faithful service, Douglass's anger makes sense in a way that it would not have in the absence of his judgment of faithful service on her part. Her unrewarded faithful service is part of the basis for his anger. That she was a slave could have angered him in any case, but it is clear that his anger justifiably has a depth to it for which there would be no basis but for his grandmother's faithfulness. If this is right, then those who would rush to deny that oppressive power arrangements are incompatible with trust should be given pause. For there are feelings of anger and resentment that can be accounted for only if one allows for the possibility of trust and goodwill to exist between victim and oppressor.

One cannot rightly accuse either a stranger whom one has not assisted in any way or someone whom one is helping only to advance one's own interest of "base ingratitude," but only someone who has been the object of a great deal of goodwill on one's part.[9] So Douglass continued: "She had rocked him in infancy, attended him in childhood, served him through life, and at his death wiped from his icy brow the cold death-sweat, and closed his eyes forever. She was nevertheless left a slave—a slave for life."[10] Douglass is angry not so much because his grandmother was a slave, but because she was left a slave after so many years of loyally caring for and serving her master, even to the very point of his death. Clearly, the implication is that she did not just care for him in the sense of mechanically attending to his needs, but that she cared for him in the sense of having feelings of affection for him.

Needless to say, if a victim can have (some) feelings of goodwill toward her oppressor, it is wildly implausible to suppose that the converse could not be true. And for the reasons just given, it would be a mistake to insist that feelings cannot exist between victim and oppressor. Some abusive power arrangements are, indeed, compatible with such feelings arising. Others are not.

Power and the Holocaust

It is clear—painfully clear, in fact—that the Nazis did not seek to have a moral relationship between themselves and the Jews. The Holocaust exemplifies what I have called a capricious power arrangement. For the most part, the Nazis' treatment of the Jews made it clear that there were no actions that Jews could perform whereby they could trust Nazis not to harm them. To be sure, it sometimes happened that Jews did not get harmed given their compliance with the demands made of them. But this was not because Nazis were desirous of being seen by Jews as people who would keep their word. In my view, a capricious power arrangement is precisely what one would expect given the conception the Nazis had of the Jews, namely that they were irredeemably evil,[11] for a relationship of trust is an inappropriate moral relationship to have with that which is irredeemably evil. This is because it cannot make much conceptual sense to want those whom one takes to be irredeemably evil to trust one not to harm them: it is not clear how it could be possible to have such a want here. And if it is conceptually possible to have this want, it seems manifestly clear that, practically speaking, the motivational structure of human beings is such that a human being could not plausibly believe that another is irredeemably evil and, at the same time, be eager not to harm that individual—where it is for the individual's own sake that one does not harm her or him, as opposed to not harming the individual for instrumental reasons.

The language of irredeemable evil gives us a sharp difference between the Holocaust, on the one hand, and sexism and American slavery, on the other. The victims of the latter two were not viewed as irredeemably evil. To be sure, when women and blacks failed to act in accordance with their supposed role, they were often subject to harsh physical abuse. But it was never held from the very outset that there simply could be no role for women to have in the lives of men and for blacks to have in the lives of whites. Some racist whites questioned the practical wisdom of slavery, holding that everyone would be better off if there were no relations between blacks and whites. These whites even thought that the moral fiber of blacks was inherently weaker than the moral fiber of whites. But this does not entail that blacks were regarded as irredeemably evil. There is a profound difference between being morally weaker than another by nature and being such that one's nature is inherently and wholly evil. The latter entails the former, but not conversely. Hence, even if it is allowed that women have been conceived of by men as a bifurcated self, as Eve the woman of seduction versus Mary the woman of purity, it nonetheless follows from this that there is a good in woman to be realized, though she may be constantly at war with her bad side and though the realization of this good may require the help of men. The Jew as irredeemably evil was not conceived of as having a good to be realized.

So, if I am right in the view that the Nazis viewed the Jews as irredeemably evil, then it could not have made any sense for the Nazis to have wanted the Jews to play a subservient role in the lives of Nazis. And this is a conceptual point: there can be no appropriate subservient role for an irredeemably evil people to play in the lives of another people. Complete and utter disassociation is the only appropriate moral attitude to have toward those who are irredeemably evil. And there is no better way to achieve complete disassociation than death itself. These considerations shed some light on why the Holocaust was a capricious power arrangement. There can be no norms of benevolence or any form of morally good behavior that is appropriate toward that individual regarded as irredeemably evil. More poignantly, it is not clear what it would mean to have a moral reason to restrict one's behavior for the very sake of those who are irredeemably evil. To be sure, one might do so for one's own sake, for it might be thought that treating the irredeemably evil in certain ways could be self-corrupting, in the way that Kant thought that being cruel to animals would have a deleterious effect upon our interactions with other human beings. But when considerations of this sort are not thought to have any weight, then it is not clear what it would mean to have a moral reason not to harm persons deemed irredeemably evil. And this point is secured, I believe, by the observation that it seems woefully inappropriate for there to be norms of benevolence toward the irredeemably evil. We take norms of benevolence to be in order when the object of them will be favorably responsive to the norms, when the norms will have an ameliorating effect. But it precisely this assumption that is ruled out of court with respect to the irredeemably evil, because, by hypothesis, the irredeemably evil are such that there is no action that another can perform that will serve to diminish their evil nature. And I suggest that when norms of benevolence are ruled out of court, then it is very difficult to make sense of having a moral reason to refrain from harming another. The point here is a Humean one. Morality can have a psychological hold on our lives with respect to others only insofar as it is possible for us to be capable of feelings of benevolence with respect to them. And this is not possible with respect to the irredeemably evil.

The implications of the Jew as irredeemably evil with respect to sexism are significant. Because the Jews were conceived of as irredeemably evil, it turns out that sexism was not a potent feature of the Holocaust. That is, the evil of the Holocaust was not exacerbated by the nature of sexism itself. It could not have been, given the conception of the Jew as irredeemably evil. Whereas it can be argued plausibly that American slavery turned out to be more evil because of the nature of sexism itself, a like argument cannot, I think, be made in connection with the Holocaust. Often enough, white slaveowners thought the privilege of owning black slaves entailed the privilege of sexual access to black females. By contrast, the Holocaust was never thought to entail any such privileges on the part of the Nazis vis-à-vis Jewish women. Fisher and Read observed that "While murdering a Jew was worth, at the most, a reprimand, 'race violation' carried a statutory penalty of ten years' imprisonment."[12]

This should come as no surprise. If, in a heterosexually oriented society, sexual relations with women, by men, is about men having their gender identity as "real" men affirmed, there is certainly a psychological incongruity, if not a conceptual one, in having one's gender identity affirmed by that which one deems irredeemably evil. When another plays an affirming role in our lives, there are limits on how negatively we can conceive of the individual without creating a tension with respect to the person playing the kind of affirming role that we want her or him to play in our lives. I am not making the foolish claim that there was no sexual abuse of Jews during the Holocaust; there clearly was. Moreover, Hannah Arendt reports that Eichmann, no less, had a Jewish mistress.[13] Rather, the point simply is that the conception that Nazis had of the Jews did not provide an independent reason for such abuse, a reason not part of the usual attitudes of male soldiers concerning women and the spoils of victory, one of which has been the raping of women. It must be remembered that the so-called Jezebel is considered an evil woman because she tempts men, often with success, to engage in acts of infidelity. But the Jew, whether female or male, was considered evil by the Nazis quite independently of tempting anyone to do anything morally objectionable. (After all, the Nazis had no compunctions about murdering even Jewish children and infants.) It is one thing to engage in sex with a person who is deemed evil only because that individual has tempted one; it is quite another to have sex with someone who is deemed inherently evil. A so-called Jezebel falls into the "right" category for affirming the gender identity of men. A Jewish female, however, is evil by nature, which means that being morally good is, and always has been, beyond her. Hence she does not fall into the "right" category for affirming the gender identity of men—Nazi men, in this instance.

Similarly, we can see that it is a mistake to think of the Holocaust as a form of slavery. A defining feature of a slave is that there are services one wants the slave to provide—and the Nazis did not conceive of Jews in this way. The irredeemably evil simply cannot be a fitting object for playing such a role in people's lives.

Concluding Remarks

What is frightening is that evil can be extremely difficult to recognize. If it is so obvious to us that sexism, racism, and anti-Semitism are wrong, we have to wonder that it has not been considered so in the eyes of those who participate in such behavior. The answer, I think, has to do with our having a very simplistic notion of evil. We often suppose that evil presents itself in sharp contradistinction to that which is good, that it is only in bizarre ways that good can be in the service of evil. This is terribly wrong, I am afraid. Further, it is simply a mistake to suppose that those who commit evil acts must, on pain of self-deception, see their acts as evil.

What both American slavery and sexism show is that it is possible for there to be some form of moral affirmation in the very context of oppression, that the oppression could not, in fact, succeed in the absence of some form of moral affirmation. What is more, when we affirm others morally, even in the context of oppression, it is not possible for us to see our actions as completely evil. There is room to see ourselves as good, under some description, even as we do that which is evil. After all, it must be remembered that no one has a claim to perfection, and seeing ourselves as morally decent individuals often turns out to be a matter of fixing upon the right description of ourselves and making salient the right aspect of our behavior or the right instances of our behavior. In his provocative essay "The Justice Motive," Melvin J. Lerner[14] has argued convincingly that seeing ourselves as morally decent people often requires downplaying the ways in which we could help others. The point I am making here is that the racist slaveowner and the sexist are not nearly as radically different from people like you and me as most of us would like to take comfort in believing.

This brings me to the Jews. I do not believe that one can talk about the Jews being perceived as irredeemably evil without making reference to Christianity. In the Gospel of John, for example, the devil is referred to as the father of the Jews (John 8:42–47). I do not want to enter into a discussion of Christianity and anti-Semitism. Rather, I want to draw attention to two things. One is that Christianity has a fundamental place in the Western narrative. The other is that our conception of another can be so much a part of the fabric of our consciousness that we fail to see that it is operating. Today, the Jew is still stereotyped as greedy and overly concerned with monetary matters.[15] These, alas, are not virtues but vices. If we subtly embrace a conception of the Jew as one given to vice, then there simply will be psychological limits to how morally responsive we will be to manifestations of anti-Semitism. Just how motivated can we be to go to the moral wall on behalf of those whose very nature we believe makes them untrustworthy?

To conclude on a positive note, I believe it is possible for people to take one another seriously and with great moral respect in spite of differences—some natural, some socially cultivated. This, however, requires the courage to listen to the other until one has been authorized to bear witness on the individual's behalf. I call this kind of listening "moral deference."[16] In its absence we will often fail to see the abusive ways in which we use the power that we have, for we cannot know how others are affected by what we do until we have heard their story. When it comes to how others are affected by our behavior, the appearances count for almost as much as the reality. Far too often we fix upon the raw behavior while determinedly ignoring its appearances to those affected by it. Therein lie the seeds for the abuse of power.

Notes

When I began this essay, *Vessels of Evil: American Slavery and the Holocaust* (Philadelphia: Temple University Press, 1993) was not even close to being completed. However, some of the main themes, such as those distinguishing the Holocaust from American slavery, were well in place, and I draw upon these differences in this essay. On the other hand, this essay very much informs the book with respect to my present understanding of sexism as it relates to power and trust, as well as my understanding of racism in this regard. I am grateful to the sponsors of the 1991 Georgia State University Conference on Racism and Sexism, Linda Bell and David Blumenfeld, for inviting me to participate, and thus giving me the opportunity to think about the connections and differences between all three forms of oppression.

1. See Elizabeth V. Spelman, *Inessential Woman: Problems of Exclusion in Feminist Thought* (Boston: Beacon Press, 1988).

2. Elizabeth Fox-Genovese, *Within the Plantation Household* (Chapel Hill, N.C.: University of North Carolina Press, 1988), 309.

3. See H. L. A. Hart, *The Concept of Law* (New York: Oxford University Press, 1963).

4. These remarks owe their inspiration to Andrea Dworkin in her *Right-Wing Women* (New York: Perigee Book, 1983).

5. The insightful remarks of my commentator, David Blumenfeld, have enabled me to see that there is a flaw in this subsection. (See his "Sexism and Gender Identity: A Reply to Thomas" in this volume.) I should have distinguished between heterosexism and a heterosexually oriented society and spoken in terms of the former rather then the latter. While I still think that a heterosexually oriented society will turn out to be a sexist one, this is far less obviously true than the thesis that a heterosexist society will be a sexist one. In the latter we perhaps have a logical entailment, whereas we have no such thing in the former, as Blumenfeld's remarks show. However, I do not see that it is ever likely that we could have a heterosexually oriented society that is not, in turn, a sexist one, even though heterosexuality does not logically entail sexism. Here one must distinguish logical possibility from practical plausibility. Consider: It is logically possible that although people always married within their own racial or ethnic group racism did not exist, just as it is logically possible that all the world should like only vanilla ice cream. This is not practically plausible, though: on the assumption that the world is nonracist, we would require quite an explanation for why everyone nonetheless marries only within their own racial or ethnic group. And the fact that this is a logical possibility would hardly count as satisfactory. My remarks about a heterosexually oriented society and sexism are to be understood in the very same vein. Further, while it is true that considerations of procreation must not be ignored, it is also true that they should not be given more weight than they deserve. The very procreative act itself takes a relatively small amount of time; whereas the rich activity of lovemaking can be a quite extended enterprise. But then lovemaking is an art form, if you will, that any two people can engage in with all of its richness. (See E. O. Wilson, ch. 6 of *On Human Nature* [Cambridge, Mass.: Harvard University Press, 1978]; see also Laurence Thomas, ch. 2 of *Living Morally: A Psychology of Moral Character* [Philadelphia.: Temple University Press, 1989], for comment on Wilson.) There is no evidence that a certain gender configuration is required. Finally, in answer to Blumenfeld's question about the relationship between my view and Andrea Dworkin's, I very much appreciate the substance of her point, though I do not accept its most extreme form.

6. See Laurence Thomas, "Sexism, Racism and the Business World," *Business Horizons* 24, no. 4 (July/August 1981): 62–68, and "Sexism and Racism: Some Conceptual Differences," *Ethics* 90, no. 2 (January 1980): 239–50.

7. See my gloss on this in note 5 above.

8. Frederick Douglass, *Narrative of the Life of Frederick Douglass: An American Slave Written by Himself* (1845), ed. Benjamin Quarles (Cambridge, Mass.: Harvard University Press, 1988), 76. Emphasis added.

9. See Claudia Card, "Gratitude and Obligation," *American Philosophical Quarterly* 25, no. 2 (1988): 115–27; see also Laurence Thomas, "The Reality of the Moral Self," *The Monist* 76, no. 1 (1993): 3–21.

10. Frederick Douglass, *Narrative of the Life of Frederick Douglass*, 76.

11. See Laurence Thomas, "American Slavery and the Holocaust: Their Ideologies Compared," *Public Affairs Quarterly* 5 (1991); see also Gavin I. Langmuir, "Introduction," in his *Toward A Definition of Antisemitism* (Berkeley, Calif.: University of California Press, 1990), for a reading of anti-Semitism that supports this characterization of how people have conceived of Jews.

12. David Fisher and Anthony Read, *Kristallnacht: The Nazi Night of Terror* (New York: Random House, 1989), 180.

13. Hannah Arendt, *Eichmann in Jerusalem: A Report in the Banality of Evil* (New York: Penguin, 1963; revised and expanded, 1973).

14. Melvin J. Lerner, "The Justice Motive: Some Hypotheses as to its Origins and Forms," *Journal of Personality* 45, no. 1 (March 1977): 1–52.

15. See Steven R. Weisman, "In a Tide of Japanese Books on Jews, an Anti-Semitic Current," *The New York Times*, February 19, 1991, A11.

16. See Laurence Thomas, "Moral Deference," *The Philosophical Forum* 24, no. 1 (1992): 233–50, and "Moral Flourishing in an Unjust World," *The Journal of Moral Education* 22 (1993): 83–96, the Fifth Annual Lawrence Kohlberg Lecture of the Association for Moral Education.

11

Sexism and Male Gender Identity: A Reply to Thomas

David Blumenfeld

Laurence Thomas has made so many important claims that it would be impossible here to give all of them the attention they deserve. In this brief reply I shall focus on only what I disagree with in his essay. But I wish to acknowledge how much of it is instructive and correct. His use of the distinction between capricious and expectations-generating power arrangements, for example, brings out fundamental differences between American slavery and the Holocaust. His idea that there can be a moral structure embedded within unjust institutions like sexism and slavery, and that this moral structure helps to stabilize and hence perpetuate them, is poignant and ironic. The role, moreover, that he assigns to trust in these contexts is a fruitful extension of the general analysis of trust developed in his rewarding book, *Living Morally: A Psychology of Moral Character.*[1]

I disagree, however, with many of his notions about gender identity and its relationship to sexism. The following quotation expresses the most central idea that I wish to dispute. "In a heterosexually oriented world, as long as there is gender identity and it can be affirmed only by a member of the other gender, and as long as there is an asymmetry in the biological capacities of women and men to affirm their gender identities, sexism is here to stay. If so, then men will always have an interest in women believing that they should be subordinate to men."[2] In Thomas's opinion, then, it is simply impossible to eradicate sexism without eliminating the sort of heterosexuality in which men's gender identity requires female affirmation. "Sexism," he says, "is deeply tied to the desire of men to assure that women affirm the gender identity of men," and in a heterosexually oriented society, the gender identity of a great many males is "inextricably tied to the act of sexual intercourse with women."[3] In view of the deep tie he describes, a heterosexual society *cannot* overcome sexism if it continues to make the attainment of masculinity depend on affirmation by women.

As a first approximation, we might set out Thomas's argument like this:

1. Sexism is deeply tied to men's need for their gender identity to be affirmed by women.

2. If premise 1 is true, then as long as there is a heterosexually oriented society in which most men's gender identity depends on affirmation by women, it will be impossible to overcome sexism.

3. Therefore, as long as there is a heterosexually oriented society in which most men's gender identity depends on affirmation by women, it will be impossible to overcome sexism.

But what exactly does it mean to say that sexism is "deeply tied" to men's need for their gender identity to be affirmed by women? And what grounds are there for thinking this deep tie entails the impossibility of overcoming sexism without undoing this kind of gender identity?

Thomas's answer is that the tie is "deep" in the sense that in any heterosexual society of the type in question most males will be unable to satisfy the need for gender identity except through female affirmation. In this respect, he notes, there is an asymmetry between the sexes: women can achieve at least some sense of their own gender identity through the capacity to give birth. But men lack any such gender-affirming biological function. In a heterosexual society, therefore, most men are dependent *exclusively* on relations with women for the achievement of gender identity. Thomas thinks it follows that they will propagate sexism as the most effective way of assuring that they attain this identity.

With this explication of the deep tie in mind, we can flesh out Thomas's argument more satisfactorily.

1. As long as there is a heterosexually oriented society in which masculine gender identity is achieved through affirmation by

women, and in which men have no purely biological way of achieving this identity, most men will be dependent for gender identity exclusively on relations with women.

2. As long as most men are dependent exclusively on relations with women for the achievement of gender identity, it will be impossible to overcome sexism.

3. Therefore, as long as there is a heterosexually-oriented society in which masculine gender identity is achieved through affirmation by women, and in which men have no purely biological way of achieving this identity, it will be impossible to overcome sexism.

The most serious problems here are with premise 2. But before we discuss them, let's look at premise 1. As it stands, I think 1 is false. Is it really true in our present heterosexual society that masculine gender identity depends *exclusively* on relationships with women? This overlooks the multitude of ways in which heterosexual men establish a sense of gender identity through relationships with other men. I will not catalogue these ways here, since they are familiar phenomena. Nor would I defend all of them, since many are sexist, homophobic, or defective in other ways. Nevertheless, it is an exaggeration to say that masculine gender identity is founded solely on men's relationships with women. It may be true, as Thomas says, that men have no biological analogue that is as effective for establishing their gender identity as giving birth is for establishing women's. But it doesn't follow that the attainment of masculine gender identity depends exclusively on relationships with women.

Perhaps it will be replied that Thomas can make his case with a more restricted claim. Heterosexual men in our society do not depend exclusively on women for gender identity, but they do depend on them in important ways. Could Thomas avoid the criticism by substituting "importantly" for "exclusively" in 1 and 2?

It is not obvious that he could. For the weaker the tie between men's gender identity and women's affirmation of it, the weaker the case for premise 2. To the extent, in other words, that men have other avenues for achieving identity, it will be just that much less clear that they will have to control women, and be sexist, in order to assure that they get this identity.

Possibly Thomas could get around the problem through some other modification. Some might argue, for example, that in our society the *fullest achievement* of masculine identity depends on relations with women, and that a modification along those lines would meet my point. I won't try to decide this issue, however, since my case doesn't turn on it: premise 2 is false for more profound reasons.

That most men's gender identity depends on affirmation by women does not in itself entail sexism. It does not entail this, I maintain, even if we postulate that men depend exclusively on women in this regard. One can easily conceive of a nonsexist heterosexual society in which this dependence relation holds and in which, furthermore, no purely biological male avenues to identity have opened up. To do so one has only to imagine a society that has given up the macho idea of masculinity and substituted a liberated conception, which stresses equality and makes true manhood incompatible with the domination and exploitation of women. Such a conception of society is clearly possible, since most of us have it. Some men, moreover, have adopted it and tried to live by it. No doubt they have succeeded only to varying degrees and seldom, if ever, perfectly. But this is true of all worthy and difficult ideals. That the number of such men has increased in recent years is one of the many debts we owe the feminist movement, which in this respect has deepened the humanity of all the men whose allegiance it has won. That this number is substantial and growing also suggests that there is no reason to think it is *impossible* for there to be such a society.

I am not claiming that there ever will be such a society. That is an empirical question to which I don't pretend to have the definitive answer. It may be, as some writers have suggested, that the sexist power structure will succeed in holding advances to small and isolated aspects of society. But if a liberated order doesn't come about, it won't be because of a deep tie that links every conception in which masculinity depends on affirmation by women to sexism. There is no such tie.

Before closing, I must mention one more argument. Thomas nowhere explicitly endorses it and it may very well be that he would not wish to do so. But there are two reasons for calling attention to it here. First, it is the kind of argument which, if sound, would block the main line I have taken against him. Second, it is an argument that appears explicitly in a writer to whom Thomas attributes the inspiration of his remarks on this topic.[4]

In her powerfully written book, *Right-Wing Women*, Andrea Dworkin claims that a system of forced sex is required to assure that women have sexual relations with men.[5] The following extended quotation expresses her position vividly.

Forced sex, usually intercourse, is a central issue in any woman's life. She must like it or control it or manipulate it or resist it or avoid it; she must develop a relationship to it, to the male insistence on intercourse, to the male insistence on her sexual function in relation to him. She will be measured and judged by the nature and quality of her relationship to intercourse. Every sign on her body, every symbol—clothes, posture, hair, ornament—will have to signal her acceptance of his sex act and the nature of her relationship to it. His sex act, intercourse, explicitly announces his power over her: his possession of her interior; his right to violate her boundaries. His state promotes and protects his sex act. If she were not a woman, this intrusion by the state would be recognized as state coercion, or force. The act itself and the state that protects it call on force to exercise illegitimate power; and intercourse cannot be analyzed outside this system of force. . . . Despite the propaganda, the mountains of it [which stresses that intercourse can give a woman pleasure if she does it right and that the right attitude is to desire men *because* they engage in phallic penetration], intercourse requires force; force is still essential to make women have intercourse—at least in a systematic, sustained way. . . .

Despite every single platitude about love, women and men, passion, femininity, intercourse as health or pleasure or biological necessity, it is forced sex that keeps intercourse central and it is forced sex that keeps women in sexual relation to men. If the force were not essential, the force would not be endemic. If the force were not essential, the law would not sanction it. If the force were not essential, the force itself would not be defined as intrinsically "sexy," as if in practicing force sex itself is perpetuated. . . . It is through intercourse in particular that men express and maintain their power and dominance over women. The right of men to women's bodies for the purpose of intercourse remains the heart, soul, and balls of male supremacy: this is true whatever style of advocacy is used, Right or Left, to justify coital access.

Every woman—no matter what her sexual orientation, personal sexual likes or dislikes, personal history, political ideology—lives inside this system of forced sex. This is true even if she has never personally experienced any sexual coercion, or if she personally likes intercourse as a form of intimacy, or if she as an individual has experiences of intercourse that transcend, in her opinion, the dicta of gender and the institutions of force. This is true even if—for her—the force is eroticized, essential, central, sacred, meaningful, sublime.[6]

If Dworkin's view were correct, then the liberated male gender identity that I have endorsed would be impossible, and indeed a hopelessly naive myth.

I think it is extremely implausible, however, to suppose that if it were not for force, women would not be drawn to men sexually (or, at any rate, not "in a systematic, sustained way"). Throughout the rest of the animal kingdom, wherever species reproduce sexually, male and female members as a rule are drawn to one another naturally by biology. And it is not difficult to understand why. It would be surprising, therefore, if the class of female Homo sapiens were an exception to this rule. Of course, there *are* some exceptions to the rule among other animals: homosexual behavior is not a uniquely human phenomenon and, in fact, can be found in other species. Nevertheless, in other species, as in our own, it is the exception rather than the rule. So the claim that men have to force—indeed to brutalize and brainwash—women in order to keep them "in sexual relation to men" seems very weak.

Certainly much more needs to be said about Dworkin's position, but that is not the task at hand. The point is that her view would supply the deep tie Thomas seeks and preclude the possibility of any nonsexist heterosexual society. Moreover, it is not clear whether any much less extreme position would do so. It would therefore be interesting to know whether Thomas is prepared to take Dworkin's line.

Notes

I am indebted throughout this chapter to discussions with Jean Blumenfeld.

1. Laurence Thomas, *Living Morally: A Psychology of Moral Character* (Philadelphia: Temple University Press, 1989).
2. Laurence Thomas, "Power, Trust, and Evil," in this volume, 161.
3. Ibid., 161.
4. Ibid., 161, 170n.4.
5. Andrea Dworkin, *Right-Wing Women* (New York: Putnam and Sons, 1983).
6. Ibid., 80–83.

Part III

Pain and Anger:
Practical Outgrowths

12

Changing the Subject:
Studies in the Appropriation
of Pain

Elizabeth V. Spelman

One of the striking features of the depiction of the situation of "women" by nineteenth-century white suffragists in the United States was their comparison of the plight of women to the plight of slaves. A not untypical formulation was this one by Elizabeth Cady Stanton: "The prolonged slavery of women is the darkest page in human history."[1] Stanton and other white women active in the movement to abolish slavery drew heavily upon the language and imagery of the experience of slavery to make sense of and bring attention to the social, legal, and economic constraints under which they lived.

In her recent book *Women and Sisters: The Antislavery Feminists in American Culture*, Jean Fagan Yellin has examined in considerable detail what she describes as the "application of antislavery discourse to the condition of women."[2] Yellin describes the ways in which and the means by which the subject of the experience of slavery was changed—from black male and female slave to white woman and, in a later development, to "humanity in general."

Jean Fagan Yellin makes clear that the linking of the condition of black female slaves and white middle-class women often was not tendered simply or cautiously as a limited analogy. Some of the most vigorous and committed of white female abolitionists came to regard themselves as slaves, came to describe their own experience in terms appropriated whole cloth from the language developed to depict slavery: as such women "expanded their discussions of the condition of slaves to include discussions of the condition of women, they continued to use the same discursive codes, but they connected them to new referends."[3] White women spoke not simply of being slaves, as in the quotation above from Stanton, but talked of being bound, fettered, having the oppressor's foot on their necks.[4] Yellin cites a passage from the diary of Angelina Grimké in which Grimké begins with a clear reference to a slave, but then proceeds, as Yellin puts it, to focus "on herself, describing her own transformation into a powerless slave. The passivity, the apprehension—the shaking knees, the sinking heart, the prayer for strength—all are her own. The suffering painfully recounted is Grimké's own. As she writes, the black woman recedes. . . ."[5] In the hands of Grimké and others, the subject changes not only from female slave to a particular white woman, but then to "women in general," though that in practice meant "white woman" in general, or rather "white middle-class Christian woman" in general.[6] In either case, the female slave is made to disappear from view. Although presumably it was her experience that originally was the focus of concern, other women's experience was made the focus.

Thus, although Yellin in no way underestimates the considerable hardship and violence to which white nonslave women were subject, her work invites us to consider to what degree such women appropriated the experience of black slaves, and black female slaves in particular—that is, the extent to which they presented themselves as occupying the same experiential territory as slaves while simultaneously erasing signs of the slaves' occupation of that territory. Yellin's concerns here are not unlike those expressed by the contemporary black feminist bell hooks, who in the opening pages of her *Feminist Theory: From Margin to Center*, insists that "feminist emphasis on 'common oppression' in the United States was less a strategy for politicization than an appropriation by conservative and liberal women of a radical political vocabulary that masked the extent to which they shaped the movement so that it addressed and promoted their class interests."[7]

Many of us no doubt share these concerns. But, as Yellin's work makes clear, there is a host of important issues that remain unexamined if all we say here is that white women illegitimately appropriated the experience of black women. Yellin's book gives us the chance to take a close look at some of the early moments in the long history of the tension between white and black women active in abolitionist, civil rights, and women's struggles in the nineteenth and twentieth centuries in the United States as they tried to make sense of their own and each other's suffering. Along the way it encourages us to look at some perplexing issues that arise when we think about the complex social and political conditions in which claims about the shared subjectivity of experiences typically are made. As Yellin's work makes clear, some white suffragists' use of the language of slavery to describe the situation of "women" had a complicated and contradictory relation to the institutionalized white racism of the time: in some ways it undermined, in some ways it sustained such racism. This paradoxical relation took at least three closely related forms, which I call the paradox in appropriation, the paradox in identification, and the paradox in universality.

The Paradox in Appropriation

What I am calling paradoxes here represent ways in which white women's comparison of themselves to slaves could both subvert and sustain the institutions of white supremacy in which the comparisons were made. The first of these paradoxes, the paradox in appropriation, is a reminder that while the self-interested appropriation by white women of the experience of black women was and is noxious, so surely would be a failure or refusal by white women to find or make anything in common with black women.

For example, Linda Brent, the voice of the ex-slave Harriet A. Jacobs in *Incidents in the Life of a Slave Girl, Written By Herself,*[8] certainly hoped the northern white women she addressed would understand the significance of their shared experience as mothers, even while expressing keen awareness that there was much about slavery the white women could not understand.

June Jordan recently made clear her astonishment at a well-meaning white woman's resolute inability or unwillingness to see or imagine that she and June Jordan have any shared experiences or concerns. Jordan describes the white woman sitting across from her in her office, "friendly as an old stuffed animal, beaming good will" toward her as she recites with bizarre envy the important problems Jordan as an African American has to face: "poverty, violence, discrimination in general."[9] Such envious glorification of Jordan's experience makes Jordan into an exotic and alien sufferer. In this connection it is instructive to remember María Lugones's reference to the "complex failure of love in the failure to identify with another woman, the failure to see oneself in other women who are quite different from oneself."[10]

Perhaps now the paradox is becoming clear: while there certainly seems to be something repugnant in seeing so much of oneself in another's experience that one completely obscures the existence of that other subject, there is something similarly repugnant in so distancing oneself from the experiences of others that one cannot see oneself as having anything to do with such an experience or thus with anyone who has such an experience.[11]

Similarly, the idea that one can slip on another's experiences, the way in which you might slip on her coat, is an almost incoherent notion that can take grotesque expressions—as in designer-line "homelessness" fashions, which according to some news reports are the next gift from Paris, and the likes of which have been seen in my neighborhood recently, in store-front mannequins draped in sleeping bags. Make a fashion statement by putting on the experience of homelessness. Or, as an ad in the *New York Times* suggests: men, wear Calvin Klein jeans, and make people think you've had the experience of being one of the workers who dug the subway tunnels of Manhattan. There are experiences we desperately don't want to have had, but we seem ready to attach ourselves, at a safe distance, to any glamour that comes to be associated with such experiences. To borrow a phrase my mother used in another context, some of us use others as "spiritual bellhops," relieved that they actually have had experiences we simply want to have the appearance of having had.

And yet, despite the ever present possibility of such exploitative sentimentality—and here again is the tension, the paradox, in appropriation—it would be absurd to deny that in some important sense people can and should try to put on the experiences of others.

Indeed—to return to the historical moment about which Jean Fagan Yellin is writing—the hope of slaves that others might understand the trouble they had seen, and be moved to do something about it, seems to be linked in some way or other with the possibility that others could be the subjects of such suffering even though in fact they were not.[12] Slaves, and the abolitionists who hoped to relieve their plight, certainly counted on the possibility that those who were not slaves could both understand claims about the horrors of slavery and be moved to act out of the belief that the experiences undergone by slaves were the kinds of experiences that *no* subject should have. That is, slaves and abolitionists presumably thought that others could know enough about what it is, or what it would be, to be the subject of such experiences, that they would act to prevent those experiences being the experiences of *anyone*.

And so it would be very odd to hope that nonslaves would understand and have compassion[13] for slaves and yet at the same time not allow that nonslaves might themselves be or become the subjects of such suffering or something very much like it. As Lawrence Blum has argued, compassion involves simultaneously both a difference in the actual situation of the sufferer and the compassionate person *and* a sense of their shared vulnerability to suffering. In compassion, I am moved by what *you* are going through, not what *I* am going through, concerned about *your* condition, not about *mine*.[14] At the same time, while I need not have gone through what you have, your "suffering . . . is seen as the kind of thing that could happen to anyone, including [my]self insofar as [I] am a human being."[15] My sense that I, too, could be a subject of such suffering, far from occluding or erasing your status as the subject of suffering about whom I am concerned, expresses my belief in our shared humanity. I not only see you as a subject of suffering, but I also see susceptibility to it as something we share. In fact, following Blum, we can say that my acknowledgment of the possibility that the subject of suffering can change distinguishes the person who has compassion from the one who merely pities: in pity, Blum says, "one holds oneself apart from the afflicted person and from their suffering, thinking of it as something that defines the person as fundamentally different from oneself." [16] While I in principle could be the subject of the kind of experience you are having, insofar as I pity you I wouldn't be caught dead in fact having such an experience—presumably because of a belief I have that goes something like this: certain kinds of experiences are had only by certain kinds of people, and by gum I'm not *that* kind of person, or at least not insofar as and in the respects in which such a person is pitiful. We will return to this interesting alleged connection between kinds of experiences and kinds of persons shortly.[17]

In sum, the paradox in appropriation reminds us that seeing one's own experience in the experience of others can all too easily lend itself to the expropriation of the experiences of others, to putting their experiences to your own use while erasing the fact of their having been subjects of those experiences. But at the same time, our jointly thinking of each other as possible subjects of the same kinds of experiences can be an important piece of our thinking of each other as members of the same human community.

If our jointly thinking of each other as possible subjects of the same kinds of experiences is part of our thinking of each other as members of the same human community, it should not be surprising to find that individuals or groups who wish to distinguish themselves from other individuals or groups try to do so by insisting that they would never be subjects of the kinds of experiences the others have, and the others could never be subjects of the kinds of experiences they have. Philosophers need look no further than Plato and Aristotle for telling examples.

Many of the paeans to Love produced by the near tipsy revelers in Plato's *Symposium* insist that the capacity for experiencing real Love is not distributed equally among human subjects. The idea that real Love involves a kind of experience that only intelligent and educated subjects can have, alluded to first in Pausanias's distinction between Common and Heavenly Love, is given more explicit articulation in Socrates' telling of the lessons he learned from Diotima. There is an experience that the lover can have only after much preparation, and Diotima's description of this culminating experience is really quite glorious: "You see," she says to Socrates, "the man who has been thus far educated in matters of Love, who has beheld beautiful things in the right order and correctly, is coming now to the goal of Loving: all of a sudden he will catch sight of something wonderfully beautiful in its nature; that, Socrates, is the reason for all his earlier labors" (210e-211a). This experience is the experience of "see[ing] the Beautiful itself, absolute, pure, unmixed, not polluted by human flesh or colors or any other great nonsense of mortality" (211e).[18] The promise here isn't anything like what one of the major television networks offered up in an advertisement a few years ago for its broadcast of the upcoming World Series: "the memories are waiting." The experience of the Beautiful that the thoroughly prepared Socratic lover will have is not something just any old person can have, not something democratically awaiting any and all who happen to turn their eyes and ears a given direction at a given time. Love is a laborious enterprise, and not something either a couch potato or a person otherwise making use of a couch can be guaranteed to have.

But Diotima's point is not simply that some experiences can only be had after long and difficult preparation. Some people just *can-*

not experience the Beautiful itself. While the lover, in "unstinting love of wisdom," that is, in *"philosophia"* (210d), finally catches sight of Beauty itself, a servant thinks beauty can be beheld in "a single example." Like the "boys and women" referred to in the *Republic* (557c), "when they see bright-colored things," the servant will "favor the beauty of a little boy or a man or a single custom" (210d). For, Diotima explains, "being a slave, of course, he's low and small-minded" (210d) and does not know, cannot know, the distinction between a beautiful thing and Beauty itself.

It is no secret that Plato thought there were different kinds of humans and that while an ideal human community is made up of many kinds—philosopher-rulers, guardians, artisans, and (though Socrates barely notes it) slaves—the kind of person you are is determined by the kind of mental capacity you have, including the capacity for certain kinds of education. Those whose natural capacities and careful education mark them out as real lovers of wisdom will have experiences that just will not be available to others.

This does not mean that Plato thought there were *no* experiences of which both philosophers and others could be subjects. Nor did Aristotle, though in his work, as in Plato's, the distinction in kind among humans is mirrored in the distinction in kind among their possible experiences (a "natural slave" of Aristotle's surely is not a possible subject of tragic experience as understood by Aristotle[19]). A danger incessantly lurking for both Plato and Aristotle is the possibility that rationally well-endowed individuals will have experiences of a kind that will erode or distort or leave underdeveloped their rationality. So, for example, as Terence Irwin recently has reminded us, Aristotle "prohibits the citizens of his ideal state from menial work, because such work is inconsistent with the virtue that is required for a happy life (*Politics* 1328b-1329a). In his view, someone who must spend most of his time and effort working for a precarious living, or in dependence on the favor of another, will never develop the right virtues of character for a citizen."[20] Aristotle insists that "no man can practice excellence who is living the life of a mechanic or laborer" (*Politics* 1278a20; cf. 1319a27)—leisure is necessary for that (*Politics* 1329a11).[21] So even though well-educated citizens could in principle have some of the same experiences as free laborers and artisans, or as slaves, they could do so only on pain of eroding crucial differences between themselves and those more "lowly" types. "Certainly the good man and the statesman and the good citizen ought not to learn the crafts of inferiors except for their own occasional use; if they habitually practice them, there will cease to be a distinction between master and slave" (*Politics* 1277b4-7).

Our inquiry into the possibility of one person or group appropriating the experience of another individual or group thus has led us to some reflections on both the ontological status of experience as the kind of thing that can have more than one subject, and the moral significance of different human beings jointly thinking of each other as possible subjects of the same kinds of experience. Just now we have seen recognition of these features of experience reflected in the insistence on the part of philosophers such as Plato and Aristotle—for whom metaphysical differences in kinds of human subjects ground claims for maintaining political distinctions among them—that some humans have important kinds of experiences that other humans just cannot have, and that while there are some kinds of experiences *any* human can have, some humans *should not* have them. Slaves just cannot have the experiences only true lovers of wisdom can; while good citizens can have the experiences menial laborers have, they *should not*, on pain of eroding the distinction between these types of human beings. (A recent advertisement in the *New Yorker* reminds us of yet another way in which claims to exclusive access to certain kinds of experiences are meant to distinguish some kinds of people from others: there are, the resort ad tells us, "pleasures few will know," since "our number of guests are [sic] limited."[22])

Having seen the investment there can be in the idea that there are sorts of experiences only certain kinds of people *can* have, and sorts of experiences only certain kinds of people *should* have, let us return to the world in which the black and white women about whom Jean Fagan Yellin writes lived and thought and did political battle. In particular, let us return to the ways in which white women's attempted identification with black female slaves had a paradoxical relationship to the white supremacy of the time, both subverting it, by conflating the experiences of whites and blacks, and yet also expressing it, by obscuring the white women's own role in the maintenance of slavery.

The Paradox in Identification

The comparison of the situation of "women" and that of slaves, which of course doesn't make sense at all as a *comparison* unless the women in question were *not* slaves, occurred in a context in which whites' alleged superiority over blacks was being affirmed in and through every major institution of the society. Even white abolitionists, male and female, did not necessarily seek to undermine white supremacy; ending slavery was fully compatible with maintaining segregation and systematic inequality between whites and blacks, with outlawing mixed-race marriages and imposing heavy sanctions on mixed-race alliances. The use of the image of slavery to describe the situation of white women involved a powerful trope intended to point to deep, significant, and compelling similarities in the experiences of two groups of people whose differences it was the main business of the dominant racial ideology otherwise to insist upon. Thus, there is good reason to believe that in the eyes of those wishing to maintain white supremacy, the conceptual miscegenation (the concept is borrowed from Toni Morrison[23]) conflating the experience of white women with that of black female slaves could have been seen as almost as damaging to the alleged purity of white experience and its crucial distinctiveness from black experience as the sexual union of whites and blacks would be to the alleged purity and distinctiveness of white blood.

But on the other hand we cannot conclude that by comparing themselves to black slaves white women could not or did not preserve their privilege vis-à-vis the female slaves with whom they said they identified, or that their appropriation of the experience of slavery was not exploitative. For as Jean Yellin reminds us,[24] if the identity of the situation of white and black women were to be taken seriously, this would mean that there were no significant differences between them—at least for the purposes of the antislavery campaign. Now, as mentioned earlier, such a claim would seem to undermine pervasive racist ideology, which cannot allow for any occasions or any ways in which skin color does not make a difference. But on the other hand—and hence the "paradox in identity"—such assertions of identity also served to reinforce racism, to the degree that the claim of identity obscured the real difference race made to the situations of the two groups of women. In particular, it obscured the role of white women themselves in maintaining the institutions of white supremacy, in helping through their everyday interactions with black slaves to add to the suffering. For the representation of one as a co-sufferer obscures whatever role one plays as a perpetrator of the misery.

The Paradox in Universality

Finally, let us turn to the third version of the paradox, which goes something like this: in the context of institutionalized racism, claims about the "universality" of a dominated group's experience can be used both to subvert and to sustain those institutions.

At least one reason for a group's calling upon the experiences of other people, even those the group considers their cultural inferiors, is to try to make sense of one's own painful situation: maybe somebody *has* known the trouble I've seen. And, as Toni Morrison has said in a related context, "comparisons are a major form of knowledge and flattery."[25] The very facts that allowed us to see the white female abolitionists' comparison between themselves and female slaves as a brazen affront to white-supremacist ideology also invite us to see the comparison as a kind of flattery—the kind of flattery no doubt intended by the editors of *The Boston Globe* when they recently described the photography exhibit "I Dream a World: Portraits of Black Women Who Changed America" as "speak[ing] to the potential inside everyone";[26] the flattery no doubt intended by a biographer of the artist Frida Kahlo when she said recently in the pages of *The New York Times* that when Kahlo "displays her wounds we immediately know that those wounds stand for all human suffering";[27] the flattery no doubt intended by those who insist that descriptions of the experiences of a historically marginalized group do not capture just their particular lives but in fact tell us something significant about the lives of all people. In this connection, Mary Helen Washington has noted the trivializing effect of black women's writing being treated as "singular and anomalous, not universal and representative."[28] It may then seem churlish to subject the white female abolitionists' comparison between themselves and female slaves to the kind of scrutiny it has gotten in Yellin's book and in these comments. The women were, after all, trying desperately to make sense of and give voice to what was without doubt a very difficult existence, and by comparing themselves to female slaves they were also suggesting that the lives of the slaves had significance beyond the slaves themselves.

However, what an analysis like Yellin's points us to is that the comparison tended neither to promote anyone's knowledge nor to honor anyone's experience. First of all, the comparison for the most part was not the fruit of discussions among white and black women about their relative situations and the meaning or meanings of their suffering. Collaboration of sorts was not entirely out of the question: Harriet Jacobs was helped by Amy Post and Lydia Maria Child, both white abolitionists; Harriet Beecher Stowe offered to include an account of Jacobs's life in *The Key to Uncle Tom's Cabin*, though Jacobs demurred precisely because she wanted to write her own story.[29] But for obvious reasons, discussions among black and white women were not likely to take place or to involve much mutual comprehension even if they did. In the absence of them, there was no way for white women to test their interpretations of the meaning of slavery for black women, especially when white women portrayed black women as reduced, either by nature or by circumstance, to virtual speechlessness about the matter.[30]

And in any event, if the situation of the white women really *were* the same as that of black women, white women could just as well speak about it as the black women. This is connected to the reason why saying that any group's experience really is the experience of everybody can easily diminish rather than enlarge the significance of that group's experience: how can they have anything special or particular to say if their experience is really no different from universal human experience? (One cannot help but think here of the anger and worry expressed by those historians of the Holocaust— many of whom are from families who directly suffered under it— who are alarmed by what one has called "the glib equation of the murder of the Jews with any disaster or atrocity, with any state of affairs one abhors or even merely dislikes."[31] The point Lucy Dawidowicz wishes to make here is not that no suffering matches that of the Holocaust; rather, she says, the facile equation of the destruction of the European Jews with any and all other atrocities "obscur[es] the role of anti-Semitism in accomplishing that murder."[32])

We can think about the lack of knowledge that prompted and was reflected in the comparison between the condition of white women and black slaves in another way: empathy and compassion are not necessarily forms of knowledge and they do not necessarily reflect or encourage relations of equality. To the extent that white women saw themselves as identifying with black women they perhaps were in effect asserting what Karl Morrison describes as the central proposition of empathy: "I Am You."[33] Morrison makes some telling points about the nature of the relationship that is affirmed thereby. The empathetic participation "in the affliction of another, making it [one's] own,"[34] is compatible with, indeed may itself enact, an imposition of the person feeling the empathy on the person for whom the empathy is felt. As Morrison reads the history of the claim, there were two powerful paradigms for understanding how an "I" can become a "You": a biological one, which involved male dominance over female, and an aesthetic one, involving "the imposition of form by the artist on recalcitrant matter."[35]

This characteristic of empathy is related to what Morrison calls the "non-dialogic" aspect of it—when empathy is "one-sided" rather than "interpersonal," when one person participates in the experiences of another but not vice versa, when the identity affirmed is so complete as to negate the very possibility of a distinction between two different people.[36] There is always the danger of the person claiming to participate in the experience of another simply being a ventriloquist.[37]

In sum, if Morrison is right, empathy does not necessarily reflect or encourage knowledge: having it does not require recognizing another as separate, nor does it require hearing what they may have to say about the empathetic gesture or about what is claimed to be understood. Inequality along almost any dimension is not at all ruled out by empathy; indeed, if Morrison is right, the paradigms out of which the understanding of "I Am You" historically was shaped are ones of domination and imposition.[38]

The point here is not to mount a campaign against compassion but simply to note some of its features. Compassion does not require trying to elicit from the afflicted their views about their pain. In this connection, early in her book Yellin points out ways in which white female abolitionists seemed to assume that the meaning of the slave's suffering was obvious. But at the same time, anyone presented as in need of compassion in this way is presented as in need of a ventriloquist, should any questions arise about her state or what ought to be done about it. To say this is not to condemn compassion but only to point out how compassion differs from what one party feels toward the other when both are actually in the same situation, when each is in a position to offer her own interpretation of her situation and to act in her own behalf.[39] In this connection it may also be useful to remember Frances Ellen Watkins Harper's address to the National Council of Women of the United States (1891): "I deem it a privilege to present the negro, not as a mere dependent asking for Northern sympathy or Southern compassion, but as a member of the body politic who has a claim upon the nation for justice, simple justice. . . ."[40]

The work of Jean Fagan Yellin and others has led us into thinking about the idea of one group's appropriation of the experience of another group. What is involved in such appropriation, and what makes it troubling?

I have sketched out three paradoxes to footnote Jean Yellin's sense of the complexity of answers to such questions. The paradox in appropriation suggests that while a danger in putting on the experiences of others is that they as subjects of such experiences will be erased, a danger in *refusing* to do so is that one may thereby deny the possibility of a shared humanity. The paradox in identification reminds us that while the formula "women are slaves" tends to subvert white supremacy by denying differences between black and white women, it sustains white supremacy insofar as it obscures white women's roles in supporting slavery. And the paradox in universality cautions that while calling on the experience of a marginalized group to represent "human experience" can be an important way of honoring that group's experience, it also can be a way of trivializing and thus further marginalizing that group.

In short, there seems to be nothing *inherently* disturbing in a person's thinking of herself or himself as the subject of the same kind of experience another person has had. Indeed, the possibility of shared experience seems in some circumstances to be part of an expression of shared humanity.

But humans are ingenious in devising ways to deny such shared status even when appearing to affirm it. Whites in the United States have made blacks undergo experiences meant to mark them as different from whites, and one of the most powerful of these was slavery. Despite the severe difficulties of their own lives, for the white women Yellin discusses to have used the language of slavery to depict their own condition was to try to reap something useful for themselves from the experience of slavery without having endured its horrors. It no doubt was a measure of their desperation that they presented themselves as subjects of such suffering. But it was also a measure of their relative power that they could so readily put on the mantle of slavery to make sense of their own condition.

All of this no doubt has something to do with what I suspect is widespread human ambivalence about suffering—a despised condition we sometimes wear as a badge of honor. But that's another paper. . . .

Notes

1. Quoted in Jean Fagan Yellin, *Women and Sisters: The Antislavery Feminists in American Culture* (New Haven: Yale University Press, 1989), 171.

2. Ibid., 44.

3. Ibid., 29, 43.

4. Ibid., 30, 39, 43.

5. Ibid., 30.

6. Yellin describes a later development in this gradual "universalizing" of the situation of black slaves in the work of the sculptor Hiram Powers. Powers's *The Greek Slave* (1841–1843), according to Yellin "the most popular American sculpture of the nineteenth century" (100), depicted an erect, bare-breasted woman with "caucasian" features; though like the black female slave still chained, this figure shows no sign of resistance. On the contrary, Yellin suggests, a small but unmistakable cross bespeaks Christian resignation to the fact of suffering. Many contemporary observers, Yellin reports, took this sculpted slave's plight to be representative of the human condition, an "emblem of all trial to which humanity is subject" (107).

7. bell hooks, *Feminist Theory: From Margin to Center* (Boston: South End Press, 1984) 5–6.

8. Jean Fagan Yellin, ed. *Incidents in the Life of a Slave Girl, Written by Herself* (Cambridge, Mass.: Harvard University Press, 1987).

9. June Jordan, "Report from the Bahamas," in *On Call* (Boston: South End Press, 1985), 43.

10. María Lugones, "Playfulness, 'World'-Traveling, and Loving Perception," in *Women, Knowledge, and Reality: Explorations in Feminist Philosophy*, ed. Ann Garry and Marilyn Pearsall (Boston: Unwin Hyman, 1989), 279.

11. Cf. Renato Rosaldo: "the modest truism that any human groups must have certain things in common can appear to fly in the face of a once-healthy methodological caution that warns against the reckless attribution of one's own categories and experiences to members of another culture. Such warnings against facile notions of universal human nature can be carried too far and harden into the equally pernicious doctrine that, my own group aside, everything human is alien to me." "Grief and a Headhunter's Rage: On the Cultural Force of Emotions," in *Play, Text, and Story*, ed. Edward Bruner. Proceedings of the 1983 Meeting of the American Ethnological Society, Washington, D.C., 188.

12. Several claims come to mind here, some of them more justifiable than others. There is the claim that unless you actually *have* gone through what I have gone through, you cannot understand what I mean when I talk about it; then the somewhat weaker claim that unless you *could* go through the kind of thing I have gone through, you cannot understand what I mean when I talk about it; then the even weaker claim that unless you know the kinds of circumstances that would verify or at least warrant what I say, or

correlatively the kinds of circumstances that would falsify or at least throw into doubt the truth of what I say, you cannot understand what I mean when I talk about an experience I have undergone (so even if you have not had, and even if you could not have, the experiences I have had, as someone who shares the language in which I speak, you nevertheless can know what I mean).

13. But see also the address by Frances Ellen Watkins Harper, "Duty to Dependent Races," National Council of Women of the United States, *Transactions* (Philadelphia, 1891), 86: "I deem it a privilege to present the negro, not as a mere dependent asking for Northern sympathy or Southern compassion, but as a member of the body politic who has a claim upon the nation for justice, simple justice. . . ." Quoted in *Black Women in Nineteenth-Century American Life*, ed. Bert James Loewenberg and Rugh Bogin (University Park and London: Pennsylvania State University Press, 1976), 247.

14. Lawrence Blum, "Compassion," in *Explaining Emotions*, ed. Amelie Oksenberg Rorty (Berkeley: University of California Press, 1980), 511.

15. Ibid., 510, 511.

16. Ibid., 512.

17. If Blum identifies a moral failure in pity as the refusal to regard oneself as a possible subject of the undesirable experience, the example from June Jordan in "Report from the Bahamas" suggests a moral failure in a certain kind of envy as the refusal to regard oneself as a possible subject in an allegedly desirable experience. It is perhaps even more complicated than that, since Jordan's account suggests that the white women's envy may in fact be a disguised form of pity.

18. Plato, *Symposium*, trans. Alexander Nehamas and Paul Woodruff (Indianapolis and Cambridge: Hackett, 1989).

19. See Elizabeth V. Spelman, "Tragedy and Slavery," in *Theory, Power, and Human Emancipation: Dimensions of Radical Philosophy*, ed. Roger Gottlieb (Philadelphia: Temple University Press, 1993), 221–44.

20. T. H. Irwin, "Generosity and Property in Aristotle's *Politics*," in *Beneficence, Philanthropy and the Public Good*, ed. Ellen Frankel Paul, Fred D. Miller, Jr., Jeffrey Paul, and John Ahrens (Oxford: Blackwell, 1987), 49–50.

21. Indeed, different kinds of pleasurable experiences are to be had by different kinds of people: there are modes of music better suited to the experiences of pleasure of "artisans, laborers, and the like," whose "minds are perverted from their natural state," than to the quite different experiences of pleasure known by the "free and educated" (*Politics* 1342a19–22).

22. *The New Yorker*, April 8, 1991, 73, advertisement top right corner.

23. Toni Morrison, "Unspeakable Things Unspoken: The Afro-American Presence in American Literature," *Michigan Quarterly Review* XXVII:I (Winter 1989): 6.

24. Yellin, *Women and Sisters*, 23–25.

25. Morrison, "Unspeakable Things," 10.

26. *Boston Globe,* Editorial, "Dreams That Changed America," September 15, 1990, 22.

27. Hayden Herrera, "Why Frida Kahlo Speaks to the 90's," *The New York Times,* October 28, 1990, Section 2, 41.

28. Mary Helen Washington, ed., "Introduction," in *Invented Lives: Narratives of Black Women 1860–1960* (Garden City: Anchor Doubleday, 1987), xix.

29. Ibid., 3, 10.

30. See Yellin, passim, for a discussion of the portrayal of the black female slave as in "speechless agony."

31. Lucy S. Dawidowicz, "Thinking about the Six Million: Facts, Figures, Perspectives," in *Holocaust: Religious and Philosophical Implications,* ed. John K. Roth and Michael Berenbaum (New York: Paragon House, 1989), 63.

32. Ibid., 63.

33. Karl Morrison, *"I Am You": The Hermeneutics of Empathy in Western Literature, Theology, and Art* (Princeton: Princeton University Press, 1988).

34. Ibid., 7.

35. Ibid., xxv; cf. 82.

36. Ibid., 30, 60, xxvi.

37. Ibid., 81, 236.

38. Morrison does not conclude, of course, that all cases of empathy involve domination. In this connection it might be instructive to try to unpack what was meant by the unnamed black woman from Harlem reported to have said of Nelson Mandela: "He is us and we are him" (*The Nation,* July 16/23, 1990, 77).

39. See María C. Lugones and Elizabeth V. Spelman, "Competition, Compassion, and Community: Models for a Feminist Ethos," in *Competition: A Feminist Taboo?,* ed. Valerie Miner and Helen E. Longino (New York: Feminist Press, 1987), 234–47.

40. Quoted in Loewenberg and Bogin, *Black Women in Nineteenth-Century American Life,* 247.

13

Speaking of Suffering:
A Response to
"Changing the Subject"

Pamela M. Hall

Elizabeth Spelman's thoughtful essay examines the ethical status of the feminist appropriation of the term "slavery" to describe oppression of women in the nineteenth century. She rightly raises a concern about the degree to which this appropriation was warranted. Spelman then addresses the following issues bearing on this question of sufficient warrant. First, she asks generally if one can appropriate or claim to share another's experience without "erasing" or de-emphasizing that other's own experience. This leads her to begin to draw a distinction between compassion and pity and to speak at length about the ambiguities, logical and moral, lurking behind claims of sameness or difference in experiences. It is in this regard that she discusses Plato and Aristotle. Second, she tries to do justice to the impetus for such historical feminist appropriation by speaking sympathetically of white women's need to "make sense" of their own experience of oppression. These feminists adopted the notion of slavery because they wished to indicate the sweeping and morally repugnant character of the prejudice under which they lived. But Spelman returns to the questionable nature of this appropriation, given the feminists' failure to recognize the way they themselves participated in the racism that buttressed slavery as a social institution. This is played out, in her view, in the way the feminists represented the female slave as without speech and, as a consequence, by their failure to elicit the slave women's own understanding of their bondage. Spelman then attempts to draw analogies between this exploitation of slavery and other forms of "offense" against suffering. In doing so, she returns to the topics of compassion and pity and to the matter of if and when claims about the "universality" or shared nature of certain experiences are justified.

I propose to reflect on this question of compassion and its proper expression, because I believe that reflection on it will lead us back to the issue of our need to "make sense" of our experiences as well. I believe Spelman's essay addresses two distinct issues: (1) whether one may ever justly lay claim to sharing *another*'s experience without in some sense pre-empting it, and (2) in what way attempts to understand or to console an individual who is suffering can succeed without giving offense. I will attempt to discuss both of these concerns while avoiding the pitfalls of each.

Spelman makes reference to certain attempts to invest particular suffering with "universality." This can serve as a useful stepping-off place for my remarks. It seems to me that there are two extremes to avoid when speaking about suffering. The first extreme is what I would term a vicious particularity: to treat one's own or another's pain as so irremediably private, so wholly impenetrable and incommunicable, that any attempt to approach such pain in order to understand or to console must founder. The second extreme might be called vicious generality: to speak of a particular suffering in such a way that one negates its particularity, its contingency, the very fact that it is happening to another and not to *you* (or to one and not to all). These are deep waters, but let me try to wade into them.

Let us begin with the experience of suffering itself.[1] Among the older meanings of the word are "receiving," "submitting," and "*undergoing*." An element of passivity, of lack of control, is implied. To suffer is to be at the mercy of something or someone, even at the mercy of the pressure of the pain itself. (I believe that this applies to psychological or emotional pain as well as to physical pain.) It is of course undeniable that suffering qua experience is private, isolated in the consciousness of the individual in pain. There is no sharing in that per se. Moreover, pain as intense as what we call "suffering" gives us the feeling of being walled in away from others, set apart by the intensity of our feeling as well as by the sense of being under duress. But the *meaning* of suffering for the sufferer is something that may be shared; this is because bound up with the immediacy of pain itself are what I might term its cognitive "resonances," that is, the meanings we attach to the pain by virtue of our personal and social histories and by virtue of the pain's origins. These may on occasion count as part of suffering insofar as certain meanings or interpretations of our experience may themselves be causes for psychic anguish. Thus my separation of pain in immediacy and in reflection might best be understood as a logical separation.

It is no accident that we so interpret and invest meaning in our experience of pain. I said earlier that to suffer is to be at the mercy of something. To be so subject to what hurts us, and hurts us keenly, is to be brought low and subject to, one feels, chaos. One then seeks to reestablish order, in part by the telling of some story about one's suffering, about its meaning. Certain stories may serve to divest particular kinds of pain of their menace or violence. I am not claiming that all forms of suffering can be so "inoculated." Far from it. But pain made meaningful is pain that is tamed, that is less and different from what I would call suffering or "affliction."[2] It is a fact about our species that we are willing to undergo great stress and difficulty when there seems to us to be a sufficient purpose for it. Think of rigorous athletic training or of lengthy academic study. But such pain is far from the loss of control and the gratuitousness that marks what I call suffering. Thus perhaps I should distinguish henceforth between pain and that psychic and epistemological disturbance I will call suffering. One might put the difference this way. Pain is a form of distress for which there is an adequate story: it is meaningful and it does not seem to disturb the due order of things. Suffering, on the other hand, is distress (often more intense) about which there is *not* an adequate story told: it feels inexplicable, absurd. This is why I call this form of pain an epistemic as well as a psychic disturbance.

This brings me to the subject of oppression as a species of suffering. I will speak of racism and sexism as forms of oppression, but in doing so I mean to imply no tight analogy between them (thus avoiding, I hope, the error of the nineteenth-century feminists). Oppression as a kind of suffering has the characteristic of submitting its subjects to *systematic* abuse, dishonor, and privation on the basis of their membership in racial groups and/or because of gender, culture, or the like. But, even more important, it is in large-scale oppression that many of the standard resources for "making sense" of one's suffering precisely serve to perpetuate the oppression. That is to say, the stock of stories that are held communally by a dominant culture, and that may serve as imaginative guides for individuals when they seek to understand their experience, themselves betray subjects of systematic oppression; this is because these stories will tell a false tale justifying or explaining the oppression.[3] Think of cultural and literary representations of blacks as ignorant and irresponsible, of women as needy and erratic. But surely such a story can give no satisfactory answer to those victimized by oppression. Indeed, part of the "true story" is that there *is* no adequate justification. The pretense that there is some good explanation is part of the insidiousness of oppression. Precisely this realization can start subjects of oppression on the road toward other explanatory options that will give them the emotional and imaginative resources to resist their oppressors. Attempts to find alternative ways of explaining the institution of slavery were being made in the debate over its abolition in the last century, ways that, rather than justifying it, sought to show its unjust and gratuitous character. And it was its unjust character that the feminists themselves were appealing to when inappropriately "borrowing" the term "slavery" to explain their own condition.

Let me now briefly remark upon some aspects of this problematic appropriation. I will return to something I sketched earlier, namely, the matter of two "vices" to be avoided in speech about one's own or another's suffering. Spelman rightly takes issue with these feminists' appropriation of the term "slavery," insofar as they never sought to elicit from slaves how they themselves understood (invested with meaning) their own suffering. But surely this is precisely what could have been shared far more than the root experience of slavery itself. Given this, the white women in question neither respected the essential particularity (and distinctness) of African Americans' suffering nor did they honor the ways in which blacks themselves had sought to understand the oppression under which they lived. As Spelman points out, the feminists' use of "slavery" when describing their suffering under sexism smacks of bad faith, insofar as they failed to recognize, and therefore to speak about, how they helped prop up a racist society. And in telling stories about our experience, what we leave out may be as important as what we include. The feminists presumed to know better than (or instead of) the slaves what slavery was like. Then again, these women were themselves struggling to find a way to understand (and to bring others to understand) their own condition. Adopting slavery as a description might be seen, not altogether naively, as at least an effort to take the evil of slavery seriously.

I think that, either in criticizing or in defending these women, we want to avoid treating any specific instance of suffering in what I called earlier a viciously particular or a viciously general way. Excessive particularity might be to hold that the experience of one form of oppression, say of slavery and systematic racist oppression, is *wholly* incommunicable; this would deny the ways in which one subject to it has told stories about it, sought to make it meaningful to oneself and to fellow sufferers. It is also such stories that *can* be shared even with those outside the circle of pain; needless to say, the immediate suffering itself, as experience, is private by psychological necessity. What I feel can only be conveyed to you; I cannot bring you to feel what I feel, insofar as that is closed within my consciousness and my sensation.

But to maintain that suffering's meaning is utterly closed to all but those who directly experience it may be neither accurate nor wise. Not accurate for the reason I have sketched, that one can share in some measure how one has sought to understand the oppression. Not wise because, if suffering and oppression isolate and alienate the ones in pain, then holding to the incommunicability of this experience only redoubles the injury, only increases the alienation. This has the possible consequence of actually cooperating with, rather than throwing off, the oppression. Why then are we so often prompted to claim that no one can possibly understand our suffering? This is, I think, in part a response of anger and in part a recognition of the reality of one's own, one's individual, suffering. Both anger and truthfulness are important responses, but it is difficult to see how one can go very far in expressing either response without *communicating* how one understands one's suffering.

But neither am I arguing for a vicious generality in speaking about one's own or another's suffering. In fact, I think this vice is far more likely to occur when speaking of a suffering that is not one's own (just as excessive particularity is likely to occur as a response of one *in* pain). Spelman gives several fine examples of such a tendency to "universalize" another's pain; she mentions a *New York Times* review which rhapsodized that the artist Frida Kahlo's wounds "stand for all human suffering."[4] Insofar as I understand this remark at all, I take it to be an attempt to say that this artist helps us to see our solidarity with her, perhaps in that we all alike are vulnerable to suffering. But this remark neglects utterly the uniqueness of the distinct experience of suffering. To leap to the "universality" of some singular experience is to miss the singular. To universalize it is to come close to treating it as simply bound up with the ordinary lot of troubles to which we are all heir. But this fails to acknowledge fully the gratuitousness, that is, the unnecessariness, of many occasions of suffering. Likewise, it is to fail to honor the part of suffering that truly is incommunicable, not its story of meaning but the suffering itself. To universalize in this way is to miss the fact that this instance of suffering was *not* universal: it happened to another, not to you.

I hope that the way I have chosen to speak of suffering, generically but also affirming that there are important distinctions in the experience of it, has not fallen into the universalizing tendency I have criticized. I have not wanted to smooth out the particular thorny manifestations of suffering in order to lump all instances together. I have wanted rather to establish epistemological constraints for speaking of suffering to clarify what can and cannot be shared. I have done this by distinguishing between immediate suffering and what can be told about it. This may, I hope, help us to understand what connections, of knowledge or of compassion, can exist between one in pain and those apart. It is, I hope, to show how a bridge is possible between them, while acknowledging the abyss that makes the bridge necessary.

Notes

1. Regarding the phenomenological reflection that follows, I wish to acknowledge a pervasive indebtedness to the work of Simone Weil on suffering. Of particular help is her essay "The Love of God and Affliction" in Simone Weil, *Waiting for God*, trans. Emma Craufurd (New York: G. P. Putnam's Sons, 1951; reprint, New York: Harper & Row, 1973), 117–36.

2. Note that I adopt here the term that is the most common translation of Simone Weil's *le malheur*, "affliction." See Weil's essay "The Love of God and Affliction."

3. It is important to distinguish here between the stories of a dominant culture and those of a marginalized or oppressed culture itself. The narratives of the latter may well provide resources for criticism of the former. But this point must not be used to minimize the damage done by the distortions in oppressive narratives.

4. See Elizabeth Spelman's "Changing the Subject," in this volume, 190, note 27.

14

Hard-to-Handle Anger

María Lugones

Anger is a form that the passion for communication takes. It is a stirring form: an urgency wishing into being an extremely delicate possibility. Incommunicative anger expresses the state of transformation. It is a cocoon, an inward motion intent on sense making. The passion that I address at you in anger is neither really different nor separate from the passion of metamorphosis. It is in the same tonality and of the same cloth.

Introduction

It is my sense that I can make more sense of anger if I capture anger in its specificity. Some of the angers I am interested in share common features; they are addressed at the same group of people or they have the same tone, the tone of rage, for example, or they are resistant angers. But the angers I will consider are sufficiently different that I want to consider each in its own right. They give rise to and answer different questions, different preoccupations. They require significantly different interpretations and conceptual schemes. There is anger that is a transformation of fear; explosive anger that pushes or recognizes the limits of one's possibilities in resistance to oppression; controlled anger that is measured because of one's intent to communicate within the official world of sense; anger addressed to one's peers in resistance; anger addressed to one's peers in self-hatred; anger that isolates the resistant self in germination; anger that judges and demands respect; anger that challenges respectability. Many of these angers can be understood as "outlaw emotions": emotions that are conventionally unacceptable. "Outlaw emotions are distinguished by their incompatibility with the dominant perceptions and values."[1] But though many of these angers are outlaw emotions, some are more outlawed than others.

Some of these angers appear irrational because it seems that one has been overcome by passion, that one is seized, possessed, in a fit. This understanding presupposes that the self is unitary. The understanding of being possessed, in a passionate, passive trance, assumes that the person who is trying to make sense within the limits of official interpretations of reality, the one exercising herself in controlled anger—attentive to the official interpretation of her movements, voice, message; asking for respectability; judging those who have wronged her—is the only person one is. But one can understand the possession as another self one is and who is doing the work of resistance. Doing so enables one to understand these angers as cognitively rich, the cognitive content understandable only in nonofficial, oppositional communities or universes of sense. In considering anger I consider questions related to the self of the angry person. Who is angry? Is the angry self the subordinate self or the insubordinate self? Is the insubordinate self resistant or asking to be seen from within the official reality by those whose subordinate she is?

I am also interested in anger and communication. I do not think all anger has a communicative intent, but rather the point of some anger is to isolate the self from others. Gloria Anzaldúa gives us a striking understanding of this anger. For each sort of anger, I will consider how other-directed the anger is, to whom it is directed, and whether its intent is to communicate. I will ask how concerned the anger is with others' feelings or with the impression one makes on others.

It has become clear to me that some angers are second-order angers. They presuppose worlds of sense against which the anger constitutes an indictment or a rebellion, worlds of sense from which one needs to separate. These angers also presuppose or establish a need for or begin to speak from within separate worlds of sense. Separate, that is, from worlds of sense that deny intelligibility to the anger.

The anger of dominators slides over me as something of no consequence. I beware of and deal with its harm, the destruction it proposes and many times succeeds in bringing about, but I pay no attention to the emotion as a source of insight or companionship. I am also unconcerned from a theoretical point of view with the anger of dominators; anger that is connected with hatred; anger that is used to mold through instilling fear for the purposes of domination, that aims at transforming its target into a function of the angry dominator's needs[2]; anger that expresses displeasure at one's not having been able to exercise complete control over one's environment for the purpose of satisfying one's own needs. But it is important to think of the manipulative power of this anger. We need to learn to exercise indifference to it, since it is a psychological tool of domination, and part of its effect depends on one's paying attention to it.

We do need to think about the manipulative effects of our own anger. Anger does create an environment, a context, a tone, and it echoes. Anger does need to be trained but not necessarily toned down. We need to think what good the anger does us with respect to oppression.

In sum, as I think about anger, I keep in mind the self who is angry, the worlds of sense that make sense of her and of her anger, the worlds of sense in which she makes no sense as angry, and whether the anger has a communicative or an incommunicative intent. I also think about the training of our angers for the purposes of resistance or for self-care. Some of our angers may be harmful, but we still need to recognize them both in order to deal with them and in order not to confuse them with the work of our selves in angry resistance.

Why Am I Worried about Anger?

"My anger has meant pain to me but it has also meant survival, and before I give it up I'm going to be sure that there is something at least as powerful to replace it on the road to clarity."[3]

"One is made angry not simply by violation. The magic of anger is a response not to injustice, but to a frustrated political impulse to speak and be heard, and the existence of anger itself is evidence of the denial of a right to social participation."[4]

In part I think about anger because I have experienced anger as a problematic emotion: on the one hand I find myself angrier and angrier; on the other I have always disliked being overwhelmed by emotion. So I have tried to contain, mold, temper my own anger. I have distrusted anger uncontained as a source of knowledge, as the impetus for political action, as the tone for my interaction with other people. But most of all I have disliked myself in deep, "overwhelming" anger. I have disliked my bodily sense, my movements, the awesome quality of myself, the largeness of my occupying other people's interior space, the strong possibility of manipulation. I have also disliked the turmoil in myself during and after "uncontrolled" anger. I have most of all disliked its effectiveness even as I have seen its political potential. It has made me think poorly of others as well as of myself, but for very different reasons. I am frightening when I am that angry and I feel somewhat possessed: the logic of my movements and of my use of space, of my use of my voice, of how I look at people is frenetic, rousing. I seem mad and sane at the same time because of the depth of passion. I lose any concern with fitting anywhere, with being appreciated, liked, respected. I am firmly marginal but I also manage to be threatening while most of the time I do not succeed in destabilizing the hold of the official on those around me or on myself. I haven't been that angry very often, but it seems to me that as years go by I am getting angrier and angrier in precisely that way. As I have a harder time containing this form of anger, I have begun to wonder about my own dislike of it and the extent to which my finding it unacceptable is not part of my indoctrination into subordination, which is of a piece with my concern with my respectability within the confines of the official, the normal.

I have witnessed women who lived this hard-to-handle anger in front of me and I found them extremely powerful, their faces expressive in extraordinary ways, their manners and words beyond containment. Awesome. Clear. This anger endangers one's hold over convention. It places one beyond the pale. It announces an emerging self toward whom the "I" tied to the official world of sense feels ill at ease. The official "I" wants to feel in control over her emotions; this is an important part of this "I." But fury, hard-to-handle anger, feels to this "I" like a fit. Its vivid embodiment seems strange to the official "I": the gestures are wild or extremely hieratic, contained; the voice loud; the use of space extensive; the body flushed. The "I" also feels a fear of cognitive lack of control. I have been taught that in a fit of anger one is cognitively at a loss. Yet, when I have observed women in hard-to-handle anger they have been outrageously clearheaded; their words clean, true, undiluted by regard for others' feelings or possible reactions.

Having considered Aristotle carefully, I have spent a great deal of my life trying to feel anger in accord with the mean, even though I have not always known where the mean might lie. I have often thought that reality has to be fairly well defined, at least coherent, for one to be able to find the mean. so I have doubted the possibility of a mean when one's reality is crisscrossed by contradiction. But I have kept a sense that it is good to look for it and that it is good to retain a sense of control over my anger.

Elizabeth Spelman refers to the "mean" when she warns us about the conflation of anger with rage. She tells us that rage is the excess and anger the mean. She also tells us that subordinate people have been discouraged from looking positively at their anger through the conflation of rage and anger.[5] I have certainly been discouraged from looking at rage positively, and maybe the point of view from which this conflation occurs is one that I have internalized. Maybe this point of view is one that devalues rage because it is troubled by the possibility of its being dismantled through rage. I will come back to this. I will prepare the way back.

Marilyn Frye tells us that anger can be an instrument of cartography. "By determining where, with whom, about what and in what circumstances one can get angry and get uptake, one can map others' concepts of who and what one is."[6] Frye's claim reveals that she is concerned with first-order anger: anger that has a communicative intent and does or does not succeed in getting "uptake" within a particular world of sense. Frye's reflection on this type of anger leads her to an understanding that women's anger may succeed in its communicative intent in an "official" world of sense only within particular womanly domains. The fact that women's anger outside womanly domains in the official world of sense doesn't get "uptake" reveals to Frye that women are not included among those who can be wronged outside those domains, that women's claims to respect outside those domains are unintelligible. "In getting angry one claims that one is in certain ways and dimensions respectable. One makes a claim upon respect."[7]

I think Frye's analysis is important because anger that doesn't get "uptake" is as interesting for what it reveals about the person who cannot countenance it as for what it reveals about the person who is angry. If she makes a claim upon respect, the angry woman must make sense of herself to herself. She must inhabit a world of sense in which she is respectable, a world of sense different from the world the one addressed through anger inhabits. It is important both to inquire into this world of sense keeping anger in mind and to question whether all anger makes a claim upon respect.

The angry woman may share the official sense and just demand her inclusion into it. The official world of sense is contradictory in this respect: it both includes her formally and excludes her in fact. As Carole Pateman argues, even the formal story is contradictory. In liberal societies, Pateman argues, women are officially individuals, people who have property in their persons. As such they can enter into contracts and commit themselves voluntarily to subordination: they can voluntarily enter into the marriage contract. But women enter the marriage contract as women, not as individuals whose sex is irrelevant to the act of contracting. It is as women that they subordinate themselves to men in exchange for benevolence, something that cannot be exchanged, because it cannot be demanded as one's right. Only subordinates enter the marriage contract to become subordinates.

So, the angry woman may be demanding respectability as an individual, a resolution of this contradiction in liberal societies toward her inclusion in them as an individual. In doing so she is expressing a different conception of who she is. If she succeeds in being given uptake, in making her anger intelligible, she will have changed. "To expand the scope of one's intelligible anger is to change one's place in the universe, to change another's concept of what one is, to become something different in that social and collective scheme which determines the limits of the intelligible."[8]

Notice that her anger is not at her not making sense in that "social and collective scheme which determines the limits of the intelligible," the official world. Her anger is about something and at someone who has wronged her outside the womanly domain. Thus her anger is first-level anger. Though it reveals that she inhabits two different domains of sense, her anger is not about this fact. The fact that she inhabits two different worlds of sense explains why her anger is not given uptake. The fact that the only, but extraordinary, difference between these worlds is that she is an individual in one but not in the other explains her communicative intent. The communicative act of anger exhibits her as someone who has the properties required for uptake. It "models" her as the right kind of person, someone who can get angry outside of womanly domains. This is one of Lyman's points when he says that "the existence of anger itself is evidence of the denial of a right to social participation."[9]

Spelman tells us that though in western cultures reason has been associated with members of groups that are dominant politically, socially, and culturally, and emotion has been associated with members of subordinate groups, anger has been excluded from the dominant group's profile of subordinates. When one gets angry, according to Spelman, one regards the person whose conduct one assesses as one's equal. So we can understand why anger has been excluded from the personality profile of the subordinate. In excluding anger from their personality profile, dominant groups exclude subordinates from the category of moral agents, since to be angry is to make oneself a judge and to express a standard against which one assesses the person's conduct, both of which are marks of a moral agent.[10] In becoming angry subordinates signal that they take themselves seriously; they believe they have the capacity as well as the right to be judges of those around them.

Spelman and Frye are talking about the same kind of first-level anger, anger that makes a claim upon respect and signals one's own ability to make judgments about having been wronged, one's own respectability. I cannot understand this anger unless I pay attention to the oppressor, since it is a communicative act and, as described by Frye and Spelman, it demands respect from the oppressor. From the inside I know this anger in its demand for respectability and both in its effectiveness and its failures. Given the contradictory nature of the official world—it treats us as subordinates at the same time that it declares us equals—this anger is useful and resistant; it has a political dimension. I will describe later an anger that is a transformation of fear that makes clear the politically resistant import of "claim upon respect" anger, and I will interpret this anger in two ways, one of which makes it an example of "claim upon respect" anger.

But the demand for respectability can become a trap against inhabiting worlds of sense that are entirely antagonistic to the "social and collective scheme which determines the limits of the intelligible," because from within them one may not be able to intend to present oneself as respectable to others who are outside of it. So if I am right in following Spelman's and Frye's analyses to my conclusion, their analyses reveal both the usefulness and the dangers of this kind of anger.

But imagine the angry woman thinking of herself as respectable in a world of sense that is entirely antagonistic to the official world of sense. The self that thinks of herself as respectable is a different self than the one she is in the official world. Her claims upon respect make sense only if addressed to herself and to others who share this world of sense. But her anger across worlds cannot be understood as a demand upon respect, because she does not respect the available domains. Her anger, then, must have a different meaning. It must be second-level anger, anger that contains a recognition that there is more than one world of sense. Anger across worlds of sense may well turn out to be rage precisely in lacking a communicative intent or in having a communicative intent of a very different, noncognitive sort.

Spelman understands rage as the "excess" in the continuum that has anger as a "mean." She thinks that dominant groups have included rage in the profile of the subordinate that allows for the identification of the subordinate with emotion. Rage is equated by dominators with hysteria or insanity. Though she does not say this outright, she implies that rage cannot be justified. She tells us that rage is an "excess." She also tells us that subordinates "have been discouraged from looking positively or clearly at their anger through the conflation of rage and anger."[11] So we can see now that the point of view from which rage is devalued is the dominator's point of view.

I find Spelman's concern with the interpretation of rage by those in the dominant group helpful in understanding our disagreement about rage, as well as in understanding my own devaluation of rage and its revaluation. She helps me understand that I had internalized the dominator's point of view in devaluing rage. As an excess, rage cannot justifiably express a judgment of having been wronged addressed to those who have wronged one, either because the manner of expression is not justifiable or the claim is not justified. I will understand Spelman as suggesting that rage cannot express, in a justifiable manner, a judgment addressed to those who have wronged one. I could not agree more since, as a noncommunicative act, rage cannot be making a claim addressed to those who share the official sense. This anger echoes or reverberates across worlds. It is a second-level anger. It decries the sense of the world that erases it precisely in that world of sense stands in the way of its possibility. It recognizes this world's walls. It pushes against them rather than making claims within them. This is the second interpretation I give to Lyman's claim that the "existence of anger itself is evidence of the denial of a right to social participation."[12] This anger speaks its sense within the official world of sense in enraged tones without the intention to make sense to those within it. Its harshness attests to the hardness of the walls against which and over which it echoes. Its intimidating power indicates that it does echo. Its inspiring power indicates that it does echo. This is separatist anger.

Once one recognizes first- and second-order anger, one can see that some anger can be interpreted both ways. It may also be possible to intend both acts, both levels of anger, through the same expression of anger. I said earlier that I would consider anger that is fear transformed. This anger also seems to possess one because there is a personality change. The oppressed, subservient person is taken over by, possessed, and becomes again the assertive, resistant person. When I asked a northern New Mexican Chicano what knowledge he had gained from his oppressed condition that he could bring to liberatory struggle, he described this mysterious transformation of fear into anger. He told us that it had been very important to him to know that this happens in him. After the Moly mine closed and he was out of a job, he decided to go back to school on the G.I. bill. The money from the G.I. bill began to run out before he was finished with his schooling. That meant that he had to talk to numerous educated, polished bureaucrats about funds for his education. He entered every one of these situations in fear. Ill at ease because of his lack of polish in these contexts, he experienced both a lack of control over his situation and the total control of the bureaucrat through the latter's use of language that could be abusively refined. The "You Chicanos are all the same" would flow into the bureaucrat's speech with ease. Reduced by the "mark of the plural"[13] and invaded by the logic of devaluation, the Chicano would find himself at a loss for words, confused, facing the inevitability of the end of his education. At this time, as he had experienced it before, the transformation came. He became self-possessed in anger: clear-headed, no nonsense, going to the core of the racist matter, immovable, determined, his muscles and his voice tense, backing up his words. The logic and the weight of oppression no longer determined him. The logic and weight of resistance were fully inspiring.

I think that in expressing this kind of anger the Chicano can be understood either as demanding uptake from the bureaucrat or as evoking a response from the bureaucrat through anger, provoking the bureaucrat into responding to his needs. He could also be intending both acts: he could be demanding respect from the bureaucrat in the terms of the bureaucrat's formal world of sense and decrying that world of sense. "I am to be treated as an equal, not as a subordinate," and "damn your world of sense which has my subordination at its core."

First-order anger seems to be consistently backward looking. In the case of subordinates, it remembers the past insubordinately. Second-order anger can be forward looking. First-order anger responds to someone's (oneself or another) having been wronged, harmed, enslaved. Audre Lorde is thinking of first-order anger when she tells us that "strength that is bred by anger alone . . . cannot create the future. It can only demolish the past."[14] But she is talking of second-order anger when she tells us of putting our anger at the service of our visions. Peter Lyman is thinking of first-order anger when he talks of "ressentiment," Nietzsche's term for anger that leads "beyond angry speech and aggressive action to a self-destructive adaptation to subordination through the internalization of rage." Lyman says that in that case "the past becomes a trauma that dominates the present and future, for every event recapitulates the unresolved injury."[15] Lyman is also talking about first-order anger when he distinguishes "being angry" from "being made angry." The latter is politicized anger, in that it recovers the origin of the anger in a social relation and thus overcomes ressentiment. But in this recovery one may be led to second-order anger, because, he thinks, the emergence of authentic political anger requires "new speech for the experience of the angry."[16]

It is as future-looking second-order anger that I interpret the anger that Gloria Anzaldúa points to in *Borderlands* and the anger that Lorde describes in her "Uses of Anger," an anger that is "a grief of distortion between peers."[17]

Anzaldúa describes a self, the self in between, as a self that is intimately terrorized by two different worlds of sense, the Anglo world and the traditional Mexican world.[18] The in-between self resists intimate terrorism—the being erased, rendered speechless, irresponsible, by the two worlds. She resists intimate terrorism by taking stock of the limits of these two worlds and inhabiting the in-between world squarely: in germination toward becoming the new mestiza. She—the self in between—uses rage to drive others away and to insulate herself against exposure. This is the reverse of what people do through anger when they can exercise their anger successfully within worlds of sense in which they are both intelligible and not subordinate. They use anger against other people and address them through anger. They engage through anger. They may

attempt to dominate others through anger or rage or they may demand rectification of a wrong done to them. In both cases intelligibility and agency are presupposed if the angry act is to succeed.
There is an expectation of being understood. But for the in-between
self, rage is a way of isolating her self, of making space for her
self, of pushing others back in creating oneself out of intimate terrorism. The in-between self cannot use rage to communicate rage:
her rage is out of character and it is unintelligible. But for the in-
between self, it is the making of space apart from harmful sense.
This anger recognizes more than one world and recognizes the need
for creating not just a different speech but a different self, and this
self cannot develop under intimate terrorism. Its germination requires separation. Since this anger is about and rejects being terrorized intimately, it is a second-order anger.

So far we have seen first- and second-order angers within or
across worlds of sense that involve the oppressor/oppressed relation. But there is also anger between oppressed people. Anger between peers.

Audre Lorde paints for us two kinds of anger between peers, the
"angers that lie between us": anger that is "a grief of distortion
between peers" and anger that keeps peers separate. These two forms
of anger are interestingly complex. The second form of anger is
built from the outside, from racist hatred, but it invades the Black
woman's self. "We have not been allowed to experience each other
freely as Black women in america; we come to each other coated
in myths, stereotypes, and expectations from the outside, definitions not our own."[19] What is so interesting about this anger is that
Lorde can recognize her love for other women as she understands
it. To understand what the anger is and what is wrong with it is to
understand her longing for the company of other Black women. She
says that the anger masks "my pain that we are so separate who
should be most together." Lorde explains the anger: "The deepest
understructure of this anger [is] hatred, that societal deathwish directed against us from the moment we were born Black and female
in america. Echoes of it return as cruelty and anger in our dealings
with each other."[20] This anger is first-order anger but it is a peculiar form of it since the judgment it exercises against Black women
is at the service of the oppressor and it is not about the past. It is,
rather, fixed in the present. A Black woman turns away from another Black woman in angry judgment of her. She is "good for nothing."[21] The Black woman is the racist stereotype turned into flesh.
She turns away because the judgment applies to her, too, unless

she is separate from the one she judges. But this is not a judgment of having been wronged by the other woman. Rather the judgment presupposes a wrong done to her by the racist oppressor, so deep that it has rendered them both, in her eyes, beyond respect, and it leads them to avert their eyes when in each other's presence. "It is very hard to look absorbed hatred in the eye."[22] Understanding this form of anger reveals the damage of racism in us. And how it keeps us apart when we need each other to heal the damage. But understanding this anger is also important to distinguish it from other, constructive anger between peers: the anger that is a grief of distortion.

This anger is particularly important to me because what has made me angriest in struggle has been the slow and terrible realization of the difficulties of working across oppressions. We are separate in difficult-to-overcome ways. This is the very subject of the anger that is a grief of distortion between peers. Lorde thinks that anger has a role to play in overcoming this separation. This is anger that echoes across different worlds of sense, sometimes across different resistant worlds that retain the oppression of others within them. Its content indicates that it is second-order anger. It recognizes the resistant world of sense of other oppressed people as resistant, but it also decries its distortion of oneself and one's own. It expresses grief at distortion in angry ways because the barriers across sense are hard to overcome. So this anger does not depend solely or mainly on recognition of cognitive content, but it calls for an emotional noncognitive response, and it further asks that the emotional response, the echo, acquire cognitive content, that is, that it become fully anger. The acquisition of cognitive content requires that we "listen to its rhythms," that we "learn with it, to move beyond the manner of presentation to the substance." This implies "peers meeting upon a common basis to examine difference, and to alter those distortions which history has created around our difference." This anger is thus also forward looking. Its object is change: "to tap the anger as an important source of empowerment." This anger "births change, not destruction, and the discomfort and sense of loss it often causes is not fatal, but a sign of growth."[23]

The propriety of this anger lies in one's expressing through it one's need for overcoming separation without distortion. It expresses love and an unwillingness to accept anything but love in return. This is a generous anger, completely extended outward over extraordinary obstacles.

Conclusions

I have interpreted anger across worlds of sense as producing emotional echoes, or emotional reverberations, in those worlds of sense. In doing so I am following Claudia Card's lead in her essay "Homophobia and Lesbian/Gay Pride." Card characterizes emotional echoing as a "picking up and feeling in oneself the joy, or sadness of others surrounding us, without any perception of the basis of these feelings, or even awareness that what we are doing is reproducing the feelings of others." The "underlying reasons are not communicated with the feeling."[24]

Anger across worlds of sense may echo as anger or it may reverberate as fear or even sadness. The echoing anger may be contagious anger or it may be counter-anger. Anger across worlds is much of the time unexpected, out of context, and out of character from the point of view of the oppressor. The oppressor may be caught emotionally off-guard.

The fact that the cognitive content of across-worlds anger is not understood does not mean that the anger is cognitively empty or expressed as cognitively empty. It means rather that it cannot be intended across worlds as cognitively straightforward, and as we saw, some across-worlds anger is precisely about lack of across-worlds intelligibility. Lorde's "grief of distortion between peers" anger demands understanding across worlds, but it depends on emotional echoing to communicate the need for understanding.

The investigation of different forms of anger shows us that since our situation requires that we move within, across, and apart from official worlds of sense, our anger strategies, the ways we train our angers, need to correspond to this feature of our situation. But since the training calls for such different ways of understanding, of feeling and expressing anger, we need to be careful with the emotional and cognitive tendencies that each produces in us. The "claim upon respect anger" creates in me a tendency toward demanding respectability as my work in liberatory struggle feeds my resistant anger away from respectability. So, I put my anger down, I tortured it, failing to understand it. In this I colluded with the oppressors' logic that would understand my rage as madness and would "mythologize" much of black women's anger as an "attitude"; my rage is a sickness that resides in me: black women just are hostile—that's part of their personality just as some people are funny.

I have considered several kinds of anger expressed by subordinates in different worlds of sense. The investigation has uncovered important differences between anger, differences that are important from a liberatory standpoint. Anger can be first-order, resistant, measured, communicative, backward looking. Or it can be second-order, resistant, raging, uncommunicative, and forward looking. Anger across worlds of sense can be generous or forbidding. And so on. The investigation shows us that we cannot understand controlled, backward looking. communicative, insubordinate anger as the only model for anger. A beginning but significant step in the political work of training our angers is understanding ourselves and each other in anger.

Notes

1. Alison Jagger, "Love and Knowledge: Emotion in Feminist Epistemology," in *Women, Knowledge, and Reality,* ed. Ann Garry and Marilyn Pearsall (Boston: Unwin Hyman, 1998), 144–45.

2. Cf. Albert Memmi, *The Colonizer and the Colonized* (Boston: Beacon Press, 1965), 86. Memmi characterizes the colonized as a function of the colonizer's needs.

3. Audre Lorde, "Uses of Anger" and "Eye to Eye: Black Women, Hatred, and Anger," in *Sister Outsider* (New York: The Crossing Press, 1984), 132.

4. Peter Lyman, "The Politics of Anger: On Silence, Ressentiment, and Political Speech," *Socialist Review,* no. 57 (vol. 11, no. 3): 55–74.

5. Elizabeth Spelman, "Anger and Insubordination," in *Women, Knowledge, and Reality,* ed. Ann Garry and Marilyn Pearsall (Boston: Unwin Hyman, 1989), 271.

6. Marilyn Frye, "A Note in Anger," in *The Politics of Reality* (New York: The Crossing Press, 1983), 94.

7. Ibid., 90.

8. Carole Pateman, *The Sexual Contract* (Stanford, Calif.: Stanford University Press, 1989), 92.

9. Lyman, *Socialist Review,* 71.

10. Spelman, "Anger and Insubordination," 262.

11. Ibid., 271.

12. Lyman, 71.

13. Memmi, *The Colonizer and the Colonized,* 85.

14. Lorde, "Uses of Anger" and "Eye to Eye," 152.

15. Lyman, 62.

16. Ibid., 68.

17. "Uses of Anger" and "Eye to Eye," 129.

18. Gloria Anzaldúa, *Borderlands/La frontera* (San Francisco: Spinsters/

aunt lute, 1987), 45.

19. "Uses of Anger" and "Eye to Eye," 170.

20. Ibid., 146.

21. Ibid., 168.

22. Ibid., 168.

23. Ibid., 129–130.

24. Claudia Card, "Homophobia and Lesbian/Gay Pride," unpublished manuscript, 1990, 8.

15

A Response to María Lugones's "Hard-to-Handle Anger

Bernadette W. Hartfield

Introduction

I was trying to understand why I was invited to participate in the symposium today. Then I read a description of law as "second-rate philosophy backed by the force of the state,"[1] and I understood a little better. I was advised, though, by a trusted friend not to try to be a philosopher for a day. Let me assure you, I will make no such attempt. Instead, I would like to affirm from my own experience much of what María Lugones has said, and to try to establish some linkages between her paradigms for considering anger, as I understand them, and some aspects of law.

I was tempted to limit my response to personal storytelling, a technique championed by Richard Delgado and employed by a number of noted and emerging legal scholars. Delgado has described many of these storytellers as members of "outgroups," which he views as groups whose marginality defines the boundaries of the mainstream, whose voice and perspective—whose consciousness—has been suppressed, devalued, and abnormalized."[2] Surely one of the masters of the genre, and possibly the first to employ it in civil rights legal scholarship, is Derrick Bell, who first published his "Chronicles" in the Harvard Law Review[3] and subsequently authored the book *And We Are Not Saved*,[4] using myth to underscore the limits of formal equality in addressing racial discrimination. I am persuaded by Delgado that

[t]raditional legal writing purports to be neutral and dispassion-
ately analytical, but too often it is not. In part this is so because
legal writers rarely focus on their own mindsets, the received wis-
doms that serve as their starting points, themselves no more than
stories, that lie behind their quasi-scientific string of deductions.
The supposedly objective point of view often mischaracterizes,
minimizes, dismisses, or derides without fully understanding opposing viewpoints. Implying that objective, correct answers can be
given to legal questions also obscures the moral and political value
judgments that lie at the heart of any legal inquiry.[5]

Delgado describes legal storytelling metaphorically as "an engine
built to hurl rocks over walls of social complacency that obscure
the view out from the citadel. But the rocks all have messages tied
to them that the defenders cannot help but read. The messages say,
let us knock down the walls and use the blocks to pave a road we
can all walk together."[6] So I will attempt storytelling. But it is my
first attempt, so I will not rely on storytelling solely.

A Story of Anger Compounded

Lugones's talk reminded me of the summer when I was twelve.
It was my first trip away from home without my immediate or
extended family. I was our Sunday school's delegate to the national council of our church denomination. I was clean and pressed,
excited and full of myself. Things were going very well. The church
ladies who were my roommates and unofficial chaperons had an
easy job. I was on my best behavior, which was nearly angelic when
you consider that I was a dedicated goody-goody most of the time,
anyhow.

Despite my shyness, I had made some good friends. A longtime
council family was there. They were delighted that their three daugh-
ters had made a new friend. We were inseparable from the time we
hit the breakfast line in the cafeteria until the time the last bene-
diction was prayed at night. Having no sisters at home, only a
worrisome, tag-along brother, I gloried in the pretend sisterhood.
So this was the north. I rather liked it.

I can't remember who broached the idea of swimming. Any right-
thinking person could have. It was nearly as hot in Westerville,
Ohio, in late July as it was in Birmingham, Alabama. I knew that
my hair would go back, but I didn't care. Between my roommates

from home and me, we'd be able to get me back to a presentable state.

We were in the car—the girls, their mom and dad, and me. We were there at the gate. We could smell the chlorinated water, maybe even feel the spray from someone's splash. Then we were back in the car. I was trying to understand and simultaneously trying not to believe that this could be happening to me. Wasn't I in the north? Wasn't I clean and pretty and smart? "Private," they were saying. "Not open to the public." Well, yes, open to the public (they could go), but not to everyone (I could not).

I cried all the way back to the dormitory. I cried up the steps, in the door. I thought I might as well just cry on. For a while, I got lots of sympathy. "There, there, dear." "Don't take it so hard." "We'll still have fun." "It's okay." But I cried on. I cried on with no intention of ever stopping. I cried on with no end in sight. (I should have heeded Lady Day's warning: help yourself, but don't take too much.)

I guess I went too far. I guess my anger was too longwinded. If I had stopped sooner, I wouldn't have tested the limits of their liberalism. The mom and dad, so unlike my own, grew impatient. One of them said, "But you're from the south. You must be accustomed to this kind of thing!" "No! No!" I protested. Anger compounded. "This has never happened to me before."

I suppose the anger component of the mass of emotions I felt at twelve was first-order anger; that is, it was backward looking and sought to demand respect for me as a little girl who deserved to have the opportunity to swim on a hot day. Who was the target of my anger? If asked then, I probably would have responded that I was angry with the proprietors of the pool who had adopted such an outrageous and cruel policy of admission. But the object of my anger soon grew to include the parents of my friends who seemed to blame me for my anger at having been mistreated. Their message seemed to be that I should not have experienced anger and pain because I must have suffered that kind of rejection and humiliation in the past. Of course it was callous of them to think that I should have developed "thick skin" to racial slights, no matter how many I might have suffered. But it was also indicative of our different worlds—theirs official, mine unofficial—that they could not comprehend the simple and well-known fact that in the black community of the 1950s and 1960s parents shielded their children from the devastation of direct confrontation with Jim Crow. (It was some months later before my mother permitted me to feel the sting of segregation via telephone. I begged and begged Mama to let me take horseback riding lessons. She finally threw up her hands in resignation and frustration. "All right! All right!" She shook her head in sadness. "If you can find a place, you can do it." Quick to the yellow pages. Dialing. "Hello." "Yes, are you open to everyone?" "Yes," came the reply, "everyone except colored." Shouldn't the answer have been "no"?) But as strangers to my world, the well-meaning parents did not know our ways, although my parents had to know theirs, and could not comprehend my anger.

So, I think I have experienced anger—mostly first-order anger— some of it communicative, demanding respect, seeking change in the official world; some of it self-destructive and debilitating. There are many stories I could tell; there are many stories of others I have read and heard that sound like mine. Our anger stories are true and credible. I am heartened by the work of Lugones and others and hope that my "old dog" anger is not too old to be trained to do new and more effective tricks.

The Law's Response to the
Anger of People Like Me

The law, both case law and statutory law, and the legal literature are doubtless full of examples of the differential treatment afforded anger and the expression of anger by dominators and those they subordinate. To begin, we may recognize that much law focuses on maintaining order, usually in the sense of maintaining the status quo. Thus, law has been a powerful instrument for enabling the dominant group to maintain its dominance. Doctrines such as *stare decisis*, mandating that courts follow precedent, have served most often to preserve the favored position of white males. The interests of white males, including their interests in expressing anger and exacting compensation or rectification for it and in suppressing or denying the anger of "others," have been protected historically by the law. Obvious examples may be drawn from the relationships of white men with African American men and women and with white women, in which white men have been afforded legal sanction for inappropriate means of expressing anger. Reportedly, a husband was permitted to beat his wife, provided the circumference of the rod did not exceed that of his thumb.[7] No corresponding right to beat a husband existed, presumably because, as Lugones noted, to give recognition to the wife's anger would be to view her as an equal. Equality was an impossibility in the common law because the wife was viewed as the subordinate of the husband.[8] This formal inequality of husband and wife has been replaced by formal equality in modern law, but the effects of past discrimination are still with us and substantive inequality prevails.[9]

The legal recognition of slavery was the ultimate subordination, and among its many evils was its failure to countenance the anger of the enslaved. Slave anger may have been impotent in some senses but its presence can still be felt in slave narratives where men and women rail at the loss of liberty and familial interests. The anger of whites faced with comparable losses was transformed by the law into legal causes of action where redress could be had. White men could protect their families and claim cognizable rights to custody of their children; African Americans could not. But slaves, as property, could be viewed as incapable of anger by rationalizing that our "inherent inferiority" justified formal inequality. Even after the legal demise of formal inequality for some subordinated groups, substantive inequality remains pervasive in affording to the dominant culture recognition and rectification or compensation for anger or anger-producing events while denying the same protection to "others."

Another area of the law that responds differentially to anger depending on who is angry or who has acted upon that anger is the criminal law. I need only say the word "rape" and note the reluctance of some states to recognize marital rape as a crime.[10] Another example is murder. A man who kills his wife may raise her adultery in mitigation, resulting in a lesser charge.[11] A battered woman who kills her husband must show her acts were in the nature of self-defense—her perceived fear, not her anger.[12]

Another example can be seen in the area of racist speech. Efforts to protect the right to be free of the cognizable harm of being the object of racist speech are challenged by many as an unconstitutional curtailment of the First Amendment rights of the racists.[13] Several critical race theorists have come forward to challenge whether the First Amendment need be interpreted in absolutes, particularly when the purpose of the speech is to maintain a position of dominance.[14]

Unfortunately, the devaluation of subordinated group anger has become easier with the resurgence of formal equality. A recent newspaper bears the headline "Fewer Law Firms Accepting Racial,

Sex Bias Suits."[15] The article recounts the opposing views of the subordinated—that lawyers are unwilling to undertake discrimination suits on behalf of plaintiffs because discrimination is less blatant (and therefore harder to prove) and because recent Supreme Court decisions, rather than recognizing advanced discrimination for what it is, have taken an approach that elevates individual rights (read the rights of whites, especially white males, and white institutions) to a more highly protected position vis-à-vis the rights of the subordinated (especially African Americans). Thus, the subordinated find would-be champions scarce, in part because today the risk of losing what would have been considered a strong case ten years ago is high, and, even if the case is won, limitations on the ability to recover attorneys' fees and costs make the decision to sue riskier still. The effect then is to deny to the subordinated a forum in which our first order anger can be vindicated. The view of the dominant culture (and interestingly this is where liberals and right-wingers enjoy solidarity) is that the anger of the subordinated must give way to the anger of dominant group members whose individual interests may suffer because of affirmative action plans. As Kimberlé Crenshaw has written:

> Formal barriers have constituted a major aspect of the historic subordination of African-Americans and . . . the elimination of those barriers was meaningful. Indeed, equal opportunity rhetoric gains its power from the fact that people can point to real changes that accompanied its advent. As the indeterminacy of doctrine reveals, however, what at first appears an unambiguous commitment to antidiscrimination conceals within it many conflicting and contradictory interests. In antidiscrimination law, the conflicting interests actually reinforce existing social arrangements, moderated to the extent necessary to balance the civil rights challenge with the many interests still privileged over it.
>
> The recognition on the part of civil rights advocates that deeper institutional changes are required has come just as the formal changes have begun to convince people that enough has been done.[16]

Crenshaw cautions that the retrenchment in civil rights presents another danger beyond the obvious. She writes:

> The lasting harm must be measured by the extent to which limited gains hamper efforts of African-Americans to name their reality and to remain capable of engaging in collective action in the fu-

ture. The danger of adopting equal opportunity rhetoric on its face is that the [constituency] incorporates legal and philosophical concepts that have an uneven history and an unpredictable trajectory. If the civil rights constituency allows its own political consciousness to be completely replaced by the ambiguous discourse of antidiscrimination law, it will be difficult for it to defend its genuine interest against those whose interests are supported by opposing visions that also lie within the same discourse. The struggle it seems, is to maintain a contextualized, specified world view that reflects the experience of Blacks.[17]

Crenshaw notes that another scholar, Mari Matsuda, has formulated this as a "'bottom up' argument—that viewing the world through the lives of subordinated minorities provides a distinct perspective on reality."[18] This is no less true when the civil rights struggle is viewed as a struggle for the recognition and rectification of our anger. It is our reality that must identify the sources of our anger and prescribe the remedy.

The supposed neutrality of legal liberalism has been assailed for its indeterminacy, which has permitted property interests to prevail over human interests and has concentrated power in the few. However, scholars like Crenshaw argue that whatever gains African Americans have made through the legal system have been made through the assertion of rights. Thus, she and others have criticized the critical legal studies movement for its failure to propose alternatives for the redress of racism and sexism to take the place of the rights doctrine it seeks to deconstruct.[19] The message is the same as that of Lugones. We know our world or worlds best. We must make the decision of how to direct our energies and anger, lest we be subordinated again.

Conclusion

I have sought to share my story of being angry and having been made angry. I have also sought to show that similar phenomena can be observed whether anger of subordinated persons is viewed from the perspective of law or of philosophy. Moreover, both disciplines impel us toward the inclusion of political remedies as we seek to harness and transform our anger. Clearly, anger has been hard to handle for me; now, I'd like to make my anger hard to handle for those who seek to dominate me.

Notes

1. Ann C. Scales, "Midnight Train to Us," *Cornell Law Review* 75, no. 3 (March 1990): 710–726.

2. Richard Delgado, "Storytelling for Oppositionists and Others: A Plea for Narrative," *Michigan Law Review* 87, no. 8 (August 1989): 2411–41.

3. Derrick Bell, "The Supreme Court, 1984 Term–Foreword: The Civil Rights Chronicles," *Harvard Law Review* 99, no. 1 (November 1985): 4–83.

4. Derrick Bell, *And We Are Not Saved* (St. Paul, Minn.: West Publishing, 1987).

5. Delgado, "Storytelling," 2440–41.

6. Ibid., 2441.

7. Homer Clark, *The Law of Domestic Relations in the United States*, 2d ed. (St. Paul, Minn.: West Publishing, 1988), 306.

8. Ibid., 286–88.

9. See Judith O. Brown, Wendy E. Parmet, and Phyllis T. Baumann, "The Failure of Gender Equality: An Essay in Constitutional Dissonance," *Buffalo Law Review* 36, no. 3 (Fall 1987): 573–644.

10. Michael D. A. Freeman, "'But If You Can't Rape Your Wife, Who Can You Rape?': The Marital Rape Exemption Re-examined," *Family Law Quarterly* 15, no. 1 (Spring 1981): 1–29.

11. Rollin M. Perkins and Ronald N. Boyce, *Criminal Law*, 3d ed. (Mineola, N.Y.: Foundation Press, 1982), 96–98.

12. Loraine P. Eber, "The Battered Wife's Dilemma: Kill or Be Killed," *Hastings Law Journal* 32, no. 4 (March 1981): 895–931.

13. See Steve France, "Hate Goes to College," *American Bar Association Journal* 76 (July 1990): 44–49.

14. See, for example, Charles R. Lawrence, "If He Hollers Let Him Go: Regulating Racist Speech on Campus," *Duke Law Journal* 1990, no. 3 (June 1990): 431–83; Mari Matsuda, "Public Response to Racist Speech: Considering the Victim's Story," *Michigan Law Review* 87, no. 8 (August 1989): 2320–81; Richard Delgado, "Words that Wound: A Tort Action For Racial Insults, Epithets and Name Calling," *Harvard Civil Rights-Civil Liberties Law Review* 17, no. 1 (Spring 1982): 133–81.

15. Douglas Lavin, "Fewer Law Firms Accepting Racial, Sex Bias Suits," *Atlanta Constitution*, May 3, 1991, E3.

16. Kimberlé W. Crenshaw, "Race, Reform and Retrenchment: Transformation and Legitimation in Anti-discrimination Law," *Harvard Law Review* 101, no. 7 (May 1988): 1331–87.

17. Ibid., 1349.

18. Ibid., Crenshaw quotes Matsuda, "Looking to the Bottom: Critical Legal Studies and Reparations," *Harvard Civil Rights-Civil Liberties Law Review* 22 (1987): 323–99.

19. Ibid., 1366.

Part IV

Where Do We Go From Here?

16

The Problem of
Speaking for Others[1]

Linda Martín Alcoff

Consider the following true stories:

1. Anne Cameron, a very gifted white Canadian author, writes several semifictional accounts of the lives of Native Canadian women. She writes them in first person and assumes a Native identity. At the 1988 International Feminist Book Fair in Montreal a group of Native Canadian writers decided to ask Cameron to, in their words, "move over" on the grounds that her writings are disempowering for Native authors. She agrees.[2]

2. After the 1989 elections in Panama are overturned by Manuel Noriega, President Bush of the United States declares in a public address that Noriega's actions constitute an "outrageous fraud" and that "the voice of the Panamanian people has spoken." "The Panamanian people," he tells us, "want democracy and not tyranny, and want Noriega out." He proceeds to plan the invasion of Panama.

3. At a recent symposium at my university, a prestigious theorist was invited to give a lecture on the political problems of postmodernism. Those of us in the audience, including many white women and people of oppressed nationalities and races, wait in eager anticipation for what he has to contribute to this important discussion. To our disappointment, he introduced his lecture by explaining that he could not cover the assigned topic, because as a white male

he did not feel that he could speak for the feminist and postcolonial perspectives that have launched the critical interrogation of postmodernism's politics. He went on to give us a lecture on architecture.

These examples demonstrate the range of current practices of speaking for others in our society. The prerogative of speaking for others remains unquestioned in the citadels of colonial administration, while among activists and in the academy it elicits a growing unease and, in some communities of discourse, it is being rejected. There is a strong, albeit contested, current within feminism which holds that speaking for others—even for other women—is arrogant, vain, unethical, and politically illegitimate. Feminist scholarship has a liberatory agenda that almost requires that women scholars speak on behalf of other women, and yet the dangers of speaking across differences of race, culture, sexuality, and power are becoming increasingly clear to all. In feminist magazines such as *Sojourner* it is common to find articles and letters in which the author states that she can only speak for herself. In her important essay, "Dyke Methods," Joyce Trebilcot offers a philosophical articulation of this view. She renounces for herself the practice of speaking for others within a lesbian feminist community, and argues further that she "will not try to get other wimmin to accept my beliefs in place of their own" on the grounds that to do so would be to practice a kind of discursive coercion and even a violence.[3]

Feminist discourse is not the only site in which the problem of speaking for others has been acknowledged and addressed, however. In anthropology there is also much discussion going on about whether it is possible to adequately or justifiably speak for others. Trinh T. Minh-ha explains the grounds for skepticism when she says that anthropology is "mainly a conversation of 'us' with 'us' about 'them,' of the white man with the white man about the primitive-nature man . . . in which 'them' is silenced. 'Them' always stands on the other side of the hill, naked and speechless . . . 'them' is only admitted among 'us', the discussing subjects, when accompanied or introduced by an 'us.'. . ."[4] Given this analysis, even ethnographies written by progressive anthropologists are a priori regressive because of the structural features of anthropological discursive practice.

The recognition that there is a problem in speaking for others has followed from the widespread acceptance of two claims. First, there is a growing awareness that where one speaks from affects the meaning and truth of what one says, and thus that one cannot assume an ability to transcend one's location. In other words, a speaker's location (which I take here to refer to their *social* location, or social identity) has an epistemically significant impact on that speaker's claims, and can serve either to authorize or disauthorize one's speech. The creation of Women's Studies and African American Studies departments was founded on this very belief: that both the study of and the advocacy for the oppressed must come to be done principally by the oppressed themselves, and that we must finally acknowledge that systematic divergences in social location between speakers and those spoken for will have a significant effect on the content of what is said. The unspoken premise here is simply that a speaker's location is epistemically salient. I explore this issue further in the next section.

The second claim holds that not only is location epistemically salient, but certain privileged locations are discursively dangerous.[5] In particular, the practice of privileged persons speaking for or on behalf of less privileged persons has actually resulted (in many cases) in increasing or reinforcing the oppression of the group spoken for. This was part of the argument made against Anne Cameron's speaking for Native women: Cameron's intentions were never in question, but the effects of her writing were argued to be counterproductive in regard to the needs of Native women because it is Cameron who will be listened and paid attention to. Persons from dominant groups who speak for others are often treated as authenticating presences that confer legitimacy and credibility on the demands of subjugated speakers; such speaking for others does nothing to disrupt the discursive hierarchies that operate in public spaces. For this reason, the work of privileged authors who speak on behalf of the oppressed is coming under criticism more and more from members of those oppressed groups themselves.[6]

As social theorists we are authorized by virtue of our academic positions to develop theories that express and encompass the ideas, needs, and goals of others. However, we must begin to ask ourselves whether this is ever a legitimate authority, and if so, what are the criteria for legitimacy? In particular, is it ever valid to speak for others who are unlike me or who are less privileged than me?

We might try to delimit this problem as arising only when a more privileged person speaks for a less privileged one. In this case, we might say that I should speak only for groups of which I am a member.

But this does not tell us how groups themselves should be delimited. For example, can a white woman speak for all women simply by virtue of being a woman? If not, how narrowly should we draw the categories? The complexity and multiplicity of group identifications could result in "communities" composed of single individuals. Moreover, the concept of groups assumes specious notions about clear-cut boundaries and "pure" identities. I am a Panamanian-American, and a person of mixed ethnicity and race: half white/ Angla and half Panamanian mestiza. The criterion of group identity leaves many unanswered questions for a person such as myself, since I have membership in many conflicting groups but my membership in all of them is problematic. On what basis can we justify a decision to demarcate groups and define membership in one way rather than another? For all of these reasons it quickly becomes apparent that no easy solution to the problem of speaking for others can be found by simply restricting the practice to speaking for groups of which one is a member.

Adopting the position that one should only speak for oneself raises similarly difficult questions. For example, we might ask, if I don't speak for those less privileged than myself, am I abandoning my political responsibility to speak out against oppression, a responsibility incurred by the very fact of my privilege? If I should not speak for others, should I restrict myself to following others' lead uncritically? Is my greatest contribution to *move over and get out of the way*? And if so, what is the best way to do this—to keep silent or to deconstruct my discourse?

The answers to these questions will certainly differ significantly depending on who is asking them. While some of us may want to undermine, for example, the United States government's practice of speaking for the Third World, we may *not* want to undermine the ability of someone such as Rigoberta Menchu to speak for Guatemalan Indians.[7] So the question arises of whether all instances of speaking for should be condemned and, if not, how we can justify a position that would repudiate some speakers while accepting others.

In order to answer these questions we need to become clearer on the epistemological and metaphysical issues that are involved in the articulation of the problem of speaking for others, issues that most often remain implicit. I will attempt to make these issues clear, and then I will discuss some of the possible responses to the problem before advancing a provisional, procedural one of my own. But first I need to explain further my framing of the problem.

In the examples used above, there may appear to be a conflation between the issue of speaking for others and the issue of speaking about others. This conflation was intentional on my part. There is an ambiguity in the two phrases: when one is speaking for another one may be describing their situation and thus also speaking about them. In fact, it may be impossible to speak for another without simultaneously conferring information about them. Similarly, when one is speaking about another or simply trying to describe their situation or some aspect of it, one may also be speaking in place of them, that is, speaking for them. One may be speaking about another as an advocate or a messenger if the person cannot speak for herself. Thus I would maintain that if the practice of speaking for others is problematic, so too must be the practice of speaking about others, since it is difficult to distinguish speaking about from speaking for in all cases.[8] Moreover, if we accept the premise stated above that a speaker's location has an epistemically significant impact on that speaker's claims, then both the practice of speaking for and the practice of speaking about raise similar issues. I will try to focus my remarks on the practice of speaking for others, but it will be impossible to keep this practice neatly disentangled from the practice of speaking about.

If "speaking about" is also involved here, however, the entire edifice of the "crisis of representation" must be connected as well. In both the practice of speaking for and the practice of speaking about others, I am engaging in the act of representing the other's needs, goals, situation, and, in fact, *who they are*. I am representing them *as* such and such, or, in poststructuralist terms, I am participating in the construction of their subject-positions. This act of representation cannot be understood as founded on an act of discovery wherein I discover their true selves and then simply relate my discovery. I will take it as a given that such representations are in every case mediated and the product of interpretation (which is connected to the claim that a speaker's location has epistemic salience). And it is precisely because of the mediated character of all representations that some persons have rejected on political as well as epistemic grounds the legitimacy of speaking for others.

Once we pose the problem as one of representation, we see that not only are speaking for and speaking about analytically close, so too are the practices of speaking for others and speaking for myself. For, in speaking for myself I am also representing my self in a certain way, as occupying a specific subject-position, having certain characteristics and not others, and so on. In speaking for myself, I (momentarily) create my self—just as much as when I speak for others I create their selves—in the sense that I create a public, discursive self, a self that is more unified than any subjective experience can support, and this public self will in most cases have an effect on the self experienced as interiority. The point is that a kind of representation occurs in all cases of speaking for, whether I am speaking for myself or for others, that this representation is never a simple act of discovery, and that it will most likely have an impact on the individual so represented. Although clearly, then, the issue of speaking for others is connected to the issue of representation generally, the former I see as a very specific subset of the latter. I am skeptical that general accounts of representation are adequate to the complexity and specificity of the problem of speaking for others.

Finally, the way I have articulated this problem may imply that individuals make conscious choices about their discursive practice free of ideology and the constraints of material reality. This is not what I wish to imply. The problem is a social one, the options available to us are socially constructed, and the practices we engage in cannot be understood as simply the results of autonomous individual choice. Yet to replace both "I" and "we" with a passive voice that erases agency results in an erasure of responsibility and accountability for one's speech, an erasure I would argue strenuously against (there is too little responsibility-taking already in Western practice!). When we sit down to write or get up to speak, we experience ourselves as making choices. We may experience hesitation from fear of being criticized or from fear of exacerbating a problem we would like to remedy, or we may experience a resolve to speak despite existing obstacles, but we experience in many cases having the possibility to speak or not to speak. On the one hand, a theory that explains this experience as involving autonomous choices free of material structures would be false and ideological, but on the other hand, if we do not acknowledge the activity of choice and the experience of individual doubt, we are denying a reality of our experiential lives.[9] So I see the argument of this paper as addressing that small space of discursive agency we all experience, however multilayered, fictional, and constrained it in fact is.

The possibility of speaking for others bears crucially on the possibility of political effectivity. Both collective action and coalitions would seem to require the possibility of speaking for. Yet influential postmodernists such as Gilles Deleuze have characterized as "absolutely fundamental: the indignity of speaking for others"[10] and, as already mentioned, important feminist theorists such as Joyce Trebilcot have renounced the practice for themselves, thus causing many people to question its validity. I want to explore what is at stake in rejecting or validating speaking for others as a discursive practice. But first, we must become clearer on the epistemological and metaphysical claims that are implicit in the articulation of the problem.

I

A plethora of sources have argued in this century that the neutrality of the theorizer can no longer, can never again, be sustained, even for a moment. Critical theory, discourses of empowerment, psychoanalytic theory, poststructuralism, feminist and anticolonialist theories have all concurred on this point. Who is speaking to whom turns out to be as important for meaning and truth as what is said; in fact, what is said turns out to change according to who is speaking and who is listening. Following Foucault, I will call these "rituals of speaking" to identify discursive practices of speaking or writing that involve not only the text or utterance but their position within a social space which includes the persons involved in, acting upon, and/or affected by the words. Two elements within these rituals deserve our attention: the positionality or location of the speaker and the discursive context. We can take the latter to refer to the connections and relations of involvement between the utterance/text and other utterances and texts as well as the material practices in the relevant environment, which should not be confused with an environment spatially adjacent to the particular discursive event.

Rituals of speaking are constitutive of meaning, the meaning of the words spoken as well as the meaning of the event. This claim requires us to shift the ontology of meaning from its location in a text or utterance to a larger space, a space that includes the text or utterance but that also includes the discursive context. And an important implication of this claim is that meaning must be understood as plural and shifting, since a single text can engender diverse meanings given diverse contexts. Not only what is emphasized, what is noticed, and how it is understood will be affected by the location of both speaker and hearer, but the truth-value or epistemic status will also be affected.

For example, in many situations when a woman speaks the presumption is against her; when a man speaks he is usually taken seriously (unless his speech patterns mark him as socially inferior by dominant standards). When writers from oppressed races and nationalities have insisted that all writing is political the claim has been dismissed as foolish or grounded in *ressentiment* or it has been simply ignored; when prestigious European philosophers say that all writing is political it is taken up as a new and original "truth" (Judith Wilson calls this "the intellectual equivalent of the 'cover record.'")[11] The rituals of speaking that involve the location of speaker and listeners affect whether a claim is taken as true, well reasoned, a compelling argument, or a significant idea. Thus, how what is said gets heard depends on who says it, and who says it will affect the style and language in which it is stated, which will in turn affect its perceived significance (for specific hearers). The discursive style in which some European poststructuralists have made the claim that all writing is political marks it as important and likely to be true for a certain (powerful) milieu, whereas the style in which African American writers made the same claim marked their speech as dismissable in the eyes of the same milieu.

This point might be conceded by those who admit to the political mutability of *interpretation*, but they might continue to maintain that *truth* is a different matter altogether. And they would be right that the establishment of locations' effect on meaning and even on whether something is *taken* as true within a particular discursive context does not entail that the "actual" truth of the claim is contingent upon its context. However, this objection presupposes a particular conception of truth, one in which the truth of a statement can be distinguished from its interpretation and its acceptance. Such a concept would require truth to be independent of the speakers' or listeners' embodied and perspectival location (except in the trivial case of a speaker's indexical statements, for example, "I am now sitting down.")

Thus, the question of whether location bears simply on what is taken to be true or what is really true, and whether such a distinction can be upheld, involves the very difficult problem of the meaning of truth. In the history of Western philosophy, there have existed multiple, competing definitions and ontologies of truth: correspondence, idealist, pragmatist, coherentist, and consensual notions. The dominant view has been that truth represents a relationship of correspondence between a proposition and an extradiscursive reality. On this view, truth is about a realm completely independent of human action, and expresses things "as they are in themselves," that is, free of human interpretation.

Arguably since Kant, more obviously since Hegel, it has been widely accepted that an understanding of truth that requires it to be free of human interpretation leads inexorably to skepticism, since it makes truth inaccessible by definition. This created an impetus to reconfigure the ontology of truth, or its locus, from a place outside human interpretation to one within it. Hegel, for example, understood truth as an "identity in difference" between subjective and objective elements. Thus, within the variety of views working in the Hegelian aftermath, so-called subjective elements, or the historically specific conditions in which human knowledge occurs, are no longer rendered irrelevant or even obstacles to truth.

On a coherentist account of truth, for example, which is held by such philosophers as Rorty, Donald Davidson, Quine, and (I would argue) Gadamer and Foucault, truth is defined as an emergent property of converging discursive and nondiscursive elements, when there exists a specific form of integration between these elements in a particular event. Such a view has no necessary relationship to idealism, but it allows us to understand how the social location of the speaker can be said to bear on truth. The speaker's location is one of the elements that converge to produce meaning and thus to determine epistemic validity.[12]

Let me return now to the formulation of the problem of speaking for others. There are two premises implied by the articulation of the problem, and unpacking these should advance our understanding of the issues involved.

> Premise 1: The "ritual of speaking" (as defined earlier) in which an utterance is located always bears on meaning and truth such that there is no possibility of rendering positionality, location, or context irrelevant to content.

The phrase "bears on" here should indicate some variable amount of influence short of determination or fixing.

One important implication of this first premise is that we can no longer determine the validity of a given instance of speaking for others simply by asking whether or not the speaker has done sufficient research to justify their claims. Adequate research will be a necessary but insufficient criterion of evaluation.

Now let us look at the second premise.

> Premise 2: All contexts and locations are differentially related in complex ways to structures of oppression. Given that truth is connected to politics, these political differences between locations will produce epistemic differences as well.

The claim here that "truth is connected to politics" follows necessarily from premise 1. Rituals of speaking are politically constituted by power relations of domination, exploitation, and subordination. Who is speaking, who is spoken of, and who listens are a result, as well as an act, of political struggle. Simply put, the discursive context is a political arena. To the extent that this context bears on meaning, and meaning is in some sense the object of truth, we cannot make an epistemic evaluation of the claim without simultaneously assessing the politics of the situation.

According to the first premise, though we cannot maintain a neutral voice we may at least all claim the right and legitimacy to speak. But the second premise suggests that some voices may be disauthorized on grounds that are simultaneously political and epistemic. Any statement will invoke the structures of power allied with the social location of the speaker, aside from the speaker's intentions or attempts to avoid such invocations.

The conjunction of premises 1 and 2 suggests that the speaker loses some portion of their control over the meaning and truth of their utterance. Given that the context of hearers is partially determinant, the speaker is not the master or mistress of the situation. Speakers may seek to regain control here by taking into account the context of their speech, but they can never know everything about this context and with written and electronic communication it is becoming increasingly difficult to know anything at all about the context of reception.

This loss of control may be taken by some speakers to mean that no speakers can be held accountable for their discursive actions. The meaning of any discursive event will be shifting and plural, fragmented and even inconsistent. As it ranges over diverse spaces and transforms in the mind of its recipients according to their different horizons of interpretation, the effective control of the speaker over the meanings they put in motion may seem negligible. However, a *partial* loss of control does not entail a *complete* loss of accountability. And moreover, the better we understand the trajectories by which meanings proliferate, the more likely we can increase, though always only partially, our ability to direct the interpretations and transformations our speech undergoes. When I acknowledge that the listener's social location will affect the meaning of my words, I can more effectively generate the meaning I intend. Paradoxically, the view that holds the speaker or author of a speech act as solely responsible for its meanings ensures their least effective determinacy over the meanings that are produced.

We do not need to posit the existence of fully conscious acts or containable, fixed meanings in order to hold that speakers can alter their discursive practices and be held accountable for at least some of the effects of these practices. It is a false dilemma to pose the choice here as one between no accountability or complete causal power. The truth, as usual, lies somewhere in between.

In the next section I consider some possible responses to the problem of speaking for others.

II

The first response I will consider is to argue that the formulation of the problem with speaking for others involves a retrograde, metaphysically insupportable essentialism that assumes one can read off the truth and meaning of *what* one says straight from the discursive context. This response I will call the "charge-of-reductionism" response, because it argues that a sort of reductionist theory of justification (or evaluation) is entailed by premises 1 and 2. Such a reductionist theory might, for example, reduce evaluation to a political assessment of the speaker's location where that location is seen as an insurmountable essence that fixes one, as if one's feet are superglued to a spot on the sidewalk.

After I vehemently defended Barbara Christian's article "The Race for Theory," a male friend who had a different evaluation of the piece couldn't help raising the possibility of whether a sort of apologetics structured my response, motivated by a desire to valorize African American writing against all odds. His question in effect raised the issue of the reductionist/essentialist theory of justification I just described.

I, too, would reject reductionist theories of justification and essentialist accounts of what it means to have a location. To say that location *bears* on meaning and truth is not the same as saying that location *determines* meaning and truth. And location is not a fixed essence absolutely authorizing one's speech in the way that God's favor absolutely authorized the speech of Moses. Location and positionality should not be conceived as one-dimensional or static, but as multiple and with varying degrees of mobility.[13] What it means, then, to speak from or within a group and/or a location is immensely complex. To the extent that location is not a fixed essence, and to the extent that there is an uneasy, underdetermined, and contested relationship between location on the one hand and meaning and truth on the other, we cannot reduce evaluation of meaning and truth to a simple identification of the speaker's location.

Neither premise 1 nor premise 2 entails reductionism or essentialism. They argue for the relevance of location, not its singular power of determination. Since they do not specify how we are to understand the concept of location, it can certainly be given a nonessentialist meaning.

While the charge-of-reductionism response has been popular among academic theorists, a second response, which I will call the "retreat" response, has been popular among some sections of the United States feminist movement. This response is simply to retreat from all practices of speaking for and assert that one can know only one's own narrow individual experience and one's "own truth" and can never make claims beyond this. This response is motivated in part by the desire to recognize difference—for example, different priorities—without organizing these differences into hierarchies.

Now, sometimes I think this is the proper response to the problem of speaking for others, depending on who is making it. We certainly want to encourage a more receptive listening on the part of the discursively privileged and discourage presumptuous and oppressive practices of speaking for. But a retreat from speaking for will not result in an increase in receptive listening in all cases; it may result merely in a retreat into a narcissistic yuppie lifestyle in which a privileged person takes no responsibility for her society whatsoever. She may even feel justified in exploiting her privileged capacity for personal happiness at the expense of others on the grounds that she has no alternative.

Opting for the retreat response, however, is not always a thinly veiled excuse to avoid the difficult work of political resistance and reconstruction. Sometimes it is the result of a desire to engage in political work but without practicing what might be called discursive imperialism.

The major problem with such a retreat is that it significantly undercuts the possibility of political effectivity. There are numerous examples of the practice of speaking for others that have been politically efficacious in advancing the needs of those spoken for, from Rigoberta Menchu to Edward Said and Steven Biko. Menchu's efforts to speak for the thirty-three Indian communities facing genocide in Guatemala have helped to raise money for the revolution and bring pressure against the Guatemalan and United States governments, who have committed the massacres in collusion. The point is not that for some speakers the danger of speaking for others does not arise, but that in some cases certain political effects can be garnered in no other way.

Joyce Trebilcot's version of the retreat response needs to be looked at separately because she agrees that an absolute prohibition of speaking for would undermine political effectiveness. She applies her prohibition against the practice only within a lesbian feminist community. So it might be argued that the retreat from speaking for others can be maintained without sacrificing political effectivity if it is restricted to particular discursive spaces.

Why might one advocate such a retreat? Trebilcot holds that speaking for and attempting to persuade others inflicts a kind of discursive violence on the other and her beliefs. Given that interpretations and meanings are discursive constructions made by embodied speakers, Trebilcot worries that attempting to persuade or speak for another will cut off that person's ability or willingness to engage in the constructive act of developing meaning. Since no embodied speaker can produce more than a partial account, everyone's account needs to be encouraged (that is, within a specified community, which for Trebilcot is the lesbian community).

There is much in Trebilcot's discussion with which I agree. I certainly agree that in some instances speaking for others constitutes a violence and should be stopped. But there remains a problem with the view that even within a restricted, supportive community, the practice of speaking for others can be abandoned.

This problem is that Trebilcot's position, as well as a more general retreat position, presumes an ontological configuration of the discursive context that simply does not obtain. In particular, it assumes that one *can* retreat into one's discrete location and make claims entirely and singularly within that location that do not range over others, that one can disentangle oneself from the implicating networks between one's discursive practices and others' locations, situations, and practices. In other words, the claim that I can speak only for myself assumes the autonomous conception of the self in classical liberal theory—that I am unconnected to others in my authentic self or that I can achieve an autonomy from others given certain conditions. But there is no neutral place to stand free and clear in which one's words do not prescriptively affect or mediate the experience of others, nor is there a way to decisively demarcate a boundary between one's location and all others. Even a complete retreat from speech is of course not neutral since it allows the continued dominance of current discourses and acts by omission to reinforce their dominance.

As my practices are made possible by events spatially far from my body so too my own practices make possible or impossible practices of others. The declaration that I "speak only for myself" has the sole effect of allowing me to avoid responsibility and accountability for my effects on others; it cannot literally erase those effects.

Let me offer an illustration of this. The feminist movement in the United States has spawned many kinds of support groups for women with various needs: rape victims, incest survivors, battered wives, and so forth, and some of these groups have been structured around the view that each survivor must come to their own "truth," which ranges only over oneself and has no bearing on others. Thus, one woman's experience of sexual assault, its effect on her and her interpretation of it, should not be taken as a universal generalization to which others must subsume or conform their experience. This view works only up to a point. To the extent it recognizes irreducible differences in the way people respond to various traumas, and is sensitive to the genuinely variable way in which women can heal themselves, it represents real progress beyond the homogeneous, universalizing approach that sets out one road for all to follow. However, it is an illusion to think that even in the safe space of a support group, a member of the group can, for example, trivialize brother-sister incest as "sex play" without profoundly harming someone else in the group who is trying to maintain her realistic assessment of her brother's sexual activities with her as a harmful assault against his adult rationalization that "well, for me it was just harmless fun." Even if the speaker offers a dozen caveats about her views as restricted to her location, she will still affect the other woman's ability to conceptualize and interpret her experience and her response to it. And this is simply because

we cannot neatly separate off our mediating praxis, which interprets and constructs our experiences, from the praxis of others. We
are collectively caught in an intricate, delicate web in which each
action I take, discursive or otherwise, pulls on, breaks off, or maintains
the tension in many strands of a web in which others find themselves moving also. When I speak for myself, I am constructing a
possible self, a way to be in the world, and am offering that, whether
I intend to or not, to others, as one possible way to be.

Thus, the attempt to avoid the problematic of speaking for by
retreating into an individualist realm is based on an illusion, well
supported in the individualist ideology of the West, that a self is
not constituted by multiple intersecting discourses but consists in a
unified whole capable of autonomy from others. It is an illusion
that I can separate from others to such an extent that I can avoid
affecting them. This may be the intention of my speech, and even
its meaning if we take that to be the formal entailments of the sen-
tences, but it will not be the effect of the speech, and therefore
cannot capture the speech in its reality as a discursive practice.
When I "speak for myself" I am participating in the creation and
reproduction of discourses through which my own and other selves
are constituted.

A further problem with the retreat response is that it may be
motivated by a desire to find a method or practice immune from
criticism. If I speak only for myself it may appear that I am immune from criticism because I am not making any claims that describe others or prescribe actions for them. If I am only speaking
for myself I have no responsibility for being true to your experience or needs.

But surely it is both morally and politically objectionable to structure one's actions around the desire to avoid criticism, especially
if this outweighs other questions of effectivity. In some cases perhaps the motivation is not so much to avoid criticism as to avoid
errors, and the person believes that the only way to avoid errors is
to avoid all speaking for others. However, errors are unavoidable
in theoretical inquiry as well as in political struggle, and they
moreover often make contributions. The desire to find an absolute
means to avoid making errors comes perhaps not from a desire to
advance collective goals but a desire for personal mastery, to establish a privileged discursive position wherein one cannot be undermined or challenged and thus is master of the situation. From
such a position one's own location and positionality would not re-

quire constant interrogation and critical reflection; one would not have to constantly engage in this emotionally troublesome endeavor and would be immune from the interrogation of others. Such a desire for mastery and immunity must be resisted.

A final response to the problem that I will consider occurs in Gayatri Chakravorty Spivak's rich essay "Can the Subaltern Speak?"[14] In Spivak's essay the central issue is an essentialist, authentic conception of the self and of experience. She criticizes the "self-abnegating intellectual" pose that Foucault and Deleuze adopt when they reject speaking for others on the grounds that it assumes that the oppressed can transparently represent their own true interests. According to Spivak, Foucault and Deleuze's position serves only to conceal the actual authorizing power of the retreating intellectuals, who in their very retreat help to consolidate a particular conception of experience (as transparent and self-knowing). Thus, to promote "listening to" as opposed to speaking for essentializes the oppressed as non-ideologically constructed subjects. But Spivak is also critical of speaking for which engages in dangerous re-presentations. In the end Spivak prefers a "speaking to" in which the intellectual neither abnegates his or her discursive role nor presumes an authenticity of the oppressed but still allows for the possibility that the oppressed will produce a "countersentence" that can then suggest a new historical narrative.

This response is the one with which I have the most agreement. We should strive to create wherever possible the conditions for dialogue and the practice of speaking with and to rather than speaking for others. If the dangers of speaking for others result from the possibility of misrepresentation, expanding one's own authority and privilege, and a generally imperialist speaking ritual, then speaking with and to can lessen these dangers.

Often the possibility of dialogue is left unexplored or inadequately pursued by more privileged persons. Spaces in which it may seem as if it is impossible to engage in dialogic encounters—such as classrooms, hospitals, workplaces, welfare agencies, universities, institutions for international development and aid, and governments—need to be transformed in order to do so. It has long been noted that existing communication technologies have the potential to produce these kinds of interaction even though research and development teams have not found it advantageous under capitalism to do so.

Spivak's arguments, however, suggest that the simple solution is not for the oppressed or less privileged to be able to speak for themselves, since their speech will not necessarily be either liber-atory or reflective of their "true interests," if such exist. I agree with her here, yet it can still be argued, as I think she herself con-cludes, that ignoring the subaltern's or oppressed person's speech is "to continue the imperialist project."[15] But if a privileging of the oppressed's speech cannot be made on the grounds that its content will necessarily be liberatory, it can be made on the grounds of the very act of speaking itself, which constitutes a subject that chal-lenges and subverts the opposition between the knowing agent and the object of knowledge, an opposition that serves as a key player in the reproduction of imperialist modes of discourse. The problem with speaking for others exists in the very structure of discursive practice, irrespective of its content, and therefore it is this struc-ture itself which needs alteration.

However, while there is much theoretical and practical work to be done to develop such alternatives, the practice of speaking for others remains the best option in some existing situations. An ab-solute retreat weakens political effectivity, is based on a metaphysical illusion, and often effects only an obscuring of the intellectual's power. There can be no complete or definitive solution to the prob-lem of speaking for others, but there is a possibility that its dan-gers can be decreased. The remainder of this essay tries to contribute toward developing that possibility.

III

In rejecting a general retreat from speaking for, I am not advo-cating a return to an unselfconscious appropriation of the other, but rather that anyone who speaks for others should only do so out of a concrete analysis of the particular power relations and discur-sive effects involved. I want to develop this point through eluci-dating four sets of interrogatory practices, which are meant to help evaluate possible and actual instances of speaking for. In list form they may appear to resemble an algorithm, as if we could plug in an instance of speaking for and factor out an analysis and evalua-tion. However, they are meant only to suggest a list of the ques-tions that should be asked concerning any such discursive practice. These are by no means original: they have been learned and prac-ticed by many activists and theorists.

1. The impetus to speak must be carefully analyzed and, in many

cases (certainly for academics!), fought against. This may seem an odd way to begin discussing how to speak for, but the point is that the impetus to *always* be the speaker and to speak in all situations must be seen for what it is: a desire for mastery and domination. If one's immediate impulse is to teach rather than listen to a less privileged speaker, one should resist that impulse long enough to interrogate it carefully. Some of us have been taught that by right of having the dominant gender, class, race, letters after our name, or some other criterion we are more likely to have the truth. Others have been taught the opposite, and will speak haltingly, with apologies, if they speak at all.[16]

At the same time, we have to acknowledge that the very decision to "move over" or retreat can occur only from a position of privilege. Those who are not in a position of speaking at all cannot retreat from an action they do not employ. Moreover, making the decision for oneself whether or not to retreat is an extension or application of privilege, not an abdication of it. Still, it is sometimes called for.

2. We must also interrogate the bearing of our location and context on what it is we are saying, and this should be an explicit part of every serious discursive practice we engage in. Constructing hypotheses about the possible connections between our location and our words is one way to begin. This procedure would be most successful if engaged in collectively with others, by which aspects of our location less highlighted in our own minds might be revealed to us.[17]

One deformed way in which this is too often carried out is when speakers offer up in the spirit of "honesty" autobiographical information about themselves usually at the beginning of their discourse as a kind of disclaimer. This is meant to acknowledge their own understanding that they are speaking from a specified, embodied location without pretense to a transcendental truth. But as María Lugones and others have forcefully argued, such an act serves no good end when it is used as a disclaimer against one's ignorance or errors and is made without critical interrogation of the bearing of such an autobiography on what is about to be said. It leaves for the listeners all the real work that needs to be done. For example, if a middle class white man were to begin a speech by sharing with us this autobiographical information and then using it as a kind of apologetics for any limitations of his speech, this would leave those of us in the audience who do not share his social location to do the work by ourselves of translating his terms into our own, appraising the applicability of his analysis to our diverse situation, and determining the substantive relevance of his location on his claims. This is simply what less privileged persons have always had to do for ourselves when reading the history of philosophy, literature, etc., which makes the task of appropriating these discourses more difficult and time-consuming (and alienation more likely to result). Simple unanalyzed disclaimers do not improve on this familiar situation and may even make it worse to the extent that by offering such information the speaker may feel even more authorized to speak and be accorded more authority by his peers.

3. Speaking should always carry with it an accountability and responsibility for what one says. To whom one is accountable is a political/epistemological choice contestable, contingent and, as Donna Haraway says, constructed through the process of discursive action. What this entails in practice is a serious and sincere commitment to remain open to criticism and to attempt actively, attentively, and sensitively to "hear" the criticism (understand it). A quick impulse to reject criticism must make one wary.

4. Here is my central point. In order to evaluate attempts to speak for others in particular instances, we need to analyze the probable or actual effects of the words on the discursive and material context. One cannot simply look at the location of the speaker or her credentials to speak; nor can one look merely at the propositional content of the speech; one must also look at where the speech goes and what it does there.

Looking merely at the content of a set of claims without looking at their effects cannot produce an adequate or even meaningful evaluation of it, and this is partly because the notion of a content separate from effects does not hold up. The content of the claim, or its meaning, emerges in interaction between words and hearers within a very specific historical situation. Given this, we have to pay careful attention to the discursive arrangement in order to understand the full meaning of any given discursive event. For example, in a situation where a well-meaning First World person is speaking for a person or group in the Third World, the very discursive arrangement may reinscribe the "hierarchy of civilizations" view where the United States lands squarely at the top. This effect occurs because the speaker is positioned as authoritative and empowered, as the knowledgeable subject, while the group in the Third World is reduced, merely because of the structure of the speaking practice, to an object and victim that must be championed from afar, thus disempowered. Though the speaker may be trying to materially improve the situation of some less privileged group, one of the effects of her discourse is to reinforce racist, imperialist conceptions and perhaps also to further silence the less privileged group's own ability to speak and be heard.[18] This shows us why it is so important to reconceptualize discourse, as Foucault recommends, as an *event*, which includes speaker, words, hearers, location, language, and so on.

All such evaluations produced in this way will be of necessity *indexed*. That is, they will obtain for a very specific location and cannot be taken as universal. This simply follows from the fact that the evaluations will be based on the specific elements of historical discursive context, location of speakers and hearers, and so forth. When any of these elements is changed, a new evaluation is called for.

Our ability to assess the effects of a given discursive event is limited; our ability to predict these effects is even more difficult. When meaning is plural and deferred, we can never hope to know the totality of effects. Still, we can know some of the effects our speech generates: I can find out, for example, that the people I spoke for are angry that I did so or appreciative. By learning as much as possible about the context of reception I can increase my ability to discern at least some of the possible effects. This mandates incorporating a more dialogic approach to speaking, that would include learning from and about the domains of discourse my words will affect.

Let me illustrate the implications of this fourth point by applying it to the examples I gave at the beginning. In the case of Anne Cameron, if the effects of her books are truly disempowering for Native women, they are counterproductive to Cameron's own stated intentions, and she should indeed "move over." In the case of the white male theorist who discussed architecture instead of the politics of postmodernism, the effect of his refusal was that he offered no contribution to an important issue and all of us there lost an opportunity to discuss and explore it.

Now let me turn to the example of George Bush. When Bush claimed that Noriega is a corrupt dictator who stands in the way of democracy in Panama, he repeated a claim that has been made almost word for word by the opposition movement in Panama. Yet the effects of the two statements are vastly different because the meaning of the claim changes radically depending on who states it. When the president of the United States stands before the world passing judgment on a Third World government, and criticizing it on the basis of corruption and a lack of democracy, the immediate effect of *this* statement, as opposed to the opposition's, is to reinforce the prominent Anglo view that Latin American corruption is the primary cause of the region's poverty and lack of democracy, that the United States is on the side of democracy in the region, and that the United States opposes corruption and tyranny. Thus, the effect of a United States president's speaking for Latin America in this way is to reconsolidate United States imperialism by obscuring its true role in torturing and murdering thousands of people in the region who have tried to bring democratic and progressive governments into existence. And this effect will continue until the United States government admits its history of international mass murder and radically alters its foreign policy.

IV

This issue is complicated by the variable way in which the importance of the source or location of the author can be understood, a topic alluded to earlier. On one view, the author of a text is its "owner" and "originator," who is credited with creating its ideas and with being their authoritative interpreter. On another view, the original speaker or writer is no more privileged than any other person who articulates those views, and in fact the "author" cannot be identified in a strict sense because the concept of author is an ideological construction many abstractions removed from the way in which ideas emerge and become material forces.[19] Now, does this latter position mean that the source or locatedness of the author is irrelevant?

It need not entail this conclusion, though it might in some formulations. We can deprivilege the "original" author and reconceptualize ideas as traversing (almost) freely in a discursive space, available from many locations and without a clearly identifiable originary track, and yet retain our sense that source remains relevant to effect. Our meta-theory of authorship does not preclude the material reality that in discursive spaces there is a speaker or writer credited as the author of their utterances, or that for example the feminist appropriation of the concept "patriarchy" gets tied to

Kate Millett, a white Anglo feminist, or that the term feminism itself has been and is associated with a Western origin. These associations have an effect, an effect of producing distrust on the part of some Third World nationalists, an effect of reinscribing semiconscious imperialist attitudes on the part of some First World feminists. These are not the only possible effects, and some of the effects may not be pernicious, but all the effects must be taken into account when evaluating the discourse of "patriarchy."

The emphasis on effects should not imply, therefore, that an examination of the speaker's location is any less crucial. This latter examination might be called a kind of genealogy. In this sense a genealogy involves asking how a position or view is mediated and constituted through and within the conjunction and conflict of historical, cultural, economic, psychological, and sexual practices. But it seems to me that the importance of the source of a view, and the importance of doing a genealogy, should be subsumed within an overall analysis of effects, making the central question what the effects of the view are on material and discursive practices through which it traverses and the particular configuration of power relations emergent from these. Source is relevant only to the extent that it has an impact on effect. As Gayatri Spivak likes to say, the invention of the telephone by a European upper-class male in no way preempts its being put to the use of an anti-imperialist revolution.

In conclusion, I stress that the practice of speaking for others is often born of a desire for mastery, to privilege oneself as the one who more correctly understands the truth about another's situation or as one who can champion a just cause and thus achieve glory and praise. And the effect of the practice of speaking for others is often, though not always, erasure and a reinscription of sexual, national, and other kinds of hierarchies. I hope that this analysis will contribute toward rather than diminish the important discussion going on today about how to develop strategies for a more equitable, just distribution of the ability to speak and be heard. But this development should not be taken as an absolute disauthorization of all practices of speaking for. It is not *always* the case that when others unlike me speak for me I have ended up worse off, or that when we speak for others they end up worse off. Sometimes, as Loyce Stewart has argued, we do need a "messenger" to advocate for our needs.

The source of a claim or discursive practice in suspect motives or maneuvers or in privileged social locations, I have argued, though it is always relevant, cannot be sufficient to repudiate it. We must ask further questions about its effects, questions which amount to the following: will it enable the empowerment of oppressed peoples?

Notes

1. I am indebted to the following for their substantial help on this paper: Eastern Society for Women in Philosophy, the Central New York Women Philosopher's Group, Loyce Stewart, Richard Schmitt, Sandra Bartky, Laurence Thomas, Leslie Bender, Robyn Wiegman, Anita Canizares Molina, and Felicity Nussbaum.

2. See Lee Maracle, "Moving Over," *Trivia* 14 (Spring 1989): 12.

3. Joyce Trebilcot, "Dyke Methods," *Hypatia* 3, no. 2 (Summer 1988): 1–13. Trebilcot is explaining here her own reasoning for rejecting these practices, but she is not advocating that other women join her in this. Thus, her argument does not fall into a self-referential incoherence.

4. Trinh T. Minh-ha, *Woman, Native, Other: Writing Postcoloniality and Feminism* (Bloomington: Indiana University Press, 1989), 65 and 67. For examples of anthropologists' concern with this issue see *Writing Culture: The Poetics and Politics of Ethnography,* ed. James Clifford and George E. Marcus (Berkeley: University of California Press, 1986); James Clifford, "On Ethnographic Authority," *Representations* 1, no. 2 (Spring 1983): 118–46; *Anthropology as Cultural Critique,* ed. George Marcus and Michael Fischer (Chicago: University of Chicago Press, 1986); Paul Rabinow, "Discourse and Power: On the Limits of Ethnographic Texts," *Dialectical Anthropology* 10, nos. 1 and 2 (July 1985): 1–14.

5. To be privileged here will mean to be in a more favorable, mobile, and dominant position vis-à-vis the structures of power/knowledge in a society. Thus privilege carries with it, e.g., presumption in one's favor when one speaks. Certain races, nationalities, genders, sexualities, and classes confer privilege, but a single individual (perhaps most individuals) may enjoy privilege in respect to some parts of their identity and a lack of privilege in respect to other parts. Therefore, privilege must always be indexed to specific relationships as well as to specific locations.

The term "privilege" is not meant to include positions of discursive power achieved through merit, but in any case these are rarely pure. In other words, some persons are accorded discursive authority because they are respected leaders or because they are teachers in a classroom and know more about the material at hand. Often, of course, the authority of such persons based on their merit combines with the authority they may enjoy by virtue of their having the dominant gender, race, class, or sexuality. It is the latter sources of authority that I am referring to by the term "privilege."

6. See also María Lugones and Elizabeth Spelman, "Have We Got a

Theory For You! Cultural Imperialism, Feminist Theory and the Demand for the Women's Voice," *Women's Studies International Forum* 6, no. 6 (1983): 573–81. In their essay Lugones and Spelman explore the way in which the "demand for the women's voice" disempowered women of color by not attending to the differences in privilege within the category of women, resulting in a privileging of white women's voices only. They explore the effects this has had on the making of theory within feminism, and attempt to find "ways of talking or being talked about that are helpful, illuminating, empowering, respectful" (p. 25). My essay takes inspiration from theirs and is meant to continue their discussion.

7. See her *I . . . Rigoberta Menchu*, ed. Elisabeth Burgos–Debray, trans. Ann Wright (London: Verso, 1984). (The use of the term "Indian" here follows Menchu's use.)

8. For example, if it is the case that no "descriptive" discourse is normative- or value-free, then no discourse is free of some kind of advocacy, and all speaking about will involve speaking for someone, ones, or something.

9. Another distinction that might be made is between different material practices of speaking for: giving a speech, writing an essay or book, making a movie or TV program, as well as hearing, reading, watching, and so on. I will not address the possible differences that arise from these different practices; I will address myself to the (fictional) "generic" practice of speaking for.

10. Deleuze, in a conversation with Foucault, "Intellectuals and Power," in *Language, Counter-Memory, Practice,* ed. Donald Bouchard, trans. Donald Bouchard and Sherry Simon (Ithaca: Cornell University Press, 1977), 209.

11. See Judith Wilson, "Down to the Crossroads: The Art of Alison Saar," *Third Text*, no. 10 (Spring 1990): 25–44, for a discussion of this phenomenon in the artworld, esp. p. 36. See also Barbara Christian, "The Race for Theory," *Feminist Studies* 14, no. 1 (Spring 1988): 67–79, and Henry Louis Gates, Jr., "Authority, (White) Power and the (Black) Critic: It's All Greek To Me," *Cultural Critique* no. 7 (Fall 1987): 19–46, esp. p. 34.

12. I know that my insistence on using the word "truth" swims upstream of current postmodernist orthodoxies. This insistence is not based on a commitment to transparent accounts of representation or a correspondence theory of truth, but on my belief that the demarcation between epistemically better and worse claims continues to operate (indeed, it is inevitable) and that what happens when we eschew all epistemological issues of truth is that the terms upon which those demarcations are made go unseen and uncontested. A very radical revision of what we mean by truth is in order, but if we ignore the ways in which our discourses appeal to some version of truth for their persuasiveness we are in danger of remaining blind to the operations of legitimation that function within our own texts. The task is therefore to explicate the relations between politics and knowledge rather than pronounce the death of truth.

13. Cf. my "Cultural Feminism versus Post-Structuralism: The Identity

Crisis in Feminist Theory," *Signs: A Journal of Women in Culture and Society* 13, no. 3 (1988): 405–36. For more discussions on the multidimensionality of social identity, see María Lugones, "Playfulness, 'World'-Travelling, and Loving Perception," *Hypatia* 2, no. 2 (Summer 1987): 3–19, and Gloria Anzaldúa, *Borderlands/La Frontera* (San Francisco: Spinsters/Aunt Lute, 1987).

14. Gayatri Chakravorty Spivak, "Can the Subaltern Speak?", in *Marxism and the Interpretation of Culture,* ed. Cary Nelson and Lawrence Grossberg (Chicago: University of Illinois Press, 1988).

15. Ibid., 298.

16. See Edward Said, "Representing the Colonized: Anthropology's Interlocutors," p. 219, on this point, where he shows how the "dialogue" between Western anthropology and colonized people has been nonreciprocal, and supports the need for the Westerners to begin to *stop talking*.

17. See ibid., p. 212, where Said encourages in particular the self-interrogation of privileged speakers. This seems to be a running theme in what are sometimes called "minority discourses" these days: asserting the need for whites to study whiteness, for example. The need for an interrogation of one's location exists with every discursive event by any speaker, but given the lopsidedness of current "dialogues" it seems especially important to push for this among the privileged, who sometimes seem to want to study everybody's social and cultural construction but their own.

18. To argue for the relevance of effects for evaluation does not entail that there is only one way to do such an accounting or what kind of effects will be deemed desirable. How one evaluates a particular effect is left open; 4 argues simply that effects must always be taken into account.

19. I like the way Susan Bordo makes this point. In speaking about theories or ideas that gain prominence, she says: ". . . all cultural formations . . . [are] complexly constructed out of diverse elementsintellectual, psychological, institutional, and sociological. Arising not from monolithic design but from an interplay of factors and forces, it is best understood not as a discrete, definable position which can be adopted or rejected, but as an emerging coherence which is being fed by a variety of currents, sometimes overlapping, sometimes quite distinct." See her "Feminism, Postmodernism, and Gender-Skepticism" in *Feminism/Postmodernism,* ed. Linda Nicholson (New York, Routledge, 1989), 135. If ideas arise in such a configuration of forces, does it make sense to ask for an author?

17

The Peculiar Position of a Woman of Color When World Fame Isn't Enough

La Verne Shelton

I stand before you as a member of an endangered species: as an African American woman in philosophy. I speak not as a political or social philosopher—my philosophical expertise lies elsewhere. But, as the person I am, I wish to make a political and social statement to you.

To our agenda for this decade, I would like to make one contribution. It concerns responsibility. I would like to address a remark, I think a considered remark, of an African American woman of considerable prestige and power—a novelist on the faculty of an Ivy League university. Since the state in which it is located is a small one, this Ivy League university is a very short distance away from the principal branch of the gigantic and unruly state university. Recently, after a number of serious "racial incidents" at the state university, she had been asked to help restore "morale" in the black student community there. Her response was that the racism of the *white* community was the cause of this poor morale and that this racism was "their problem," not hers.

I do not wish to question her claim that she could not help with the morale of the student community of that state university. But I question the *reason* she gave. Does the white community bear the responsibility for racism? Or, analogously, do males bear the responsibility for sexism?

We wish to eradicate these cancers of our society. Whose prob-

255

lem is it? We wish for women, of all colors, not just to be hired in our best universities, but to receive promotion and all benefits that their male colleagues of no more than equal ability receive. Whose responsibility is that?

The novelist I mentioned might point the finger at "them." "We" need to indicate, by our actions (especially our publications) that, as scholars, "we" are quite as good as "them." But the racism they exhibit is "their problem." This agenda for change is one that each of us participates in every day. We want change. But who is to change? It has been my perception that it is not just their problem.

The peculiarities of my own experience do not begin with my work in philosophy, although the clear awareness of the difference my being "nonstandard" made began then. In my first year of graduate school, I went to the office of an instructor (who later became my advisor) to discuss a paper I had written for his course. Fond of drama and good at timing, this instructor queried, at a crucial point in our discussion, "Do you realize what a position of *power* you are in?" He went on to detail my prospects for employment (just how long does it normally take to get a degree in philosophy: two quarters?), indicating that all top universities would be actively seeking a woman of color who was good in her field.

My advisor was not a maniac—though it may be that he spoke more openly than others did at that time of what many thought would be the result of an end to discrimination in hiring and the beginning of affirmative action. The message he gave, graphically and explicitly, was the same as a covert message I had been receiving most of my life. Today, this and other "messages" help define my perspective as an African American woman philosopher. The initial observation from this perspective is:

1. I'm going to do a lot better than I deserve to do.

From childhood I had already learned:

2. I'm (already) doing a lot better than I'm supposed to do.

African American children were not supposed to be able to spell, do computations, draw, sing (except black spirituals), think, or talk. Teenage girls were not supposed to be interested in science and medicine or to show a better comprehension of it than their male colleagues. The things I could do that I was not supposed to be able to do were all (fortunately, I suppose) good things. Unfortunately, most of the things I was supposed to do as a black girl—

sing spirituals, flirt, laugh and talk nonsense—I could not do well. But these behaviors, *which were allegedly "part of my nature,"* were BAD. So it was fine that I couldn't do them. In fact, I had better take steps to insure that I would make no improvements in this quarter. Or my BAD nature would show. For my primary lesson of socialization was:

3. Underneath it all I am irredeemably BAD.

In the context of doing philosophy, these radically false beliefs, which I believe to be part of the worldview of anyone who is oppressed because of race or gender, may long be held at bay. But in the context of being part of the profession of philosophy, they are bound to have a strong influence—one that is stronger and more negative to the degree that the beliefs are consciously ignored.

This perspective of oppression had at least the following negative influences on my career:

A. I attempted to disguise what I felt to be an inappropriate lack of understanding—where this might mean not asking questions at crucial points or not sharing earlier drafts of papers with the colleagues who might offer the most helpful criticism.

B. I deliberately handicapped myself by undertaking projects/ teaching courses for which I was inadequately prepared.

C. I relied, almost completely, on external measures of approval, even when I "knew" this was irrational (to the degree I practiced it).

D. I was ashamed of my own interests and achievements when I was around people of my "own sort." The other side of this coin: I was proud of my own interests and achievements and "confronted" people who were *not* of my "own sort" with them.

E. I believed I could shake the philosophical world in the way that a Hume or a Wittgenstein has done and thought I was a failure when this did not happen.

Such behavior will result in a bumpy career, at best. It can result in ultimate failure if the practitioner becomes adept at this sort of undermining of herself.

It seems, then, that pernicious discrimination is a cooperative enterprise. Those who discriminate instill in those who are discriminated against attitudes such as those I described, and the behavior following upon such attitudes has the result of justifying the discrimination as a mere reflection of the abilities and achievements of the person against whom discrimination is practiced.

1. I'm going to do a lot better than I deserve to do.

2. I'm doing a lot better than I'm supposed to do.

3. I am BAD.

This might best be called the "Three-Step of Institutional Racism."

I have survived this education of lies. But what has it done to me? What message can I give to my sisters who follow me? *Not* that they should let *the others* worry about "their" racism and sexism. Unless my sister is insensitive, her growth has been fed and poisoned by the lies of their racism. But what, now, should she *do*? Eradication of their racism and sexism will not heal her wounds.

I have no message except my own existence. For many of my responses and modes of action are damaging to society. They tend to exacerbate the racism and sexism of those around me. Not in any simple way: I do not seem to be an inferior person. But I have watched, in my professional life, scores of white males defending their "turf" and being *assisted* by the defense mechanisms that I have developed. For example, one way I have of defending myself is to be overly, often misappropriately, exact in my reasoning. In the past, some of my colleagues have described my exactness as being acerbic: "This woman just isn't playing our game right." Their conclusion, as chauvinists: SHE CAN'T PLAY RIGHT.

Clearly, this is an illustration of their sexism (a male colleague with exactly the same behavior would be quick-witted and rigorous). It's true that my male colleagues have a lot of work to do. But, so do I.

Each of us has to work to rid ourselves of the damage that pernicious discrimination has done.

Note

This essay was prepared for the Central Division Meetings, 1991 panel, "Problems Facing Women in Philosophy: Towards an Agenda for the Nineties."

Index

About the Contributors

Linda Martín Alcoff teaches philosophy and women's studies at Syracuse University. She has published articles in *Signs*, *Hypatia*, and *Philosophical Forum* and has coedited an anthology entitled *Feminist Epistemologies* (Routledge). Her book, *Real Knowing*, will be published by Cornell University Press in 1995, and she is now working on problems of subjectivity and identity for mixed-race persons.

Kwame Anthony Appiah is Professor of Afro-American Studies and Philosophy at Harvard University and the author of *In My Father's House: Africa in the Philosophy of Culture*, *Necessary Questions: An Introduction to Philosophy*, *For Truth in Semantics*, and *Assertion and Conditionals*, as well as three novels, of which the latest is *Another Death in Venice*. His interests are reflected in the range of his journal publications: in the philosophy of language and mind, African philosophy, philosophical problems of race and racism, and Afro-American and African literature and literary theory.

Linda A. Bell is Professor of Philosophy at Georgia State University in Atlanta, Georgia. In addition to feminist theory, she studies, teaches, and publishes in the areas of existentialism, ethics, and continental philosophy. She has published numerous articles and three books: the first, an anthology of philosophers' statements about women, *Visions of Women* (Clifton, N.J.: Humana Press, 1983); the second, a development of an ethics from the writings of Jean-Paul Sartre, *Sartre's Ethics of Authenticity* (University of Alabama Press, 1989); and the third, an existentialist feminist ethics, *Rethinking Ethics in the Midst of Violence: A Feminist Approach to Freedom* (Rowman & Littlefield, 1993).

Bernita C. Berry received her Ph.D. in sociology from Kent State University in 1988. Her special areas of expertise are race and ethnic relations, gender, and aging. She is expanding her research interests to include mass communications. In her forthcoming publication, "Life Satisfaction and the Older African American Woman," she explores the impact of race, gender, age, and social class for this particular group in our population. She has been employed as an Assistant Professor of Sociology, most recently at John Carroll University and before that at Agnes Scott College. She is a powerful motivational speaker and frequently lectures on topics such as racism and sexism, gender and social class issues, youth motivation, aged African American women, African American families, and African American history.

David Blumenfeld is Associate Dean for the Humanities at Georgia State University. He has also taught at the University of California at Santa Cruz, the University of Illinois at Chicago, and Southwestern University. His interests are in the free will problem, ethics, and seventeenth-century philosophy (especially the philosophy of Leibniz). His most recent publications are "Perfection and Happiness in the Best Possible World" and "Leibniz's Ontological and Cosmological Arguments, (both in *The Cambridge Companion to Leibniz*, ed. Nicholas Jolley, 1995).

Claudia Card (Ph.D., Harvard) is a Professor in the Department of Philosophy at the University of Wisconsin–Madison and Faculty Affiliate in Women's Studies and the Institute for Environmental Studies. She is the author of *Lesbian Choices* (Columbia University Press, 1994) and more than fifty articles and reviews, editor of *Feminist Ethics* (University Press of Kansas, 1991) and *Adventures in Lesbian Philosophy* (Indiana University Press, 1994), and member of the editorial or review boards of the *Journal of Homosexuality, Social Theory and Practice, Hypatia: A Journal of Feminist Philosophy*, the *APA Newsletter on Feminism and Philosophy*, and the book series *Between Men, Between Women* for Columbia University Press. Her research and teaching interests are in philosophy, environmental philosophy, and lesbian culture.

Blanche Radford Curry is a visiting faculty member of the Women's and Gender Studies Program at Eckerd College. She is a graduate of Clark Atlanta University with a Ph.D. in philosophy from Brown University. Her research and teaching areas include moral and social value inquiry, African American philosophy, feminist philosophy, and multicultural theory. She is an assistant editor of the American Philosophical Association's "Newsletter on Philosophy and the Black Experience" and a member of the editorial board of *Hypatia: A Journal of Feminist Philosophy*.

Victoria Davion (Ph.D., University of Wisconsin–Madison) is an Assistant Professor of Philosophy at University of Georgia. Her research areas include ethics, feminist philosophy, and political philosophy.

Marilyn Frye is a Professor of Philosophy and teaches Women's Studies at Michigan State University. Her essays are collected in two anthologies, *The Politics of Reality* and *Willful Virgin*, both published by The Crossing Press.

Pamela M. Hall is Associate Professor of Philosophy and Women's Studies at Emory University. Her interests are primarily in ethics, moral psychology, and feminist thought. She has a book on Aquinas's ethics forthcoming from the University of Notre Dame Press, entitled *Narrative and the Natural Law*.

Bernadette W. Hartfield is Associate Professor of Law at Georgia State University. Her areas of interest include legal issues affecting children and families, especially African Americans, and interstate adoption law. In addition to numerous chapters in continuing legal education publications, she has published articles on interstate adoption in the *Nebraska Law Review* and the *Oklahoma Law Review* and coauthored a paper on homosocial reproduction in academic institutions in the *American University Journal of Gender & the Law*.

Marsha Houston is Associate Professor of Communication and holder of the Nancy Reeves Dreux Chair in Women's Studies at Tulane University, New Orleans. Her scholarship focuses on intercultural communication, feminist communication theories, and the communication of African American women. Her recent publications include "When Black Women Talk With White Women: Why Dialogues are Difficult," in the anthology *Our Voices: Essays in Culture, Ethnicity, and Communication*, edited by Marsha Houston, Alberto Gonzalez, and Victoria Chen (Los Angeles: Roxbury Press, 1994). She is currently editing "Women and the Language of Race and Ethnicity," a special issue of the journal *Women and Language* (Spring 1995), and completing *Talking Proper: Communication, Culture, and the Black Middle Class Woman*, which is under contract to Temple University Press.

María Lugones is a feminist philosopher and folk educator who teaches at the Escuela Popular Nortena and at State University of New York–Binghamton. Her work centers on theorizing oppressions and resistance to oppressions as intermeshed.

Lucius Outlaw is T. Wistar Brown Professor of Philosophy at Haverford College (Haverford, Pennsylvania), where he teaches, researches, and writes about African philosophy, African American philosophy, Marx, critical social theory, and the history of philosophy in the west. He is a graduate of Fisk University, W. E. B. Du Bois's alma mater, and of the Graduate School of Arts and Sciences of Boston College. Recent essays have been published in *Philosophical Forum, Journal of Social Philosophy, Man and World*, and several anthologies, and he is at work on a book on race and philosophy entitled, tentatively, *Race, Reason, and Order.*

Stephen Prothero is an Assistant Professor in the Department of Philosophy at Georgia State University, specializing in American religious history. His first book, *The White Buddhist: Henry Steel Olcott and the American Encounter with Asian Religions*, is forthcoming from Indiana University Press.

La Verne Shelton was born in Louisville, Kentucky. She attended college at New York University, received a B.A. in mathematics and music from Goddard College, did a year of graduate study in mathematics, and received a Ph.D. in philosophy from the University of Minnesota. She has published papers in philosophy of language, philosophy of mind, philosophy of mathematics, and gender- and race-related issues. She is currently an Assistant Professor at the University of Wisconsin at Madison.

Elizabeth V. Spelman is Professor of Philosophy and chair of the department at Smith College. Her teaching and research interests include social and political thought (particularly gender and race theory), ethics, philosophy of mind, and jurisprudence. The author of *Inessential Women: Problems of Exclusion in Feminist Thought* (Beacon Press, 1988), she presently is at work on a new book, *Unworthy Subjects: Suffering and the Economy of Attention.*

Laurence Mordekhai Thomas teaches philosophy, political science, and Judaic studies at Syracuse University. He has published numerous articles on ethics and is the author of *Living Morally: A Psychology of Moral Character* and *Vessels of Evil: American Slavery and the Holocaust*, both published by Temple University Press, 1989 and 1993, respectively.